JUDSON PRESS

PUBLISHERS SINCE 1824

COMING TOGETHER
IN THE
21ST CENTURY

**The Bible's Message
in an Age of Diversity**

CURTISS PAUL DEYOUNG

Foreword by Cain Hope Felder

JUDSON PRESS
PUBLISHERS SINCE 1824
VALLEY FORGE, PA

Coming Together in the 21st Century: The Bible's Message in an Age of Diversity

Library of Congress Cataloging-in-Publication Data

DeYoung, Curtiss Paul.
Coming together in the 21st century : the Bible's message in an age of diversity / Curtiss Paul DeYoung. -- [Newly rev. & expanded ed.].
p. cm.
Rev. ed. of: Coming together. c1995.
Includes bibliographical references.
ISBN 978-0-8170-1564-0 (pbk. : alk. paper) 1. Christianity and justice. 2. Jesus Christ--African American interpretations. 3. Multiculturalism--Biblical teaching. 4. Race relations--Religious aspects--Christianity. I. DeYoung, Curtiss Paul. Coming together. II. Title. III. Title: Coming together in the twenty-first century.
BR115.J8D48 2009
270.8'308--dc22

2009032210

To *my children,*
Rachel Maria DeYoung and Jonathan Paul DeYoung
You are artisans of reconciliation in the twenty-first century.

In memory
of my dear friend Terry Coffee (1951–2009)
Your spirit and life exhibited the essence of reconciliation.

In honor
of Cain Hope Felder
Your exemplary scholarship on the Bible and multiculturalism
has inspired many, and particularly me.

CONTENTS

FOREWORD

When *Coming Together* was first published in 1995, we were witnessing one of the most profound sociopolitical revolutions in biblical interpretation that the world had seen since the Protestant Reformation. Instead of the Bible being presented to the world as a compelling compendium of ancient European spirituality designed to "civilize" pagan cultures and preserve European cultural domination, increasing numbers of contemporary interpreters were breathing new life into ancient biblical texts no longer accepted as tools for oppression but as divine promptings for human liberation. It is striking that the decade that closed the twentieth century reopened an almost forgotten vision of racial and ethnic pluralism and reconciliation that dates back to events that culminate in the first century.

The first decade of the twenty-first century began with the tragic destruction of the World Trade Center on September 11, 2001, which fueled anti-Arab and anti-Muslim sentiments.

Public commentators spoke of a war of civilizations, and hatred and xenophobia were on the increase. Yet the public discourse of ethnocentrism and bigotry did not slow the strong and steady work started by biblical scholars and interpreters at the end of the twentieth century. In fact, the work of these artisans of cultural hermeneutics continued to gain momentum especially at the grassroots. I believe these efforts by so many of us laid the foundation, in part, for the unbelievable event that occurred near the end of this first decade of the twenty-first century—the election of Barack Obama as President of the United States.

What was proclaimed as a dream in August 1963 by Martin Luther King Jr. is taking on flesh in the vision and ideals of Barack Obama. The dream is now physically manifested in reality. What was once seen as impossible is now visible. We are at the beginning of a remarkable new set of possibilities. The election of Barack Obama signals to the United States and the world that the time has come for us to move forward beyond traditional approaches to race and culture. We must move from ethnic confrontation to heroic efforts at inclusion. It seems so timely that this newly revised volume, aptly titled *Coming Together in the 21st Century*, is released as we find ourselves in such a season when hopes for real and authentic reconciliation have emerged.

As I said fifteen years ago, one voice that deserves to be widely heard is that of Curtiss Paul DeYoung. Here are the fruits of the scholarship and praxis of a European American minister and social activist who has uniquely chosen to sit where many so-called minorities have had to sit. He thereby writes as one who knows what it is to be an alien in your native land and to some extent marginalized because of choosing to break from the pack and to look at the social chaos and injustice of those below who hurt. In these past fifteen years he has made numerous visits to South Africa, as well as to other places outside of the United States, exhibiting a consistent spirit and witness. With this provocative and timely revision Curtiss DeYoung joins the ranks of persons like the late William Stringfellow, Jim Wallis, and other white males who, rather than resisting constructive and needed social change, have mustered up the courage to witness on its behalf in open dialogue with the Bible.

DeYoung's revised edition, *Coming Together in the 21st Century*, presents much more than a mere collection of interpretations of the ancient biblical world, typical of many traditional biblical interpreters. Instead of such standard fare, DeYoung offers a daring attempt to glean insights from the biblical past as he relates them to contemporary aspirations of a diverse array of racial and ethnic Bible interpreters among God's people. This book shows that many of us are being heard and that our struggles with the Bible are having a telling effect. We have an ally and friend in Brother DeYoung—we who are Native American, African, Latina/o, and Asian, and the socially sensitive European American as well. How instructive it is to find one such as DeYoung reminding us that the Bible is far from being a relic of the distant past, designed only for the maintenance of power and superiority of one group! In his literature review, analysis of specific biblical passages, and his provocative prescriptions for the church today, DeYoung has performed a great service for us all. In this new edition, DeYoung goes even a step further by actually including significant contributions from an array of diverse biblical commentators right in the pages of this volume.

The African American eclectic scholar and social critic W. E. B. DuBois, in his often quoted *The Souls of Black Folk*, declared many decades ago that "the problem of the twentieth century would be the problem of the color line." Curtiss De-Young's wide reading and disciplined writing help us to see that DuBois was essentially correct, but in the twenty-first century clarification and expansion of the color line is necessary. The "color line" turns out to involve what we may call a "culture line," with Eurocentrism on one side of the line (the realm of the honorific) and all other cultures on the other side of the line (the realm of the pejorative). Even the ways in which the Bible has been interpreted by the so-called mainline Bible scholars (overwhelmingly white males), we have seen the triumphalism of Western culture and a certain captivity of the Bible maintained through technical linguistic and historiographic tools applied to preserve narrow parameters for biblical interpretation.

New visions and prophetic perspectives have arisen in the United States and the world, reclaiming the vitality of the Bible's agenda for social transformation. Some of my own research and writing has moved in this direction, as has the work of extramural colleagues such as Justo Gonzalez, Ivone Gebara, R. S. Sugirtharajah, and Anne Nasimiyu-Wasike among others whom Curtiss DeYoung cites in this work. Let the reader be advised: this is not a book written from detached lofty places! No, this book is a true labor of love, emerging out of the heart and social praxis of a minister who has sought aggressively to bring together diverse racial and ethnic groups so that they may better understand one another and form coalitions of helping solidarity informed by new read¬ings of the Bible itself. I am proud of my former student at the Howard University School of Divinity who has remained so faithful to a mission and sense of Christian witness that he has produced this marvelous window of biblical opportunities that enables us to return again and again to the Bible rejoicing!

Cain Hope Felder
Professor, New Testament Language and Literature
Howard University School of Divinity
Chairman, The Biblical Institute for Social Change, Inc.

PREFACE

Designating groups of people by culture, race, geographic location, and other factors is always a tentative task. This book
uses terminology that reflects the accepted usage at the time of
writing. A few years from now these designations may change.
Of course, each of these classifications includes a broad range
of cultural expressions. For example, *Asian* would include
people from China, Iran, Japan, India, and Laos. The terms
Latino and *Latina* are used to identify people whose origins
are found in Mexico, Central America, and South America.

I do not use the word *Caucasian*. This identifier for whites of
European descent was used to designate whites as superior in
a biological race hierarchy. Caucasians were superior to Mon-
goloids who were superior to Negroes by birth and genetic
makeup. Since I reject the notion of biological race, I also reject the use of these terms. While the terms *Negroid* and *Mon-
goloid* have not been used for quite some time, the designator
Caucasoid has continued to be used. Since *Caucasian* implies

white racial superiority, I wonder if its continued use points to something very deep within in our cultural psyches. I prefer *white*, but Anglo and European American are also in use.

I use the term *people of color* when speaking of people who are not white. This is an imperfect term given that white is a color. But when discussing historic injustices based on white racial superiority, we need a term that includes all who are not white. The term *nonwhite* has greater negative connotations. The term *minority* is not accurate in a global sense and soon in the United States. It also can be interpreted as diminishing one's value. When I use the term *multicultural*, I use it as inclusive of all members of the human family, including whites.

I rarely use the word *America* for the United States or *American* to identify a citizen of the United States. America includes people from North, South, and Central America. I make an exception in the case of *African American*, *Asian American*, and *Native American*, because these terms are used by members of these communities. I do not use the word *slave* to identify a person. Identifiers carry power, and no person's identity should be that of a slave. I use the term *enslaved African* to note individuals from the continent of Africa who were kidnapped and sold into slavery. Gender inclusive language is employed throughout. The primary exceptions to all of the above are found when quoting sources.

INTRODUCTION

When Judson Press published the first edition of *Coming Together: The Bible's Message in an Age of Diversity* in 1995, the church, the academy, and grassroots community leaders were seeking guidance regarding how to navigate the increasing cultural diversity in the United States and around the world. There were few resources from a biblical perspective addressing the growing multiculturalism, and few, if any, of these brought together voices from multiple cultures. Most resources focused on one racial/ethnic group, and nearly all of these volumes had a theological outlook (rather than biblical). *Coming Together* was one of the only books to take a decidedly biblical view of multiculturalism using the lenses of many cultures. In the foreword to the first edition, Cain Hope Felder called *Coming Together* "a significant step forward in what has come to be called cultural hermeneutics of the Bible."

When *Coming Together* was published in 1995, demographers had projected that whites would drop below 50 percent

1

of the population in the United States by the year 2050. We now know that the shift is taking place at a faster pace than expected. The United States Census Bureau revised their estimate in 2008. They now project that whites will no longer be in the majority by 2042. By 2050 people of color will make up 54 percent of the population in the United States. Non-Hispanic whites, who made up 66 percent of the U.S. population in 2008, will drop to 46 percent in 2050. From 2008 to 2050 the percent of the population will increase for Latinos from 15 percent to 30 percent, blacks from 14 to 15 percent, Asians from 5 to 9 percent, with increases also for Native Americans and multiracial individuals. The working age population (ages eighteen to sixty-four) will be 50 percent persons of color by 2039 and 55 percent by 2050. By 2023 children of color will make up more than 50 percent of all children.[1] Similar trends are found throughout much of the world. According to evangelism professor Soong-Chan Rah, this demographic shift is occurring even faster in the racial and cultural composition of the church in the United States.[2]

The effects of this demographic transition are already being felt in the United States. The diverse constituency that came together to elect Barack Obama as president of the United States in November 2008 revealed the political power of this new reality. The expansion of political influence by Latinas/os in the 2008 election was another sign. Perhaps *Coming Together* was ahead of its time when it was originally published. With diversity rapidly increasing in the United States and globally, the release of a revised and expanded volume is very timely. One of the greatest needs in the next few decades is to equip leaders to guide the church and society through the massive cultural transitions that are occurring. Leaders will seek cultural awareness integrated with biblical wisdom.

I want to thank Judson Press for publishing a new edition of *Coming Together* in time for the fifteenth anniversary of its original release. Thanks also to Robin Bell for encouraging this effort by regularly telling me that *Coming Together* was ahead of its time and a new edition should be released. I also appreciate the wonderful cover artwork prepared by my former student Kyle Johanson. Much of the original content of the book has been retained, while new material has been developed. All of the original content has been revised, updated, and condensed. This revised and expanded edition also features contributions from scholars and activists of color to further strengthen its resourcefulness. These new contributors are Asian American, Native American, Latina, African American, Palestinian, Lebanese-American, and South African. The growing diversity in our world is not limited to ethnicity and race. This expanded edition of *Coming Together* places a greater focus on women and the Bible, and socioeconomic class issues are woven throughout. The closing chapter explores how we must further expand the diversity discussion in the twenty-first century.

Coming Together addresses diversity from a biblical perspective. The findings presented are biblically based and incorporate the research, insights, and perspectives of female and male scholars who are African, Native American, Latina/o, African American, Asian, and European, as well as from many other contexts. These many cultural viewpoints on the Bible are brought together and synthesized in some very unique ways. At times the ideas presented are constructed by an intertwining of cultural standpoints. This powerfully demonstrates that what is "human" can cross any cultural divide.

The first three chapters delve deeply into culture and ethnicity. Chapter 1 explores the wide cultural mosaic of the Bible itself through a look at the fundamental oneness of humanity (and the oneness found in Christ) and the cultural variety of this one human family. An acceptance of our shared humanness and our unique cultural identities is a necessary prerequisite for understanding the Bible in an age of diversity. Specific attention is given to discovering how people today in various settings, who have often felt left out of God's salvation story, see their story intersecting with the biblical story of old. In chapter 2 Frank M. Yamada and Leticia A. Guardiola-Sáenz present an essay on culture and identity. The chapter opens by defining culture and examining identity formation (as it relates to culture). Subsequent sections illustrate how culture and identity are observed in the Bible and how they affect one's reading of the Bible. I close this chapter with a sampling of approaches used by people of color when interpreting the Bible. These wide-ranging understandings found in our world provide for a more inclusive biblical interpretation. The focus of chapter 3 is a critical examination of the racial and cultural background and social location of Jesus of Nazareth and his universal presence as the risen Christ. Any discussion of biblical faith for Christians rests on the central issue of how we understand Jesus Christ. We will also analyze the effects of a "white Europeanized Jesus" and explore the various ways the universal Christ is presented in cultures today.

The next two chapters shift our attention from a focus on culture to a closer look at injustice. In chapter 4 Mimi Haddad directly addresses the apostle Paul's view of women. She uses Galatians 3:28 as a lens for understanding Paul's seemingly contradictory viewpoints. The Galatians passage places gender alongside socioeconomic class and ethnicity. Chapter 5 then explores some biblically based strategies for addressing three forms of injustice—racism, sexism, and classism.

The three following chapters consider liberation, reconciliation, and community. Chapter 6 examines liberation as a central message of the Bible that resonates with the cry of a majority of the world's population. The worldwide significance of the biblical themes of freedom and empowerment is highlighted as vitally important to the mission of the community of God. Chapter 7 is a roundtable on the Bible, liberation, and reconciliation. In a world that needs both liberation from injustice and reconciliation across wide divisions caused by injustice, more perspectives on the interrelationship between liberation and reconciliation are needed. This chapter brings together voices from places where these issues are debated.

Four people write from four perspectives—two men and two women, two from North America and two from international contexts: Brenda Salter-McNeil, Richard Twiss, Jean Zaru, and Allan Boesak. Chapter 8 discusses biblical images of community and then offers some approaches for developing community in a world that is becoming increasingly fragmented. It also offers key insights for moving toward true reconciliation.

The final chapter reminds us that diversity is far more than culture, race, gender, and class. Age, disability, sexual orientation, lifestyle, and religion are important aspects of diversity discussions. Often children and seasoned adults are marginalized in society and the church. People with disabilities find themselves and their issues invisible to many Christians and churches. Debates about sexual orientation are dividing the Christian community. Religious diversity is becoming more commonplace in the United States and much of the world. What is the Bible's message regarding these aspects of diversity?

A group reflection and action guide has been developed by Robin Bell to help readers become active citizens who are committed to working on diversity issues for ministry education and social change. The purpose of the study and action guide is to help readers understand the content of *Coming Together*, prepare readers to present an argument for how the future of diversity can be different, and enlist readers to work on issues of diversity in their own communities. Each session corresponds with the content of a particular chapter.

As a result of rapidly changing demographics and enhanced communication systems, the people of our world are increasingly interacting with one another. The United States, along with many other countries, is a microcosm of heterogeneous perspectives from around the world. For many, these extensive changes have brought escalated tensions and heightened fears. In this age of diversity, we have the opportunity to breathe new life back into the message of God found in the Bible and revitalize its potency for our world. We need to be set free from narrow and sometimes oppressive ways of interpreting the Scriptures and be challenged to embrace a multicultural approach. All people need to hear their own stories in the Bible and gain an appreciation for the stories of others. I believe that faith in the twenty-first century depends on our ability to embrace the multicultural message of the Bible. That message, in short, calls us to come together as the people of God despite our differences. The twenty-first century could be a time of great conflict because of increased diversity *or* followers of Jesus could take the lead as catalysts, using diversity as a reason for coming together.

1

ONE HUMAN FAMILY, MANY CULTURAL EXPRESSIONS

In the late 1970s while I was a college student in Anderson, Indiana, the Knights of the Ku Klux Klan (KKK) marched through the town recruiting new members. A student majoring in journalism interviewed a KKK member during the march. The Klansman attempted to instruct the young journalism student regarding the origins of the black race by using the Genesis account of Cain killing Abel and then being sent away by God (Genesis 4:1-16). The Klansman said that "Gabe" killed his brother Abel. Because of the killing of Abel, "Gabe" was sent away by God and found an ape for a wife. This was the beginning of the black race. Even though the Klan member did not seem to know the right name for Cain, and stretched beyond the truth of the text into his own imaginings, he was certain the Bible proved that people who were not white were less than human. In fact, they were half ape! The Bible has been misused and abused in the dialogue on diversity—sometimes overtly, as in the case of the Ku Klux Klan leader. Other times the Bible has been assumed to support a lesser status for women in the church and society or as speaking against interracial marriages.

What does the Bible offer a dialogue concerning cultural diversity? The ancient Israelites often found themselves struggling with ethnocentrism and the resulting tendencies to feel superior and uniquely special. The early church proclaimed the message of Jesus in a world where diversity in culture (Jew and Gentile), gender (male and female), and social class (slave and free) caused tensions. In the midst of these challenges, the biblical authors recorded how followers of God not only coped but also made surprising contributions to showing the importance of diversity.

The Bible addresses issues of diversity, but not by starting with the differences in the human family. Rather, it begins with the oneness of humanity. In Genesis 1 the author records God saying, "'Let us make humankind in our image, according to our likeness. . . .' So God created humankind in his image, in the image of God he created them; male and female he created them" (vv. 26-27). The Bible announces that all of humanity flows from one couple, Adam and Eve. All women and men are created in the image of God. This theme of the oneness of the human family is found throughout the Bible. It was the bedrock of Jesus' ministry as he called humanity to a re-creation experience. The apostle Paul echoed this theme when he told the philosophers in Athens that "from one ancestor [God] made all nations to inhabit the whole earth" (Acts 17:26).

While the Bible begins with the unity of humanity, it clearly demonstrates that God values the diversity that emerged within the human family. A rich mosaic of people is acknowledged and celebrated by the biblical authors. The Bible is a confessional and historic document written primarily from the perspective of the ancient Hebrews of Israel and the Diaspora, and Christians in the region of Palestine. Yet the Hebrew Scriptures and the New Testament also present the universal message of God's salvation. Therefore, by necessity, a variety of people from outside the particular cultural focus of those writing the story were included. If we emulate the biblical authors, then our starting point for discussion is our oneness rather than our differences. Faced with fears that push us to separateness, our common ancestry must challenge us to recognize those who seem different from us as sisters and brothers. Even if we want to forget our relatedness, the God revealed in the Bible does not.

Written after the time described in the text, the first eleven chapters of Genesis are devoted to explaining the origins of humanity and how this one family came to be so culturally diverse. The author began by identifying the location of Eden where the first family lived:

> A river flows out of Eden to water the garden, and from there it divides and becomes four branches. The name of the first is Pishon; it is the one that flows around the whole land of Havilah, where there is gold; and the gold of that land is good; bdellium and onyx stone are there. The name of the second river is Gihon; it is the one that flows around the whole land of Cush. The name of the third river is Tigris, which flows east of Assyria. And the fourth river is the Euphrates (2:10-14).

The writer of Genesis named four rivers to describe the location of the home of the first humans. The Pishon and Gihon have been identified as the rivers known today as the Blue Nile and White Nile in the eastern portion of the continent of Africa.[1] The Gihon is clearly in Africa, because it was said to circle Cush, the ancient black African nation often identified in the Bible as Ethiopia, located south of Egypt (currently the Sudan and surrounding areas).[2] The Pishon was listed as flowing around Havilah. In Genesis 10:7 Havilah was identified as a descendant of Cush, therefore placing it geographically near Cush.[3] So the western boundaries of Eden were found on the African continent. The second two rivers mentioned in Genesis 2 are the Tigris and Euphrates. They are in the western part of the continent of Asia (currently Iraq). So the eastern boundaries of Eden are in Asia. Palestine is located in what would have been the center of Eden.

When the Hebrews heard the creation account and the location of Eden, they understood that the home of the first family encompassed the world they knew—from Africa to Asia. All the diversity of humanity that they had encountered came from one original homeland and from one original family. Similarly, when God made a covenant with Abraham, the land that his descendants would live in would be "from the river of Egypt to the great river, the river Euphrates" (Genesis 15:18). The river of Egypt was the Nile. Therefore the boundaries were nearly the same as those of Eden—from Africa to Asia.

The fundamental oneness of this diverse human family was once again reasserted by the writer of Genesis after Noah and his family left the ark following the flood: "The sons of Noah who went out of the ark were Shem, Ham, and Japheth. . . . These three were the sons of Noah; and from these the whole earth was peopled" (9:18-19). According to the Bible, all of the nations and cultures known to the Hebrews found their ancestral source in the family of Noah, and ultimately in the family of Adam and Eve. In Genesis 10 the writers provided a table of nations descending from Noah's sons to further demonstrate this fact. The story of the Tower of Babel (11:1-9) was included by the author at the end of the prologue in Genesis as an explanation for how this one family, at the time of writing, had taken on such wide diversity in culture, ethnicity, and language.

The first eleven chapters of Genesis helped the Hebrews understand themselves as one group among the many people who came from this original human family created in the image of God. The universality of God's concern for the human family is restated throughout the Scriptures. The psalmist wrote, "Glorious things are spoken of you, O city of God. . . . Among those who know me I mention Rahab and Babylon; Philistia too, and Tyre, with Ethiopia—'This one was born there,' they say" (Psalm 87:3-4). Using the language of faith, God's love was stated as inclusive of the world known to the Hebrews, from the continent of Africa (Rahab, which was Egypt, and Ethiopia) to the continent of Asia (Babylon).

We see this same spirit of inclusiveness repeated in the writings of the prophet Isaiah: "On that day Israel will be the third with Egypt and Assyria, a blessing in the midst of the earth, whom the LORD of hosts has blessed, saying, 'Blessed be Egypt my people, and Assyria the work of my hands, and Israel my heritage'" (19:24-25). Here the prophet is reminding Israel that God's love is not restricted to them but includes all people, from Africa (Egypt) to Asia (Assyria). Isaiah has God using terms of affection for all three nations: "my people," "the work of my hands," "my heritage."

This theme of God's universality is also evident in the New Testament. At Jesus' birth his family was visited by magi from Asia (the East) (Matthew 2:1-12) and sought safety in Africa (Egypt) (vv. 13–21). In his teaching Jesus acknowledged God's love for all people. In one parable he proclaimed: "Then people will come from east and west, from north and south, and will eat in the kingdom of God" (Luke 13:29; see also Matthew 8:11). At the crucifixion Jesus again found support from Africa in Simon of Cyrene (Matthew 27:32; Mark 15:21; Luke 23:26), and faith from Europe, a part of the world not well known to the early Hebrews, in the Roman centurion (Mark 15:39). After the resurrection, Jesus challenged his followers to "go therefore and make disciples of all nations" (Matthew 28:19; see also Mark 16:15; Acts 1:8).

The story reached a climax at Pentecost when people from nations in Africa, Asia, Europe, and Palestine received the gift of the Holy Spirit after hearing the disciples of Jesus speak to them in their native language and dialect: "Parthians, Medes, Elamites, and residents of Mesopotamia, Judea and Cappadocia, Pontus and Asia, Phrygia and Pamphylia, Egypt and the parts of Libya belonging to Cyrene, and visitors from Rome, both Jews and proselytes, Cretans and Arabs—in our own languages we hear them speaking about God's deeds of power" (Acts 2:9-11).

Just as the Babel story in Genesis sought to give an explanation for diversity, Pentecost clarified God's desire for oneness. The postresurrection experience of inclusiveness at Pentecost, in a sense, reversed Babel. This message of the oneness of humanity and God's universal love for all people finds its fitting conclusion in the book of Revelation. The author of the Revelation writes about a vision of "a great multitude that no one could count, from every nation, from all tribes and peoples and languages" (7:9).

Seeing Today's Diversity in Yesterday's Text

Unfortunately, the oneness of the human family and the universality of God's love have been distorted in postbiblical times. Instead of living as one human family with many cultural expressions, we have divided ourselves by many classifications. By way of example, the modern invention that we call "racism" created a system of racial hierarchy that undergirded the superiority of one "race" of people, white Europeans, for the purpose of cultural and economic domination.[4] One result of this artificial racial hierarchy has been the portrayal of nearly all of the biblical people as white.[5] Certain biblical interpreters, in an attempt to keep the Hebrews white, regarded the people of North Africa and biblical Ethiopia as white during the time of the Genesis accounts.[6] The lack of knowledge regarding the biblical authors' inclusion of people from a wide variety of cultures and with a wide range of skin colors was the result of the dominance of biblical translation and interpretation by whites from Europe and the United States together with only a slow, halting effort on the part of much of the church to confront and eradicate racism.

Interpretation based on preconceived notions of white racial superiority is further illustrated by how few scholars have even been able to consider the possibility of Eden extending into

Africa.[7] It has been suggested that the Pishon River referred to the Ganges River in India.[8] This would locate Eden exclusively in Asia and keep the first family far away from Africa. This notion of a white Hebrew race has been taken to such extremes that it has been suggested that Noah's sons were the ancestral originals of three biological races: Shem (Caucasian/white European), Ham (Negroid/black African), and Japheth (Mongoloid/Asian). It is amazing how few serious scholars questioned how Noah and his wife could give birth to children of three different races.[9]

Ham, Shem, and Japheth (and their offspring) descended from the one human family that emerged from Eden and initially settled in Asia, Africa, and Palestine. In Genesis 10 we are given an approximate geographic placement of these brothers' families. The children of Japheth were found in Palestine, Asia Minor, and perhaps Europe. The descendants of Ham lived in Africa (Egypt, Put [Libya], and Cush [biblical Ethiopia]), Palestine (Canaan), and probably Arabia. The offspring of Shem settled in West Asia and Palestine. These "cousins" lived as neighbors, often intermingling and intermarrying (as we shall see). The transposing of modern racial categories onto the sons of Noah is untenable.

We must see beyond the biases of past and present interpretations in order to uncover the truth. In today's context of racial and ethnic fragmentation, it is essential to rediscover the wide cultural diversity of biblical peoples if we are ever to find our way back to the oneness of the human family. Discovering one's people in the biblical story can be empowering. This is particularly true for persons whose identity has been battered by societal prejudices. After repeatedly being told that persons of your race or culture are cursed by God or are somehow created as less than the dominant group, it revives your soul and renews your spirit to learn that people of your race and culture can be found in the biblical salvation story and were not afterthoughts or mistakes of God. What follows is a focus on the stories and contributions of people in the Bible who are representative of the cultural categories used today in the United States. Persons of African, Asian, and European descent in the Bible will be highlighted. Latinas/os, Native Americans, and people with multicultural and multiracial heritages will also discover how their stories can interact with the biblical story. The process of identifying the people of the Bible by the ethnic or cultural designations used today is often imprecise, and the following attempt should be considered a suggested approach for interpretation.

The Biblical Hebrews
We begin with a discussion of the "racial" type of the biblical Hebrews. The Hebrews did not have any concept of being a "race" other than the human race. What made them distinct was not their race but their religion. The Bible was content to leave it at that. Had our modern world been content to do the same, a focus on the racial/ethnic background of the Hebrews would not have relevance. But the recasting of the Hebrews as a white Northern European people requires that the issue be pursued. Too many generations have used the white pictures of biblical characters in their Bibles to make certain assumptions about the racial type of the biblical Hebrews and the superiority of the white race. Cain Hope Felder has put forth the contention that the Hebrews were an Afro-Asiatic people. He writes, "Scholars today generally recognize that the biblical Hebrews most likely emerged as an amalgamation of races, rather than from any pure racial stock. When they departed from Egypt they may well have been Afroasiatics."[10] Felder further argues that since Palestine extends from Africa and connects with Asia, it was at the center of the constant migration of people back and forth between these two continents, Therefore, the people of Palestine, and perhaps other surrounding areas, were "essentially Afro-Asiatic peoples."[11]

We have already established that Eden began in Africa and extended into Asia (an Afro-Asiatic homeland). Abraham and Sarah, the parent figures of the Hebrew people, were born and raised in Ur (Asia; Genesis 11:31) and traveled into Egypt (Africa; Genesis 12:10) before settling in Palestine. There are many references to Hebrews taking refuge in Egypt, and of course the Hebrews lived there for over four hundred years. In Exodus 12:38, the writer described the Hebrews leaving Egypt as a "mixed crowd."[12] This implies that the Hebrews who left Egypt were a much more diverse people than the folks who entered with Jacob. Later, the Hebrew people were taken captive and moved into Asian lands such as Babylonia. Certainly the culture of the Hebrews felt the impact of their residence in both Africa and Asia.

With Abraham and Sarah coming from the region around the Tigris and Euphrates, the Asian-ness of the Hebrew people seems clear. Also, Palestine has been called "West Asia." The African-ness of the Hebrews has been difficult for many in the modern world to accept, and the fact that Palestine was also considered "Northeast Africa" is rarely noted.[13] Before the Suez Canal was constructed, Palestine was a part of the African land mass. It can also easily be demonstrated that African blood flowed through the veins of Hebrew people. A few high-profile examples will corroborate this fact.

Intermarriage to people of other races and cultures was not uncommon among the Hebrews. Some of the most honored leaders among the Hebrew people were married to Africans. In addition to Sarah, Abraham was married to Hagar, an Egyptian (Genesis 16:3). Their union bore a son, Ishmael. Hagar and Ishmael were eventually sent away from the Hebrews. But from the time of Jacob on, when there was intermarriage, the spouses and the children were integrated into the family, with the children simply becoming Hebrew.[14] Joseph married Asenath, an Egyptian woman, during his time as a ruler in Egypt (Genesis 41:45). Their two sons, Ephraim and Manasseh, were blessed by Jacob and became tribes of the nation of Israel (Genesis 41:50-52; 48). All the members of these Israelite tribes had African genes. Moses married a woman from Cush (Numbers 12:1), and Solomon married the daughter of an Egyptian pharaoh (1 Kings 3:1). If we include the Canaanites among African peoples (because they are from the Hamitic line), there are many more Hebrews of African descent. Among these are two unions that are significant: Judah and his Canaanite daughter-in-law Tamar had twins, Perez and Zerah (Genesis 38), and King David and Bathsheba, had a son, Solomon, who became the next king of Israel (2 Samuel 11-12). Bathsheba's first husband was Uriah the Hittite, implying that Bathsheba was also a Hittite. The Hittites were descendants of the Canaanites.

Another clue to the fact that the Hebrews had an African heritage was the fact that they were often thought to be Egyptians. This would tell us that the physical appearance of the Hebrews was very similar to that of their African neighbors. Three notable cases of this ethnic confusion are Joseph (Genesis 42:8), Moses (Exodus 2:19), and the apostle Paul (Acts 21:38). Moses and Joseph were probably dressed as Egyptians when they were misidentified, although it was Joseph's own brothers who did not recognize him as a Hebrew. In Paul's case, he was debating fellow Israelites when a Roman military officer confused him with an Egyptian rebel. It seems very reasonable to assume that the ancient Hebrews, as well as the Jews of the New Testament, were an Afro-Asiatic people who would today be considered people of color.

Africans

With the first geographic references mentioned in the Bible being found on the continent of Africa, we have demonstrated an African presence in the Bible that began in Eden and infused the ethnic identity of the Hebrews. Yet even without an understanding of the Hebrews as an Afro-Asiatic people, the African presence in the Bible is significant both numerically and spiritually.[15] African people and countries are mentioned over eight hundred times in the Hebrew Bible and over fifty times in the New Testament.[16] Yet the significance of Africa and African people in the Bible has been denied by many in

16

modern history because of the economic benefits of slavery, colonialism, segregation, apartheid, and racism.

The cornerstone of this pseudobiblical polemic against people of African descent has been the "curse of Cain," as noted earlier, and the "curse of Ham."[17] The so-called curse of Cain comes from Genesis 4:15: "The LORD put a mark on Cain, so that no one who came upon him would kill him." This mark has been interpreted by some as black skin. There is nothing in the text that would lead to such an interpretation. In fact, the mark was meant as a sign of protection, not a curse. Even if it was a curse, it would no longer be in effect at the time Genesis was written, because all of Cain's descendants would have died in the flood of Genesis 7. If the mark was indeed black skin, this would not explain the existence of black-skinned people after the flood. Of course, black skin would not be a mark that set Cain apart, because the original humans were dark-skinned. Therefore black skin would not be a curse; rather, it would be a blessing.

The so-called curse of Ham is a fabrication, because Genesis 9:25-27 actually records that Canaan was cursed. The so-called curse of Ham is a much later adaptation of the text for use in developing a rationale for enslaving and exploiting the children of Ham in Africa. As a result of this curse mentality, the people of Egypt (and Put [Libya]) have often been made white or assumed to have a culture influenced by Europe, and ancient Cush has been disregarded or demeaned. Of course Egypt has always been in Africa, and Cush was one of the most powerful nations of the ancient world.

Cush, presently the Sudan (and surrounding areas), was called "Aethiopia" by the Greeks and Romans and was translated in the King James Version and some other Bibles as "Ethiopia." Cush was also known as "Nubia." According to historian David Roberts, "Nubian civilization lasted far longer than either classical Greece or Rome."[18] The height of Nubian culture was 3800 BC to AD 600. At times in history, Cush controlled Egypt.[19] Among the pharaohs of Egypt are

Nubians. One of these Cushite pharaohs, King Tirhakah is mentioned in the Bible (2 Kings 19:9). There is no doubt that the nation of Cush/Ethiopia was highly regarded by the biblical authors. The prophet Isaiah described it this way: "Ah, land of whirring wings beyond the rivers of Ethiopia, sending ambassadors by the Nile in vessels of papyrus on the waters! Go, you swift messengers, to a nation tall and smooth, to a people feared near and far, a nation mighty and conquering, whose land the rivers divide" (18:1-2).

In addition to the many references to nations of Africa in the Hebrew Bible, there are individuals who played significant roles in biblical history. One of the books of the Hebrew Bible, Zephaniah, was most likely written by an African. The book of Zephaniah begins by introducing the prophet as "Zephaniah son of Cushi" (1:1). Cushi usually refers to one from Cush.[20] In 2 Samuel 18 we are told about one of King David's elite soldiers, a Cushite, who was given the responsibility of bringing the news to David that his son, Absalom, had been killed in battle. Solomon was visited by the queen of Sheba (1 Kings 10:1-10, 13; 2 Chronicles 9:1-9, 12). She was the queen of a Nubian empire that extended from Nubia into southern Arabia.[21] It is possible that the Song of Solomon was written for Solomon's Egyptian wife. In Jeremiah 38 and 39, Ebed-melech the Ethiopian saved the life of the prophet Jeremiah.

African people continue to play a significant role in the New Testament and in the life of Jesus. In Matthew 2:13-22 we are told that Jesus' family fled to Egypt to save his life. The gospel writer interpreted this to be a fulfillment of the prophet Hosea's prophecy that "out of Egypt I called my son" (11:1). An African, Simon of Cyrene, carried the cross of Jesus (Matthew 27:32; Mark 15:21; Luke 23:26). Jesus also illustrated one of his recorded sermons by referring to an African. He said that the queen of Sheba ("queen of the South") will rise up at the judgment and condemn the wickedness of first-century religiosity in Israel (Matthew 12:42; Luke 11:31).

The early church included people from Africa. This is first stated at Pentecost. Listed among the people who heard the disciples speaking in their native language and dialect are persons from "Egypt and the parts of Libya belonging to Cyrene" (Acts 2:10). Acts 8:26-39 records the story of the first Gentile convert after Pentecost, an Ethiopian finance minister who was traveling down the Gaza road back to Africa and his Nubian queen, Candace. Believers from Cyrene helped start the church at Antioch (Acts 11:20), and African prophets and teachers were a part of the leadership team in the church at Antioch: "Now in the church at Antioch there were prophets and teachers: Barnabas, Simeon who was called Niger, Lucius of Cyrene, Manaen a member of the court of Herod the ruler, and Saul" (Acts 13:1). Lucius was from Cyrene in Libya, and Simeon was called "black." Another great leader in the early church was the African-born preacher Apollos, from Alexandria in Egypt (Acts 18:24-28; 1 Corinthians 1:12; 3:4-6, 22; 4:6). Some scholars think that the book of Hebrews may have been written by Apollos.[22]

The presence of Africans in the Bible is an important reminder that God's concern for persons of African descent did not begin with the colonizer's missionaries in Africa or the slave master's preacher in the United States and the Caribbean. Africans, Caribbean islanders, African Americans, others of African descent, and the rest of the human family can read about African foremothers and forefathers in the Bible and celebrate a heritage that reaches back to the very beginning in Eden and continues through the Hebrew Bible and New Testament into the present.

Asians

While the first geographic reference in the Bible is to Africa, it is closely followed by a reference to two rivers found on the continent of Asia. Biblical writers mention people and nations on the continent of Asia from Asia Minor (present-day

Turkey) to India. The ancient Asian empires of Assyria, Babylonia, and Persia played significant roles in the Hebrew Bible. Noah's ark came to rest on the Asian mountain called Mount Ararat (Genesis 8:4). As mentioned earlier, Abraham and Sarah, the parents of the Hebrew nation, came from the city of Ur in the heart of the Fertile Crescent, near where the Tigris and Euphrates meet and empty into the Persian Gulf (Genesis 11:31). They found a wife for their son, Isaac, among their relatives in Asia (Genesis 24:4). Isaac and Rebekah followed the same tradition and sent their son Jacob back to Asia, where he found two wives, Rachel and Leah (Genesis 28:2).

The book of Ezra tells of an Asian king whom the Lord used. "In order that the word of the LORD . . . might be accomplished, the LORD stirred up the spirit of King Cyrus of Persia" (Ezra 1:1). Three Asian kings acknowledged the power of God because of mighty acts done in their presence. King Nebuchadnezzar saw Shadrach, Meshach, and Abednego survive a fiery furnace (Daniel 3). King Belshazzar saw what appeared to be the fingers of a human hand write a message to him on the palace wall about his impending death (Daniel 5). King Darius saw Daniel still alive after being thrown into a den of hungry lions (Daniel 6). A number of Jews acknowledged God while serving in the governments of great Asian kings. Most notable was Esther, who was married to King Ahasuerus of Persia. She was the queen of an empire that stretched from India to Nubia. Others who served in Asian governments were Nehemiah, Daniel, Shadrach, Meshach, and Abednego. The book of Jonah describes how the prophet Jonah was sent by God to preach in the heart of Asia at Nineveh, the capital of Assyria.

There is also an extensive Asian presence in the New Testament. It began with a visit to the home of the infant Jesus by some magi from the East, most likely from Persia (Matthew 2:1-12). Among the people from the continent of Asia at Pentecost who heard the gospel in their own language and dialect were "Parthians, Medes, Elamites, and residents of Mesopotamia . . . Cappadocia, Pontus and Asia, Phrygia and Pamphylia"

(Acts 2:9-10). The Parthians, Medes, and Elamites resided east of the Tigris and Euphrates. Large portions of Acts are devoted to descriptions of the apostles' ministry in Asia (13:13-52; 14:1-28; 16:1-8; 18:19-28; 19:1-41; 20:6-38). Paul's ministry to the Gentiles had its first real success in Asia (Acts 13:46-49). The apostle Paul himself was born in the city of Tarsus in Asia Minor (Acts 22:3). The letters to the Ephesians, Galatians, Colossians, and Philemon all were sent to churches or people in Asia. The province of Asia, which was the farthest-west section of Asia Minor, is mentioned often in the Bible (Acts 20:4; 1 Corinthians 16:19; 1 Peter 1:1). Acts 19:10 says that "all the residents of Asia, both Jews and Greeks, heard the word of the Lord." The first three chapters of Revelation include letters to seven churches in the province of Asia: Ephesus, Smyrna, Pergamum, Thyatira, Sardis, Philadelphia, and Laodicea.

Regarding the outreach into Asia by the early Christians, R. S. Sugirtharajah writes that "early on, there was a strong eastward thrust of the Jesus movement through Persia and Afghanistan."[23] He adds that this effort even reached into South India and China. Long before European missionaries visited Asia, Asians were at the forefront of the movement of God in this world. God's concern for Asia, which began in Eden and continued with Abraham and Sarah in Ur, can be found throughout the Hebrew Bible and the New Testament.

Europeans

References to Europe in the Hebrew Bible are limited. In the prophetic literature, mention is made of some of the countries on the continent of Europe. The book of Daniel mentions Greece several times (8:21; 10:20; 11:2), and Daniel 11:3 refers to the rise of a "warrior king," most likely Alexander the Great.[24] In Jonah 1:3 the prophet Jonah tries to flee to Tarshish, a city probably located in southern Spain.[25]

People and places from Europe play a more significant role in the New Testament. During Jesus' ministry a Roman centurion asked Jesus to heal his servant (Matthew 8:5-13; Luke

7:2-10). Jesus said of this European, "I tell you, not even in Israel have I found such faith" (Luke 7:9). Jesus was also sought out by Greeks who were in Jerusalem for the Passover festival. They said to Philip, "We wish to see Jesus" (John 12:20-21). As Jesus died on the cross, a Roman centurion remarked, "Truly this man was God's Son!" (Mark 15:39). At Pentecost there were "visitors from Rome" and "Cretans" (Acts 2:10-11). Nicolaus, one of the seven deacons appointed in Jerusalem, was a Greek convert to Judaism before becoming a follower of Jesus Christ (Acts 6:5). In Acts 10 we find the story of Cornelius, a centurion of the Italian Cohort, who converted to the Christian faith. The books of Luke and Acts were both addressed to Theophilus, possibly a Roman official.

The apostle Paul had a vision of a man in Macedonia beckoning him to come and help (Acts 16:9-10). Extensive portions of Acts describe Paul's ministry in Europe (16:11-40; 17:1-34; 18:1-17; 20:1-6; 27:1-44; 28:1-31). The first convert in Europe was a businesswoman named Lydia (Acts 16:14-15, 40). There were also the Philippian jailer (Acts 16:23-34), Jason (17:5-9), Dionysius the Areopagite (17:34), and others. In the last reference to Paul in Acts, he is in Europe under house arrest for two years in Rome (Acts 28:30-31). Among his many letters were those written to European churches in Rome, Corinth, Philippi, and Thessalonica. One of Paul's faithful colaborers was a Greek named Titus (Galatians 2:3); a Pauline letter bears his name. While there are few references to Europe in the Hebrew Bible, God's concern for persons of European descent is clear. Jesus ministered to Roman centurions, the early church put a prime focus on outreach in Europe, and the apostle Paul was last heard of preaching in Rome, the center of European influence.

Latinas and Latinos
The arrival of Columbus and other Europeans in the Americas produced a new race and culture of people—Latinas/os. Justo Gonzalez describes the birth of this new race as "an

act of violence of cosmic proportions in which our Spanish forefathers raped our Indian foremothers."[26] Many Latinas/os are a mixture of European, African, and Native American heritage, with the blood of three continents flowing through their veins. The history of Latinas/os often parallels the history of the biblical Hebrews, who became a multiracial people through enslavement, colonization, and captivity, and in the process created a new ethnic and cultural identity. Orlando Costas described a somewhat different situation for Latinas/os in the United States when he wrote: "Hispanic Americans are the offspring of a double process of mestizaje (from mestizo, "hybrid," a racial and cultural mixture). This process has encompassed the triple encounter between European (Iberian), Native American, and African peoples . . . [and] the encounter between the Anglo-American civilization and the civilization of Latin America."[27]

Virgilio Elizondo believes that the Galilean Jews of the New Testament are the biblical people closest to this double mestizaje experience. Throughout its history, Galilee experienced domination by many nations, including Assyria, Babylonia, Persia, Macedonia, Egypt, and Syria. By the first century, Galilee was home to people originating from each of these nations and cultures, as well as Jews.[28] Fernando F. Segovia noted, "As a mestizo people, Mexican Americans represent a Galilee of the contemporary world, a modern example of a marginalized and oppressed people."[29]

By using the Galilean experience as a point of departure, Latinas/os in the United States have a powerful vehicle for hearing their story in the Bible. The ministry of Jesus and his disciples takes on a whole new significance. Jesus was raised in Nazareth of Galilee (Matthew 2:22-23; Mark 1:9; Luke 2:39-40, 51), and his ministry headquarters were in Capernaum of Galilee (Mark 2:1). He was known as "Jesus the Galilean" or "Jesus of Nazareth." Most of Jesus' followers were from Galilee, including the Twelve, the women who followed him (such as Mary and Martha), Lazarus, and others. Their Galilean accent caused them to stand out when they were in Jerusalem. Peter could not hide his accent when he denied knowing Jesus, and some bystanders commented, "Certainly you are also one of them, for your accent betrays you" (Matthew 26:73).

Galileans, like Peter and John, were at the forefront of spreading the gospel. At Pentecost those gathered recognized the Galilean accent of the disciples who were preaching: "Are not all these who are speaking Galileans?" (Acts 2:7). Galilee was at the center of a movement that would ultimately change the world because God took on flesh and experienced humanity as a Galilean.[30] God's concern for Latinas/os did not begin with modern-day missionaries. Latinas/os can hear their story today through the history of the mestizo Hebrew people and in the Galilean experience of Jesus and his disciples.

Native Americans

There are no direct references to Native Americans in the Bible since the Americas were not known to the authors of the Bible. Robert Allen Warrior believes that "the obvious characters in the story for Native Americans to identify with are the Canaanites, the people who already lived in the promised land."[31] Warrior's suggestion does open up some creative methods of interpretation. Certainly the experience of Native Americans and other indigenous people around the world can be compared to that of the Canaanites. The Canaanites were the indigenous people of Palestine. Included among the Canaanite people were the Hittites, Hivites, Perizzites, Girgashites, Amorites, Arkites, Sinites, Arvadites, Zemarites, Hamathites, and Jebusites. For much of biblical history, the Hebrews dominated the Canaanites in their own land. This was not true in the beginning of their relationship, however. When Abraham and Sarah moved into the land of the Canaanites, they lived in peace with the indigenous peoples. Abraham even gave a tithe to and received a blessing from a Canaanite holy man, Melchizedek (Genesis 14:18-20; see also Psalm 110:4;

Hebrews 7:1-17), whom Genesis 14:18 identifies as a "priest of God Most High."

When Sarah died and Abraham needed to find a burial plot for his wife, he went to the Hittites and acknowledged that he was "a stranger and an alien" in their land and needed a burial plot (Genesis 23:4). They responded by inviting him to take the best place available. Ephron the Hittite was the person who helped Abraham arrange for Sarah's burial. The next few generations of Hebrews and Canaanites continued to live in a peaceful coexistence. As was mentioned earlier, there was much intermarriage between the Canaanites and the Hebrews. So there was a definite trace of indigenous Canaanite blood in the veins of the Hebrews.

When the Hebrews returned to Palestine after their enslavement in Egypt, they came as conquerors of the land of Canaan. Perhaps the most celebrated person of Canaanite heritage in the Bible was a prostitute named Rahab (Joshua 2:1-21; 6:23-25). She helped the Israelites by hiding two spies sent by Joshua. Rahab made a deal with the spies to save her family in return for her kindness. When the walls of Jericho fell, Rahab and her family were the only ones in the city spared. After the conquest, she and her family lived with the Hebrews. Rahab was probably considered a traitor by the Canaanites because she hid Israelite spies who were on a mission that was key to the conquest of Canaan, but she was among ancient Israel's heroes of the faith (Hebrews 11:31; see also James 2:25).

Two other Canaanites mentioned in the Hebrew Bible are Uriah the Hittite and his wife, Bathsheba (2 Samuel 11:1–12:25). By this time in history, most of the Canaanites who had survived the conquest by ancient Israel had been assimilated into Israelite society. Uriah was a soldier in King David's army. While Uriah was at battle, his king, David, ordered Bathsheba into the king's bedroom. Bathsheba discovered she was pregnant as a result of this rape. So David recalled Uriah from the battlefield, hoping he would lay with his wife and thereby believe he was the father. But as a faithful member of King David's army, he could not enjoy such a pleasure while his fellow soldiers were at battle. So King David intentionally transferred Uriah to the front lines where he would be killed. Then David took Bathsheba as his wife.

The experiences of Rahab, Uriah, and Bathsheba are not unlike the Native American experience. Rahab was accepted into ancient Israelite society as a hero because she betrayed her own people. Uriah and Bathsheba had been assimilated into the dominant society and yet were treated horrendously— Bathsheba was raped and Uriah was killed. In the midst of this disregard for the indigenous people of Palestine, God redeemed the Canaanite heritage. Solomon, the most powerful of Israel's kings, was the son of Bathsheba and therefore half Canaanite (2 Samuel 12:24-25). Both Rahab and Bathsheba (also Tamar) were ancestors of Jesus (Matthew 1:3, 5-6). Jesus had the blood of indigenous people running through his veins.

The indigenous people of Palestine also appear in the New Testament. Two of the Gospels record an episode of a Canaanite woman interacting with Jesus:

> Just then a Canaanite woman from the region came out and started shouting, "Have mercy on me, Lord, Son of David; my daughter is tormented by a demon." But he did not answer her at all. And his disciples came and urged him, saying, "Send her away, for she keeps shouting after us." He answered, "I was sent only to the lost sheep of the house of Israel." But she came and knelt before him, saying, "Lord, help me." He answered, "It is not fair to take the children's food and throw it to the dogs." She said, "Yes, Lord, yet even the dogs eat the crumbs that fall from their master's table." Then Jesus answered her, "Woman, great is your faith! Let it be done for you as you wish." And her daughter was healed instantly (Matthew 15:22-28; see also Mark 7:24-30).

The interaction between Jesus and this Canaanite woman is significant for indigenous people seeking to relate to Jesus. The woman is presented in the text as a mother who is greatly concerned for her daughter. She is identified as a Canaanite, perhaps one of the few remaining descendants of a proud people who had experienced genocide, assimilation, and domination. When she comes to Jesus for help, she is rebuffed with the same ethnocentrism that Canaanites had often experienced. It is shocking to see Jesus ignore her and compare her to a dog. Was Jesus, in his humanity, revealing his ethnocentrism and prejudice? This is certainly possible. Or was Jesus illustrating prejudice for his disciples, who wanted Jesus to send her away? The reasons Jesus responded the way he did can be debated. But what is most inspiring about this text is the strength and wisdom of this Canaanite mother. She refused to accept a narrow view of God's love. She demanded to be included by challenging Jesus' exclusive ethnic focus regarding who should receive his ministry. Jesus was so moved by her unyielding faith that he invited her to participate in the blessing of God, and her daughter was healed.

Native Americans can hear their story in the Bible through the experience of the indigenous Canaanite people. Melchizedek, Ephron, Rahab, Uriah, Bathsheba, and the Canaanite woman, like the indigenous people of today, represent varied responses to different times, yet all are honored by God because of the Canaanite blood that flows throughout the veins of Jesus.

Multiracial and Multicultural

With a growing number of people identifying themselves as biracial, interracial, multiracial, or multicultural, it is important to acknowledge the presence in the Bible of multiracial people. We have already demonstrated that the biblical Hebrews were multiracial and multicultural. That is why the Hebrews have been identified as Afro-Asiatics, a racially and culturally blended people. While the Hebrew Bible regulated marriages outside of the faith, it expressed little concern about marriage outside of ethnic group. The list of multicultural unions in the

Hebrew Bible includes Abraham and Hagar, Moses and his Cushite wife, Judah and Tamar, Joseph and Asenath, Salmon and Rahab, Ruth and Boaz, David and Bathsheba, Solomon and Pharaoh's daughter, and Esther and Ahasuerus. Their offspring included Ishmael, Perez, Zerah, Ephraim, Manasseh, Boaz, Obed, and Solomon.

The best-known multiracial and multicultural person in the New Testament was Timothy. His father was Greek and his mother was Jewish (Acts 16:1-4). Timothy must have experienced some cultural prejudice due to his interracial heritage. He was circumcised as an adult so he would be accepted culturally among Jews. It was well known that his father was a Greek. Interracial, biracial, multiracial, and multicultural people can find themselves in the Bible as reflected in the lives of the Hebrew people and in followers of Jesus Christ like Timothy. In fact, the Hebrew Bible is the story of a multiracial and multicultural people seeking to follow God. The New Testament is the story of a culturally segregated people (Jew and Gentile) coming together through the Spirit of Jesus Christ.

Oneness in Christ

Much more could be written regarding the cultural diversity of the people in the Scriptures. The Bible includes people representative of the worldwide human family. "One human family, many cultural expressions" is a biblical truth that needs to be reclaimed and proclaimed in this age of diversity. The Bible is a multicultural document. The Hebrew Bible proclaims God's universal love for humanity from the very beginning. This message of oneness keeps emerging even in the midst of ancient Israel's ethnocentrism. The New Testament declares a faith initiated by Jesus that was truly multicultural at its core.

2

CULTURE AND IDENTITY

Frank M. Yamada and Leticia A. Guardiola-Sáenz

If there is one clear commonality between twenty-first-century readers of the Bible and the peoples of the biblical world, it is that each of us, like each of them, belongs to a culture and has an identity.[1] Of course, our contemporary cultures and identities also set us apart, in various ways, from the peoples of the Bible. How, then, can understanding culture and identity help us understand the biblical text, considering our sameness but without losing sight of our differences?

Our initial encounter with culture and the process of identity formation is subtle and imperceptible; it begins with our first breath. Our first interactions with those who care for us and with the environment we share with them give us our first appreciation of sameness and difference; we learn to reject or to accept certain differences in other people. Later, as we grow and pass through the stages of life, participating in new cultural spaces such as school, church, workplace, and community, we encounter other ways to value diversity, which can either affirm or challenge our earlier perceptions. Sadly, more often than not, we are socially trained to assimilate that which is similar to us and reject that which is different from us. What is similar and familiar appeals to our trust, but what is different and strange tends to trigger fear and suspicion in us. But as nations are becoming more and more culturally diverse because of immigration and political, social, and economic factors, the face of the world is changing and new identities and cultural spaces are emerging. With these changes we are offered an opportunity to gain a new appreciation for the richness of diversity.

Within this new social reality, understanding culture and the process of identity formation not only can give us new light to appreciate the social complexities of the biblical text; it can also help us realize how our own cultural diversity as readers affects the ways we read the Bible and live in a multicultural world.

Defining Culture

Culture is a word we commonly use but rarely define. Culture can be explained as the sum total of our everyday practices and "texts"—the ways we live everyday life, our behavior, beliefs, social interactions, and all human production, such as food, clothing, art, ideology, institutions, and, most importantly, language. Culture is the collective space where the meanings we produce are assimilated or resisted; it is the battleground where the ideologies of those in power are established or dissolved; it is the public and private terrain where we create our personal and social identities. Culture—with its values, points of view, and traditions—shapes the way we see life, understand the world, define ourselves, think, act, create community, relate to others, and express our sense of belonging to family, groups, and nations.

All the creation, expression, and transmission of culture and identity is only possible through the fundamental vehicle of language. Through language we create meaning to express ourselves, and because meaning can only be understood in context, language is intrinsically connected to culture. Through the acquisition of language we enter into a cultural dialogue already in progress as we go through a process of socialization.

Language is fundamental for cultural identity: it shapes our perception of reality, past and present. Our native languages express our identity and culture in ways that no foreign language can. Language is a maker of identity; when languages disappear, cultures die. Losing a native language means losing aspects of a culture and an identity. On the other hand, speaking other languages creates the opportunity for different or multiple identities as we immerse ourselves into other cultures. As a strategy of colonization, native languages were suppressed in order to undermine a native people's sense of nation, community, culture, and therefore identity. In some other instances, immigrants who arrive in a new country, or later generations of their offspring, have refused to speak their native language to avoid being identified with a certain group. This is a way of erasing an identity that is not equally valued in a new context.

With the help of technology, we have managed to increase our mobility in the world more than ever before. Now we find ourselves negotiating our identities in a new world where multiple cultures converge in neighboring spaces in most big cities. With an abundance of new cultural traits around us, we find ourselves constantly modifying our identities, looking for new ways to communicate with others in a changing world.

Identity Formation

Identity, or how we speak about ourselves, can be defined in different ways. The spectrum of definitions ranges from those that assign autonomy and power to the self—as a being not only in control of the process of self-definition but also capable of changing social structures—to those that barely recognize the existence of the individual. The latter definitions assert that the multiple external forces at play in the formation of our identities hardly give us any control over the ways we define ourselves, let alone any power to create change apart from what current social structures allow.

Identity formation is complex and not easily defined, but three main ideas are crucial in this process. First, identities are shaped by power relations; they are created in relation to outsiders (thus Western representations of the non-Western "other" in terms of ethnic identities are often seen as subordinated to the West). Second, identities are not unified; they are fragmented, ruptured, discontinuous, and contradictory. We are split among political allegiances; we have multiple identities that sometimes struggle within us. Third, identities are constantly in flux; they are always changing, not fixed products; they are productions in process.

By and large, although we could say that there are some genetic predispositions involved, the formation of identity is mostly a social process. Even identity markers such as ethnicity, skin color, gender, sexual orientation, or physical disabilities cannot really be said to affect our identity because of biological predispositions; rather, they are identity markers because of the cultural value we have assigned to such characteristics. Identity is formed within culture and in relation to those around us. We learn to become ourselves by observing others, mirroring behaviors, trying out new patterns of action, following in the steps of those we admire, or those we feel pressured to imitate. Our identity is formed in community, and therefore understanding others helps us understand ourselves.

Even before we can speak, the formation of our identity has already started. We come into a world that has a culture and a language with ready-made labels, names, and expectations that begin to shape our identity even without our knowledge. At first, our existence is automatically explained through those labels. Later on, once we have acquired language and a sense of the culture that surrounds us, we can escape some of those labels and choose others on our own. Our power to define who we are is limited, however, by language, a system already established by society before we participate in it.

Despite the sense of being trapped by language, identity is fluid and dynamic. It changes as we move in life and adopt new cultures, new ideologies, new beliefs, new languages. Identity is in constant motion, just as culture and language are, which in turn helps us create new and complex identities shaped by our cultural heritage, family, geography, religion, and social identity. Identity is a *process*. At any moment, identity is only a snapshot of a person who continues to grow, develop, and identify herself or himself in diverse ways. We are not born with an essence of identity within ourselves that we need to discover; identity is rather a social and public process linked to the personal and emotional ways we define ourselves at different conscious and unconscious levels.

The construction of our identity is not an abstract process in a vacuum; it is historically grounded in culture and involves a lot of emotions and feelings. For many it can be traumatic as we move from childhood to adulthood, if we do not find the support to be ourselves in the face of stressful or even harmful social and cultural expectations. Our identities are also grounded in larger histories. Just as our nations are characterized geographically by specific terrains shaped by natural forces over time—mountains, rivers, deserts, and plains—so our identities are affected by government, religious, educational, and other cultural institutions that have been shaped by the sweep of history.

Culture, Identity, and the Bible

As complex as it may sound, we all experience culture and identity in our daily lives, and it is through these social realities that we learn to understand the world that surrounds us. As we read the Bible, we should keep in mind that although we may find some stories very familiar because of our experiences in life, it is still important to ponder the stories in their own cultural context before translating their message into our own. Just because we find a point of correlation between a biblical story and our own lives does not mean that we can ignore the temporal and cultural gap between us and the Bible. Some of the most oppressive readings of the Bible arise, for example, when we lose track of the liberating message of a text and seek instead to reproduce the cultural settings of the text—trying, say, to reproduce the social mores of the first-century church in a twenty-first-century context.

As we explore aspects of culture and identity in the Bible, we should also keep in mind that just as we are constantly negotiating our identity in complex cultural settings, the people of the Bible were also negotiating their own identities in the midst of different cultures. In the First Testament we see the Hebrews forming a new identity as the people of God in the midst of a hostile environment, surrounded by cities and nations with different and often opposing cultures and customs. Later we see a similar struggle in the Second Testament when those who believed in Jesus were called to adopt a new identity in the midst of political, cultural, and religious opposition. In both cases, the process of identity formation as people of God became a constant struggle as men and women seemed at times to adopt the identity of those around them as a strategy of survival, and at other times to strive to establish a clearly different identity that distinguished them from their neighbors—even when that might have implied oppression, violence, and death.

Culture and Identity in the Bible

Most discussions among biblical scholars about cultural identity focus on the issue of ethnicity. For example, scholars tend to understand Israelite identity in relationship to Israel's emergence and history as a nation—from a confederation of tribes to a monarchy, from a divided monarchy to Assyrian and

Babylonian deportations, from exile to repatriating peoples in the province of Yehud (Judah). In contemporary North America, especially in the United States, while ethnicity also plays an important role for cultural groups, the issue of race is one of the key identifying marks of cultural identity, especially for people of color. "Race" usually refers to particular physical traits (for example, skin color) around which groups understand a common culture. However, the division of peoples into racial categories is arbitrary, varying from one Western society to another and having no basis in human genetics. The practice developed among the pioneers of the social sciences in the West and had racist underpinnings and assumptions. In spite of this history, African Americans, Latina/o Americans, and Asian Americans have continued to use these racial designations strategically to build community and to obtain a collective political and social voice.

Contemporary understandings of racial identity are not used as prominently in the Bible to mark identity as are ethnicity or religion. Historically, "ethnicity" tends to refer to issues of identity that are related to the identity of a people or a nation. In biblical terminology, the Greek word *ethnos*, from which we derive the word *ethnicity*, refers to a people or a nation (although in the New Testament the NRSV consistently translates the plural *ethnē* as "Gentiles"). In early Judaism, and in the New Testament (where early Christians of whatever ancestry often considered themselves to be in continuity with Judaism), other "peoples" or "nations" fell under the generic collective term *ethnē*.

The writers of the Hebrew Bible assumed that their place in and perspective of the world was normative for all humankind. The contemporary reader of the biblical text must recognize, however, that the Hebrew Bible is told from the perspective of a small, colonized group of peoples who lived in successive generations in the land first called Canaan. Most of these writings were compiled in the sixth and fifth centuries BCE, though some books, sources, and texts were written earlier in Israel's history. Moreover, most of the biblical authors wrote from the perspective of the Southern Kingdom of Judah (928–586 BCE), which had its capital in Jerusalem. Northern traditions are still present in a significant way, but the point of view is heavily skewed toward that of the Southern Kingdom. All these factors influence the way that a people understood its identity as Israel and how Israel came to be represented in relation to other peoples in the biblical text.

National identity, or ethnicity, certainly plays a large role in Israel's self-understanding. Israelite traditions show an awareness of different national identities within Canaan and beyond, represented in the various nation lists that appear in biblical narrative and law (Genesis 10; Deuteronomy 7:1) and in oracles against the nations within prophetic materials (Jeremiah 46–51; Amos 1–2). As far as the biblical text indicates, Israelite cultural identity tends to understand itself as fundamentally different from these foreign "others." Hence, in Deuteronomy 7, part of what makes Israel a chosen nation before its God is its religious and cultural distinctiveness from the surrounding peoples. Israelites are not to worship as those other peoples do, nor are they to make covenants with them or intermarry with them (see Deuteronomy 7:1-6). Thus the people are called to be holy, that is, separate or set apart to their God. This language of religious and cultural distinctiveness must be understood in light of Israel's status as a small nation in the shadow of great empires. Archaeologists and biblical scholars now recognize that the cultural artifacts and religious traditions of earliest Israel were actually very consistent with the traditions from surrounding Canaanite society. In fact, on the basis of its similarity in material culture, many scholars now hold that early Israel was ethnically indistinguishable from the Canaanites. They further contend that the sharp differentiation that later biblical writers, living under the aegis of the Persian Empire, sought to maintain between Israelite and "Canaanite" is not as much related to an actual ethnic difference between their ancestors and the people of Canaan as it is a cultural, social, or religious construction serving particular purposes in the sixth and fifth centuries BCE. We can certainly understand the perceived need for constructing such a difference. When small groups or peoples feel the impact of larger empires (such as the Egyptian, Assyrian, Babylonian, or Persian empires), the need for cultural identity and particularity increases. Thus, in the Hebrew Bible we see ancient Israel constructing its self-understanding as religiously and culturally unique: they are a chosen people who are in a special relationship to their God.

Within the New Testament, the language of cultural specificity and religious uniqueness takes on a similar tone. Even though some early Christians saw their missionary activity as being inclusive of the whole world (Matthew 28:19; Acts 1:8), cultural identity in early Christian groups was often maintained by dividing the world into two parts—God's chosen people (the elect, understood as the church) and outsiders, who are often described as the "other" nations (the "Gentiles"). While the early apostolic communities sought to join Jews and non-Jews together in the circle of those who were considered chosen (a process that plays out in different ways through the letters of Paul and the book of Acts), that very distinction shows that the cultural assumptions of Roman-era Judaism remained strong among these communities. We see in Paul's letters the concern to establish a new identity for non-Jewish believers that is neither Jewish nor "Gentile" (see, for example, 1 Corinthians 5:1, where the NRSV translates *ethnesin* as "pagans"). When later New Testament writings begin to speak of Jews (or "Judeans"; in Greek, *Ioudaioi*) as the "other," scholars see evidence that the composition of the early Christian movement shifted decisively from a Jewish to a non-Jewish majority, probably soon after the fall of Jerusalem in 70 CE. The reader of biblical material must remember that, similar to what we find in the Hebrew Bible, the New Testament writings represent the perspectives of small groups of people living under an imperial authority (so the traditions

of Jesus' birth are set within an environment of Roman oc-
cupation: Matthew 2; Luke 2:1-2). Even though the Christian
church was later accepted by the Roman emperor Constan-
tine, the New Testament writings show a more conflicted relationship between early Christian identity and empire. But
the drive to establish group identity by distinguishing insid-
ers from outsiders, whether those outsiders are "Gentiles" or
Jews, may be understood as different responses to the pressures of an imperial culture.

Culture and Identity of Readers

It is well beyond the scope of this essay to address the multiplicity of contemporary readers and the cultural contexts in which
they seek to find meaning in the Bible. However, one of the
important features of *The Peoples' Bible* is that it represents
a shift in the way scholars approach the biblical writings. Indeed, in recent decades, scholars of both the Hebrew Bible and
New Testament have increasingly recognized the importance
of identifying the cultural and social location of readers in a
more disciplined and concrete way. For most of the nineteenth
and twentieth centuries, a method of investigation known as
historical criticism had been the dominant mode of scholarly
exploration of the biblical text. In its basic form, historical
criticism, which emerged in Europe among other intellectual
developments in the Enlightenment, believed that contemporary readers must set aside their own self-understanding in order to examine the historical contexts of the biblical authors
and readers. In this way, historical critics understood that
contemporary readers' biases could substantially influence the
ways they read the text. Hence, historical critics recognized
the importance—and in their minds the potential danger—of
people reading their own self-interest into the Bible.

What historical critics often failed to recognize, however,
was that their own ways of reading were not universal principles through which the biblical text became evidently clear

to all peoples of the world. Historical criticism itself is a culturally contextualized approach to the biblical text—one that is heavily shaped within the context of post-Enlightenment Europe, especially Germany. It served the purpose of helping biblical scholars to be objective in their approach to the biblical text. This objectivity had at least two functions. First, similar to broader trends within theology, biblical criticism was seeking to define itself as a legitimate form of "scientific" inquiry (in German, *Wissenschaft*). Within this methodology, objectivity became an important value in presenting biblical criticism as a legitimate form of knowledge within European intellectual life. Second, biblical scholarship during this time sought to distance itself from the traditional and confessional interpretations that emerged from faith traditions. Hence, objective, disinterested inquiry was championed as a way to create a safeguard against interpretations of the Bible that sought to reinforce the positions of the church in an age of increased secularization.

During the last third of the twentieth century, which saw the emergence of racial and cultural identities following the Civil Rights era, biblical scholars and theologians began to understand the vitality and importance of new perspectives from African Americans, Latinas/os, Asian Americans, Native Americans, and many other historically marginalized groups. In his important essay "Toward a Hermeneutics of the Diaspora: A Hermeneutics of Otherness and Engagement" (1995), Fernando Segovia argued that biblical scholarship must take seriously the "real reader" of the Bible. Segovia's argument represents a larger trend in biblical scholarship that moves beyond historical criticism's objective reader and fully engages the social and cultural location of real readers with the same disciplined rigor that has been a hallmark of biblical scholarship from its inception. This shift highlights the important role that a reader's cultural context plays in generating meaning in relation to the biblical material. Hence, within culturally contextual biblical interpretation, scholars and readers find importance not only in the cultures of ancient Israel, Judaism, and early Christianity, but they also highlight the significant contributions of people of color to the interpretation of the biblical text. All interpreters, regardless of their social location, benefit from the powerful interpretative insights of African Americans and Latin American liberation theologians in their expositions of the exodus and liberation narratives of the Hebrew Bible. Native American and Palestinian perspectives on the conquest narratives, in which readers often find themselves sympathizing with invaded Canaanites, help all of us to understand the problematic side of the language of chosenness that is so prevalent in both the First and Second Testaments. Asian American interpretations of the Ruth and Esther stories help all of us to see the various cultural nuances and conflicting responses that happen when a group seeks to establish their identity in a dominant culture that sees them only as foreign others.

Culture and Identity in Our Reading of the Bible

Culture, whether it is understood through identity markers such as race, ethnicity, class, gender, or sexual orientation, affects the way we understand the biblical text. But this does not lead us toward a negative understanding of Babel—the confusion of too many tongues all speaking different languages. Rather, this great polyphony of different cultural voices challenges the assumption that one can learn only through the limited experience of voices similar to one's own. Within all of the great religions of the world that assume some form of god or gods, we find a common theme: human beings do not learn from what is similar to them but from what is different. Within the Bible, people of faith also maintain that humans have a great capacity to be transformed when they come in contact with the holy Other, whose desire it is to dwell among human beings. What goes for human interactions with the divine holds true as well for human-to-human interactions. We learn from difference. We can be mutually transformed as we listen attentively to our very different understandings of the God that we may encounter in and through the biblical text.

As we read the Bible, let us keep in mind that culture shapes our faith and how we read. Since meaning is bound to context, there is no single general understanding of the Bible that will be valid for everyone; understanding is always particularized, modified by our context. Cultural diversity is an integral part of who we are. Learning to appreciate its richness can help us overcome our biases, our racism, and our discrimination, so that we can see our interdependency with others. We are formed in light of others who have preceded us. Devaluing or seeking to destroy cultural diversity hinders and limits our understanding of the world and of the Word. Valuing diversity and the richness that it brings makes us stronger as a people and allows us to discover and respect the otherness in ourselves as well.

Addendum by Curtiss Paul DeYoung

Frank M. Yamada and Leticia A. Guardiola-Sáenz speak wonderfully of the richness of cultural diversity for biblical interpretation. A fuller understanding of the modern relevance of the ancient mysteries of God is gained when the Bible is interpreted by people living in different social settings, with wide ranges of cultural experiences. Certain aspects of the biblical story invariably will have greater meaning in particular social, historical, and cultural settings. James Earl Massey describes this effect:

> Despite a common confession as Christians, members of communities that have experienced oppression or marginalization read the Bible from a different perspective, always wary of so-called objective approaches and interpretations that are insensitive to human need and problems resulting from exploitation of others. Communities that have a remembered history of

injustices perpetrated against them by the dominant society do not find meaning, identity, or affirmation in "mainstream biblical interpretations" that overlook or disregard their social location.[2]

When one cultural interpretation dominates, it also restricts our ability to understand the multiple dimensions of truth contained in Scripture. Without the diverse perspectives of God's rainbow of humanity, we cannot grasp the true universalism of the biblical story. We may not be able to understand certain aspects of the biblical story because we lack the necessary points of reference. We may miss the nuances that someone else can see clearly because his or her life experience is more closely aligned with that of the story being examined. Perhaps a culture or society's "historical experience . . . can identify better with the content of the Bible."[3] We really do need diverse perspectives to gain holistic understandings.

Impact of Culture on Rules of Interpretation

When seeking to understand the Bible from cultural perspectives other than our own, it is important to note that our cultural and social settings shape the rules or methods we use for interpretation.[4] What we bring to the text from our culture, economic status, race, denomination, gender, theological assumptions, faith experience, and other markers of our identity are often taken for granted and not challenged or even acknowledged. When we begin to examine the Scripture from other social locations, we must learn to recognize our tacit, self-serving rules of interpretation and set them aside, at least temporarily, so that we can become familiar with the approaches used by others. In order to gain a greater appreciation for how culture shapes the rules of interpretation, we will observe two examples: the perspective of Latin American women (Latinas) for interpretation as defined by Elsa Tamez[5] and some rules for interpretation in an Asian context as suggested by Stanley Samartha.[6]

For Elsa Tamez, rereading the Bible from the perspective of Latin American women is necessary because of the way the Bible has been used to limit the opportunities of Latinas. She writes, "In truth, the problem would not be serious if everybody considered the Bible for what it is: a testimony of a Judeo-Christian people with a particular culture, for whom holy revelation works always in favor of those who have least."[7] Reading the Scriptures from the perspective of Latinas, according to Tamez, requires the interpreter to first gain distance from the text. This means reading the Bible as though one has never read it before. This is difficult because we often accept traditional interpretations of texts. Yet one must attempt to read without referencing these understandings. After removing the traditional understandings, one needs to come closer to the text by reading with the eyes of life experience. "This is the process of coming closer to daily life, which implies the experiences of pain, joy, hope, hunger, celebration, and struggle," states Tamez. "In Latin America the Bible is not read as an intellectual or academic exercise; it is read with the goal of giving meaning to our lives today."[8] This gives the interpretative task a sense of urgency and a need for relevance.

Latinas read the Bible with the poor as a point of departure, because this is where most find themselves. Elsa Tamez writes, "In a context of misery, malnutrition, repression, torture, Indian genocide, and war—in other words, in a context of death—there is no greater priority than framing and articulating the readings according to these situations."[9] A majority of the world's people find themselves in this context. This is particularly true for the women of the world. As the Bible is read from the perspective of the poor, it gains greater power for this majority of the world's people. The entire Bible is read with the eyes of women, with a feminist consciousness. Yet this way of reading the Scriptures is not limited to women. Tamez believes that men can learn to read the Bible in a way that can perceive the viewpoint of women in the Bible and women today. Since biblical interpretation has traditionally been done by men, most women have the ability to view the Bible from a male vantage point. Unless men attempt to read the Bible with the eyes of women, they will not have a balanced understanding of Scripture. Elsa Tamez believes that the deepest longings of Latin American women are touched as their reading of the Bible intersects with their experiences as women whose daily lives are familiar with struggle.

Like Tamez, Stanley J. Samartha is committed to discovering rules of biblical interpretation that make sense in his setting. He states:

> Every time a Biblical scholar in Europe sneezes, theologians in Asia should not catch a cold and manifest the symptoms all over the footnotes! To depend on rules of interpretation developed in countries alien to Asian life is a hindrance to the Church's growth in maturity. It reduces our credibility, diminishes our spirit, and distorts the universality of Jesus Christ to whom the scriptures bear witness.[10]

Samartha notes that the countries of Asia have much longer traditions of indigenous religions (Hinduism, Buddhism, Taoism, and Confucianism) with their own well-loved scriptures. Therefore, biblical interpretation needs to be done in an atmosphere of respect for and willingness to dialogue with other religious traditions.

It must be acknowledged that people in Asia have been sustained by these other religions for thousands of years. Tissa Balasuriya adds, "As an Asian I cannot accept as divine and true any teaching which begins with the presupposition that all of my ancestors for innumerable generations are eternally damned by God unless they had been baptized in or were related to one of the Christian institutional churches."[11] The multiple faith traditions of the East create a very different interpretive challenge from that in the Judeo-Christian West. Because Christianity is a newcomer religion among some of the most ancient religions, Asian interpreters "try to take Jesus out of the study into the dusty streets of Asia and let him mingle with other seers and savior figures."[12]

This difference of approach required in the East can be further observed when speaking about the authority of the Bible. In the West, it is not unusual to hear a preacher exclaim, "The Bible says," to underscore her or his point. An emphasis on the "authority" of the Bible is not always helpful for biblical interpretation in Asia because of the many other competing "authoritative" scriptures. Samartha says that the Bible "must *become* authoritative to us in our life as we grapple with our problems today."[13] An understanding of a biblical text comes as one responds in faith to the God to whom the biblical text points. Kwok Pui Lan supports Samartha's contention: "For most Chinese, the truth claim of the Bible cannot be based on its being the supposed revealed Word of God, for 99 percent of the people do not believe in this faith statement. They can only judge the meaningfulness of the biblical tradition by looking at how it is acted out in the Christian community."[14] In other words, the Bible has authority in direct proportion to how Christians live the faith proclaimed in its pages.

The rules of biblical interpretation will differ, sometimes radically, from culture to culture.[15] So the greater the number of perspectives we take into account on a scriptural passage or theological concept, the stronger our interpretation. Examining the various methods used for interpreting the Bible around the world helps us acquire the tools necessary for developing a framework for multicultural understandings of Scripture.

The Effect of Traditional Spirituality on Biblical Interpretation

The rules of interpretation that emerge within a particular culture greatly affect the insights that can be gained in Bible study. Sometimes these viewpoints come from traditional understandings of God and humanity within a culture and provide new perspectives on the Bible. We must respect and seek to understand indigenous forms of spirituality. The effect of the spirituality of a cultural context on the way the Bible is interpreted can be observed in the context of Native America. George Tinker contends that the Native American beliefs that God is revealed in place or space, the Creator is in relationship with the created, and the created are in relationship with each other affect biblical interpretation.[16]

Tinker states that a Native American understanding of God is that "God reveals God's self in creation, in space or place and not in time."[17] This idea that God is revealed in space or place is radically different from the Western linear concept of history. Western spirituality is about periods of time and historic events. Traditional Native American as well as Asian and African spirituality is concerned with sacred experiences, holy places, and a faith lived in community. Tinker explains that "personal transformation is not the goal of Native ethic religion; one feels called not to transcend one's natural humanity, but to live it, and live it in the context of a particular community and that community's particular geography."[18] This emphasis on the spirituality of "place" explains why many Native Americans are traumatized when they are forced to leave the land their families have lived on for centuries or watch as their burial places are desecrated. For native peoples, "at the core of their self-understanding [is] the sense of having been created in kinship with the land."[19] These are the lands where they and their forefathers and foremothers met God.

According to Tinker, the effect on biblical interpretation of this way of thinking can be observed in Jesus' teaching on the kingdom of God. The first question asked by the Western approach to Scripture is, "When?" The first question asked by the Native American approach to the Bible is, "Where?" The question of when is answered in Jesus' statement that "the time is fulfilled, and the kingdom of God has come near; repent, and believe in the good news" (Mark 1:15). The question of where is answered in Jesus' statement that "the kingdom of God is not coming with things that can be observed; nor will they say, 'Look, here it is!' or 'There it is!' For, in fact, the kingdom of God is among you" (Luke 17:20-21).[20] Which question we ask determines which passage is emphasized in our faith understanding. A multicultural approach would ask both questions and thereby gain a fuller understanding of the kingdom of God. As we have just seen, Jesus answered both questions.

The traditional understanding of God as Creator affects one's perspective on God's relationship with the created. Tinker writes, "Each Native American tribal community in North America had a relationship with God as Creator that was healthy and responsible long before they knew of or confessed the gospel of Jesus Christ."[21] He further states that "this relationship began with the recognition of the Other as Creator, the creative force behind all things that exist, and long predated the coming of the missionaries."[22] According to Tinker, then, Jesus' call to repentance (*metanoia*) in Mark 1:15 is a call to return to one's relationship with God the Creator rather than a call to change one's mind. To repent is "to return to the ideal relationship between Creator and created."[23]

Not only are we to be in relationship with the Creator, according to Tinker, but we are to be in relationship with others in God's creation. The Lakota and Dakota peoples of North America pray *mitakuye oyasin* ("for all my relatives").[24] Relatives include all of creation. Homer Noley writes, "Among Native American concepts, humankind is seen as a part of the continuum of spiritual existence which involves all of Creation."[25] This is represented in many Native American tribes by a circle. "The Native American concern for starting theology with Creation is a need to acknowledge the goodness and inherent worth of all of God's creatures," George Tinker explains. "We experience evil or sin as a disruption in that delicate balance, which negates the intrinsic worth of any of our relatives."[26]

George Tinker and Steve Charleston write of an "Old Testament" of Native America.[27] Regarding spirituality of Native American people, Charleston writes:

> They have their own original covenant relationship with the Creator and their own original understanding of God prior to the birth of Christ. It is a tradition that has evolved over centuries. It tells of the active, living, revealing presence of God in relation to Native People through generations of Native life and experience. It asserts that God was not an absentee landlord for North America. God was here, on this continent among this people, in covenant, in relation, in life. Like Israel itself, Native America proclaims that God is a God of all times and of all places and of all peoples.[28]

George Tinker warns that when the Hebrew Bible is imposed on Native Americans, it has two "dysfunctional" effects: "First, it functions to proscribe (explicitly or implicitly) the validity of Native American traditions. Second, it inherently prescribes replacing one's own history with someone else's history as a prerequisite for conversion."[29] Steve Charleston contends that the biblical interpreter who is from a setting with a traditional form of spirituality in the culture needs to include the Hebrew Bible while working with that traditional spirituality and the New Testament in developing understandings of God.[30] The Hebrew Bible is important for understanding the history and spirituality of the people into which Jesus of Nazareth was born. "There was much in the memory of Israel that Jesus confirmed; there was also a great deal that he sought to correct. The same applies to the Old Testament memory of Native America. There is much that the Christ confirms and much that stands corrected," states Charleston.[31]

Ancient cultural traditions, the "old testament" of indigenous cultures, can pave the way for the New Testament message of Jesus. The preexisting understanding of a Creator God revealed in space or place in Native American spirituality and culture allowed for fresh insights in biblical interpretation when Native Americans encountered the Bible. These unique cultural perspectives are not only of value for persons from the particular culture; they offer new approaches and insights for all who seek biblical truth. Cultural and spiritual categories that exist in the Old Testament of Native America and in present-day settings in Native America help us develop tools for biblical interpretation. While it may be difficult for some, Charleston asserts that "as Christians, we're going to have to make some elbow room at the table for other 'old testaments.' Not only from Native America, but from Africa, Asia, and Latin America as well."[32]

3

JESUS CHRIST: CULTURALLY HUMAN, INCLUSIVELY DIVINE

If we are asked to close our eyes and imagine what God looks like, we often visualize the Almighty as being from a particular culture or ethnicity. Sometimes this mental image of God corresponds to our own race and culture. For some, visualizing God as from their culture and ethnicity strengthens their ability to relate to God in the vertical dimension through prayer. But an exclusive image of the Divine weakens the possibility of experiencing God in the horizontal dimension through one's relationships with others. A monocultural image of God develops from a faulty understanding of the biblical teaching that humans are created in the image of God. A theological reversal occurs that reasons, *If I am created in the image of God, then God must look like me.* Instead of seeing themselves as being created in the image of God, some have tried to create God in their own image.

This reversal becomes even more problematic when the group that is in power creates God in its own cultural and ethnic image and then imposes that image of God on others. It could be argued that the United States was founded on the premise that God is a white male. When the United States Constitution was written with the words "We the people," the "we" referred to white men. Only white men could vote; no women or people of color were included in that "we." When the idea that God is male and white was accepted, women and people of color were not only left out but were treated with contempt because they were not created in the image of God. Degrading and harassing women and dehumanizing and humiliating people of color were considered permissible because God was perceived as being a white male. Women and people who were not "white" functioned in society in a role that relegated them to a less-than-human status.

The genocide of indigenous people and the enslavement of Africans were based on the contention that Native Americans and Africans were not really human in the fullest sense of the word. Enslaved Africans were even designated as three-fifths of a human being in the United States Constitution. Someone who was not fully human could be brutalized without engendering guilt. Society gave whites permission to torture, rape, and kill people of color because, according to the Constitution, they were only three-fifths human. They were not created in the image of the white male God. While the more blatant forms of expression have been reduced, this thought process can be found in the deeper realms of our consciousness. The image of a white male God still shapes attitudes and inhibits one's ability to interact with people who appear different from us. A distorted image of God not only hurts the person who is being marginalized by the image; it also affects the person who benefits from the image. Feeling "superior" or "chosen" because of one's whiteness or maleness causes a spiritual and psychological isolation from the rest of the family of God.

One way to address this concern about the whiteness of the image of God is to accept the perspective of Albert Cleage, who in the 1970s said: "If God created man in his own image, then we must look at man to see what God looks like. There are black men, there are yellow men, there are red men and there are a few, a mighty few, white men in the world. If God created man in his own image, then God must be some combination of this black, red, yellow and white. . . . In America, one drop of black blood makes you a black. So by American law, God is black."[1]

Cleage's statement, perhaps shocking to some, moves us in the right direction. If all of humanity is created in the image of God, then God's image includes all ethnicities, races, and cultures, both genders, and so on. If we were to ask what color or what culture God is, our answer must be that God is multicolored or multicultural. God's signature, the rainbow, symbolizes the biblical teaching that God's image embraces all of humanity.

Yet the image of a white God and the idea that Christianity is a religion for white people remains pervasive in many parts of this world. This is directly linked to the reality that for hundreds of years the dominant image of Jesus around the world has been a white male. The most effective way of projecting an image of God in Christianity is through the use of images of Jesus in art and more recently in the media. William Mosley writes, "Art, then, functions as a kind of visual preaching, frequently with the express purpose giving concrete form to abstract or theological notions."[2] What image or picture do we visualize in our minds of the historical Jesus? Perhaps we have a mental image of one of the previous centuries' many famous paintings of Jesus that portrays him as a white European. A discussion of the race and culture of the historical Jesus is important, because images of Jesus ultimately affect our view of God and, therefore, our perception of who is created in the image of God.

The Racial and Cultural Identity of Jesus of Nazareth

We can all agree that Jesus of Nazareth, while living on this earth as a human being, had a particular "ethnic" look and lived his life as a cultural being. The Jesus of history was culturally exclusive in his human existence. Since Jesus has been cast in a white image, it is important to discover if this is an accurate portrayal of the race and culture of the historical Jesus. We must consider whether Jesus would share the Afro-Asiatic heritage of the Hebrew people. This problem could easily be solved if we had a portrait of Jesus dating back to the time that he spent on earth or descriptions from people who saw Jesus in the flesh. We have no such paintings or even written descriptions of the physical appearance of Jesus in his human form dating back to the first century.

The only physical description of Jesus in the New Testament is found in the vision of John on the island of Patmos, as recorded in the book of Revelation. In recounting the vision, John uses symbolic language to describe the resurrected and glorified Christ. Considering the tradition that John of Patmos had been among the Twelve who had seen Jesus in the flesh or the alternate possibility that the author was a disciple of someone else who had seen Jesus in the flesh, certain aspects of the description could be based on historical fact. John described Jesus Christ this way: "His head and his hair were white as white wool, white as snow; his eyes were like a flame of fire, his feet were like burnished bronze, refined as in a furnace, and his voice was like the sound of many waters" (Revelation 1:14-15). The vision describes a person with coarse white hair and reddish brown (burnished bronze) skin. The glorified Christ, as described by John, certainly did not appear in the vision as a white European.[3]

In Matthew 2 the writer records an event in the life of Jesus that sheds some light on the physical appearance of Jesus and his family. Joseph, Mary, and the infant Jesus fled Palestine into Egypt to escape the death threats of Herod. The purpose for traveling to the continent of Africa was to hide from Herod's soldiers. For Jesus and his family to blend in with African people, their appearance must have been quite similar to that of the people living in Egypt at that time. Jesus and his family would not have easily hidden in Africa if their skin color was white and they bore features found in Northern Europe.[4]

Along with most other Jews of Palestinian Hebrew ancestry, Jesus no doubt had a distinct Asian-ness and African-ness about his culture and probably his physical features. Jesus also had Hamitic (African) ancestors. Three women from the line of Ham were included in his genealogy: Tamar, Rahab, and Bathsheba (Matthew 1:1-16).[5] Although this information comes from the genealogy of Joseph (Jesus' earthly adoptive father), Jesus' mother was also a descendant of David and would have shared Tamar and Rahab as ancestors, if not also Bathsheba.[6] When the angel Gabriel was explaining to Mary how she as a virgin was going to become pregnant, he referred to David as an "ancestor" of Jesus (Luke 1:32). Therefore Mary must be of the line of David, since the angel was explaining to her how she would be the only human parent. Throughout the Gospels, Jesus is presented as a son of David. We can only reconfirm our earlier contention that Jesus, like other Jews in Palestine who had descended from the Hebrew people, was Afro-Asiatic. He had a multicultural and multiracial ancestry.[7] In the United States the historical Jesus would presently be called a person of color. Given his African heritage, he might be considered black.

How Did Jesus Become a White European?

Given that Jesus was an Afro-Asiatic Jew, how did his image become white? The process that painted Jesus white is a critical issue. Why was the image of the historic Jesus of Nazareth, born in Palestine to a people at the crossroads of Asia and Africa, transformed into a geographically distant one? The earliest representations of Jesus do not even include human characteristics. They were symbols, such as a fish or a lamb.[8] The first images of Jesus in human form were of a young "good shepherd," often with a Roman look. These first appeared in the third century in the Roman catacombs.[9] Eventually adult representations of Jesus began to appear. The earlier ones pictured Jesus with "an Oriental cast" and "a brown complexion."[10]

Soon European artists were attempting to develop images of Jesus Christ that were culturally appropriate for their settings. The Byzantine artists in the fourth century created a white image of Jesus with a beard and his hair parted down the middle. This likeness became the standard.[11] Also in the fourth century, a letter circulated claiming to be written in the first century by Publius Lentulus, a friend of Pilate. The letter, later determined to be a fourth-century forgery, described Jesus as follows: "His hair is the colour of wine [probably meaning yellow] and golden at the root—straight and without lustre—but from the level of the ears curling and glossy, and divided down the centre after the fashion of the Nazarenes [Nazarites]. . . . His beard is full, of the same colour as His hair, and forked in form: His eyes blue extremely brilliant."[12]

Europe, like other regions, developed culturally appropriate representations of Christ. But why did Europe's culturally appropriate Christ become cast in stone as the dominant image of the historical Jesus? It would seem that Jesus was permanently cast in a white image to support European colonial expansion and the capture and enslavement of black Africans. A white Jesus served the purpose of being God's stamp of approval on the actions of white people. Such an image was also useful for demonstrating that white people were superior to people of color by virtue of the whiteness of Jesus. The propagation of white images of Jesus continues even into our own time through media portrayals in movies and television, as well as in the pictures of nearly every Bible produced for use around the world.[13]

A culturally appropriate image of Jesus for Europeans was co-opted by the ruling class to serve its pursuit of power and economic gain. The white image Jesus is a product of Europe that was exported to the rest of the world to facilitate the domination of people of color. The white image of Jesus has been a powerful tool for undergirding European colonialism, enslavement of Africans, genocide of indigenous peoples, and white racial superiority. Otherwise, Jesus Christ would have been presented in racially and ethnically appropriate ways in other cultures. Missionaries from Europe would have discarded the Western images of Jesus upon arrival in Africa, the Americas, Asia, and the islands of the great oceans. With the help of the indigenous people, new images of Jesus Christ would have been shaped that spoke powerfully to the people encountered.

The Effects of a White Jesus

The effects of a Western white Jesus on people of color have been far-reaching. A white depiction of Jesus prevented images that were culturally appropriate from appearing. In contexts outside of Europe, the whiteness of the image made Jesus seem like a foreigner or a stranger. In describing the image of Jesus that was presented in Latin America by Spanish colonizers, J. A. Mackay spoke of this Jesus as an impostor. The real Jesus Christ "sojourned westward, went to prison in Spain, while another who took his name embarked with the Spanish crusaders for the New World."[14]

The extreme foolishness of using white and Western images of Jesus can be further illustrated by the comments of R. S. Sugirtharajah, who writes that "when Jesus made his belated second visit to the eastern part of Asia, he did not come as a Galilean sage . . . he came as an alien in his own home territory."[15] The image of the historical Jesus would have been culturally appropriate for Asia, but the Asian-ness of Jesus had been stripped away so successfully that he appeared as a stranger even in Asia. When Jesus comes as a stranger or an alien, we lose the significance of the incarnate Jesus who came as Emmanuel, "God with us."

Nowhere has the "strangeness" of a white Jesus been more dramatic than in Mexico and much of Latin America. The effect was the emergence of the image of Mary as the dominant symbol of faith and, in a sense, a replacement for Jesus. In 1531 the Virgin (Mary) of Guadalupe appeared near Mexico City "to an Indian convert named Juan Diego. And she appeared as a young, brown-skinned Aztec woman who spoke Nahuatl, the language of the conquered Aztecs."[16] Because they could not embrace the white Jesus brought by the conquerors, when Mary appeared as a brown-skinned Aztec, religious revival broke loose with "a spontaneous explosion of pilgrimages, festivals; and conversions to the religion of the Virgin."[17] Aaron Gallegos writes that "until Our Lady of Guadalupe appeared in 1531, there were very few Mexicas who converted to Christianity, as opposed to the eight million who did so in the next seven years."[18] A culturally inappropriate white image of Jesus produced an image of Mary as "la Morenita ('the brown Lady')."[19]

Virgilio Elizondo believes that this image of a Mary who was indigenous to Mexico synthesized Spanish Catholicism and the face of the indigenous people "into a single, coherent symbolimage."[20] He further states: "The cultural clash of sixteenth-century Spain and Mexico was resolved and reconciled in the brown Lady of Guadalupe. In her the new mestizo people finds its meaning, its uniqueness, its unity. Guadalupe is the key to understanding the Christianity of the New World, the self-image of Mexicans, of Mexican-Americans, and of all Latin Americans."[21] Elizondo makes the case that the most powerful image for Christian faith in Latin America is Mary rather than Jesus. The brown Mary became the doorway to faith in God because Jesus was presented in the white image of the oppressors.

A white Jesus has not only seemed foreign; he has often been perceived as the enemy by people who encounter the message of Christianity. Sometimes this white image of Jesus has been used to signify that God was on the side of those who were conquering or enslaving people of color. "When Western Christians brought Jesus to Asia, many also brought with them opium and guns," writes Chung Hyun Kyung. "They taught Asians the love of Jesus while they gave Asians the slow death of opium or the fast death of a bullet."[22] If the Jesus of the oppressor appears to endorse your domination or your death, he hardly seems like your savior.

The impact of portraying Jesus as one who sides with the oppressor intensified because he looked like the enemy. The fact that this Jesus' white skin contrasted with the darker skin of those who were being oppressed has had a dramatic effect. Many of the young African American activists of the 1960s and 1970s "loathed the Christ who supported the ravage of Africa, fostered the bondage of Black people, stood silently by during the rapes of Black women, and shamed Black people by his 'pigmentation so obviously not [their] own.'"[23] The white Jesus became identified with the white racist. The biblical Jesus of love was transformed into the enemy and despised by those who experienced the brutality of their oppressors. Mosley comments on this effect, saying that "for a Black person to love the White version of God is to hate self (Black self) because in Western color symbolism white and black connote polar opposites."[24]

When Jesus appeared in contexts outside of Europe, he seemed a captive of the West. People failed to understand Jesus as separate from those who brought him from Europe. Christian faith and Western culture appeared to be synonymous. This remains a difficult legacy for Christians outside of Western contexts as they try to interpret the message of Jesus for their setting. Efoe Julien Penoukou writes, "Even today, many African Christians continue to think that the West has delivered Christ to them bound hand and foot."[25]

Not only has a white image of Jesus made Christianity seem like a captive of the West, it has subtly given the impression

that European and Euro-American ways of thinking and acting are normative for Christianity. Kosuke Koyama writes:

> Languages, such as Spanish, French, English and German, are
> center languages in this Christian enterprise [and] these "center-
> theologies" (of the "blond Jesus") are irrelevant to the world
> outside of the West, and most likely to the West itself. Even to-
> day most of the world's Christians, including their theologians,
> believe that somehow Jesus Christ is more present in America
> than in Bangladesh, and therefore, America is the center and
> Bangladesh is a periphery. By thus thinking, they unwittingly
> entertain the idea that . . . America is the standard for all.[26]

Any attempt to understand the message of Jesus Christ outside of the realm of Western thought is somehow considered
not normative and therefore inferior or an exception to the
rule. This demeans other forms of Christianity, including the
ancient rites of the Orthodox and Coptic churches.

The white image of Jesus also reduced the Christian faith's
ability to proclaim a message of liberation. The Jesus who
preached good news to the poor and freedom for the oppressed
was altered in order for systems of exploitation to be put in
place. While it is difficult to change the words of the Bible,
one can easily modify and manipulate the interpretation of
Scripture to the benefit of those in power. This is illustrated by
looking at the Christian religion of slaveholders in the United
States. One former enslaved African recounts the actions of
the minister at her church: "Why the man that baptized me
had a colored woman tied up in his yard to whip when he
got home, that very Sunday . . .We had to sit and hear him
preach. . . . And he had her tied up and whipped. That was
our preacher."[27] Slaveholders developed a form of Christianity
that allowed for "the justification of slavery," for "Christians
to be slaves," and for Christianity to be compatible "with the
extreme cruelty of slavery."[28]

The Christian religion of the slaveholder focused on a belief in the incarnation, that God was made flesh in Jesus Christ. It was by believing that God came in Christ that one gained salvation. Little emphasis was placed on the historical Jesus, but rather on God's act in Jesus Christ. Christianity became a religion of right belief. You could enslave people as long as you had the right belief. You did not have to worry—you were free to be as brutal to the people you enslaved as you felt necessary.[29] The primary action orientation of this form of Christianity was "evangelism," which was understood as introducing people to a right belief about Christ. Many were convinced that Africans were enslaved because God wanted them to be saved. Slavery, therefore, allowed Africans the opportunity to gain the right knowledge and belief.

To allow for slavery and justify the slave master's desire for domination, Christianity was stripped of its liberating power. The Jesus who preached freedom and liberation was replaced with a Christ who served as a symbol of right belief (which included the white person's divine right to own enslaved Africans). Furthermore, slaveholders forced their enslaved Africans to worship a white Jesus who looked like a slave master, where "a white God, a white savior and a white master functioned as one."[30] The tragic contradiction in this formulation of Christian faith was that the slaveholder enslaved and beat people who looked much like the Afro-Asiatic Jesus of history. Every time the slave master beat, raped, or killed enslaved Africans, he or she was symbolically beating, raping, and killing Jesus. One can hear the voice of Jesus echoing through time, "Truly I tell you, just as you did it to one of the least of these who are members of my family, you did it to me" (Matthew 25:40).

Another effect of the religion of the slaveholder was that two forms of Christianity developed side by side: the slave master developed a faith based on right belief and the incarnation of God in Christ, while enslaved Africans developed a faith that emphasized the message of liberation in the Bible, with Jesus as the liberator par excellence. The slaveholder had a white Christ, and enslaved Africans had a black Christ. "According to slaveholding Christianity, knowledge of God's act in Jesus was sufficient for salvation," writes Kelly Brown Douglas. "According to slave Christianity, however, salvation was not linked necessarily to God's act of becoming incarnate in Jesus, but to what Jesus did in history on behalf of the downtrodden." She further states, "Salvation is tied to liberating activity, not to knowledge. In order for Christians to receive salvation, they must engage in liberating acts, not enslaving acts."[31]

The ill effects of a white Jesus have been many on both people of color and whites. The development of culturally appropriate images of Jesus was significantly stifled in Africa, Asia, the Americas, and the islands of the great oceans. So the Jesus that was presented in these settings appeared as a stranger, a foreigner, an enemy, an oppressor, and a captive of the West. The white image of Jesus has encouraged the emergence of a brown Mary as a symbol of Christian faith, made the ways of Europe and Euro-America seem normative, led to the rejection of Christianity by many, reduced the Christian faith's ability to liberate, caused the development of multiple forms of Christianity, and inhibited true reconciliation across racial and cultural lines. The wholesale propagation of the white image of Jesus has been a tragedy of monumental proportions in our world. Many generations have lived and died without knowledge of the truth about Jesus.

The Importance of an Afro-Asiatic Jesus

To counter the effects of the white image of Jesus, it is important to proclaim that the Jesus of the Bible, who lived in Nazareth, was an Afro-Asiatic Jew. This is a case in which if you know the truth, the truth will make you free (John 8:32). "Indeed, for Blacks to walk across the bridge from a Jesus of white symbolic distortions to Jesus as He was and is," writes Mosley, "Black imagery must necessarily be employed."[32]

People of color need to visually see that Jesus was not white. Although the messages of the colonizer, the slaveholder, and the white supremacist were lies, the image of a white Jesus is deeply imbedded in the psyche.

An Afro-Asiatic image increases Jesus' relevancy for people in Africa, Asia, the Americas, and the islands of the great oceans. Jesus will no longer be perceived as a stranger, a foreigner, an enemy, an oppressor, a captive of the West, or in any other way that is threatening or unapproachable. Many have lifted up the white Jesus as proof that Christianity is a "white man's religion." An Afro-Asiatic Jesus returns Jesus to his rightful place as the founder of a faith that has its roots in Africa and Asia. Jesus came for all nations representing the God who created all peoples.

True reconciliation across racial and cultural lines becomes a stronger possibility with an Afro-Asiatic Jesus. Just the designation "Afro-Asiatic" makes a multiracial, multicultural, multiethnic statement about faith. People of color may be more trusting of an image of Jesus that is relevant and more authentic. The white image of Jesus carries with it the excess baggage of a history of racial and cultural prejudice. Also, white people may need a Jesus of color to be set free from racism. If white people are able to visualize the Jesus of the Bible as Afro-Asiatic, brown or black, perhaps this will facilitate the removal of the blinders of prejudiced attitudes. If white people can pray to and express love for an Afro-Asiatic Jesus, something profound will happen to their souls. This could lead to a heartfelt understanding of people of color as sisters and brothers in the human family. Whites who intellectually assent to an Afro-Asiatic Jesus cannot then experientially accept society's racial hierarchy. Renewed perceptions of Jesus must lead to transformed realities in the world in which we live.

Proclaiming an Afro-Asiatic Jesus is more than just reclaiming a truer visual image of the historical Jesus. We must not just "paint the statues brown and keep the Western cultural prejudices intact."[33] Embracing an Afro-Asiatic image of Jesus also means addressing the cultural baggage that came with the white image. A white image of Jesus was used to propagate the thought that the ways of Europe and Euro-America were normative and superior to other cultural perspectives. An Afro-Asiatic Jesus declares that cultures that are not Euro-centered are equally valid and valuable.

Where Is Jesus to Be Found Today?

The acceptance of Jesus of Nazareth as Afro-Asiatic is vitally important for the future of the Christian faith around the world. Yet Jesus as the Christ must not be confined to the context of a human being who lived and breathed at the gateway to Africa and Asia in the first century. The image of Christ must be free to take on new cultural appropriations in order to speak in all cultures. As the early disciples shared the message about the life, death, and resurrection of Jesus, they found new ways to speak of the Christ when they entered cultures that were not influenced by Judaism. This was critical if the faith of Jesus was to expand beyond the confines of Palestine and be understood in other geographical, cultural, and historical contexts. In the prologue of the Gospel of John (1:1-18), the author uses the term *logos* as a word picture for Jesus Christ. This rhetorical image helped Greek readers understand the implications of who Jesus was.[34]

We can discover visual images and word pictures that describe Jesus Christ for our time. As Steve Charleston writes, "In the Pauline sense, I can assert that while as a man Jesus was a Jew, as the risen Christ, he is a Navajo. Or a Kiowa. Or a Choctaw. Or any other tribe."[35] We will now briefly look at four diverse images of Jesus Christ. These have been selected because they are rooted in the culture of their origin, but they also speak to the broader issues facing our world in this age of diversity. They attempt to make Jesus Christ relevant for our time by highlighting an aspect of Jesus' ministry or a particular cultural need. The following images of Jesus Christ are not examined in their fullness, nor are they necessarily the most popular image of Christ within that particular culture. The images to be examined are the Gold-Crowned Jesus, the Galilean Jibaro Jesus, Jesus the One Crowned with Thorns, and Jesus the Great Healer. While each image speaks to a different theme, together they present a broad picture of how people around the world embrace Jesus Christ.[36]

The Gold-Crowned Jesus

R. S. Sugirtharajah says that the key question "is not what the historical Jesus looked like but what he means for Asia today."[37] Korean poet Kim Chi Ha has attempted to answer the question of Jesus' relevancy to Asia in a play called *The Gold-Crowned Jesus*.[38] The play opens with the display of a cement statue of Jesus Christ wearing a gold crown on his head. The play revolves around a number of conversations that take place near the Christ statue. A company president, a police officer, and a priest discuss their common belief that "success" demonstrates God's blessing. A beggar, a leper, a prostitute, and a sympathetic nun are heard dialoging about their desperate circumstances. In both of these cases, the concrete Jesus is silent.

The gold crown on the head of Jesus is meant to signify his allegiance with the rich and powerful elite. The beggar and the leper are unable to accept this understanding of Jesus, so throughout the play they question where the real Jesus is. The query comes out of their need for Jesus. C. S. Song comments: "When a beggar turns to the question, it is not his head or his faith that turns to it. It is the stomach, his empty stomach! . . . When a leper asks the question, his immediate concern is not the defense of the faith and correct doctrine. What is at stake is his humanity—his humanity eaten away by the horrible disease and himself excluded from human community."[39] Despite their intense longings to discover a Jesus who will respond to their cries, the Jesus statue remains silent.

As the play continues, the leper notices the gold crown on the head of Jesus and, considering the possibility of a life free from poverty, removes the gold crown. It is at this point that the concrete Jesus comes to life and says: "I have been closed up in this stone for a long, long time . . . entombed in this dark, lonely, suffocating prison. I have longed to talk with you, the kind and poor people like yourself, and share your sufferings. I can't begin to tell you how long I have waited for this day . . . this day when I would be freed from my prison, this day of liberation when I would live and burn again as a flame inside you, inside the very depths of your misery."[40]

The rich and powerful people are surprised to discover Jesus conversing with the beggar, the leper, and other marginalized people. Shocked by what they see, they grab the gold crown from the leper. Then the priest places it back on the head of Jesus. Instantly Jesus becomes a silent cement figure again and remains this way through the end of the play.

The Gold-Crowned Jesus is an image that presents Jesus as a captive of the powerful elite. The church, in league with powerful economic interests, has often promoted an image of a Jesus who sides with the status quo. "The golden crown on his head is the ideology of the established Church, which was forced on Jesus in order to make him support the Church institution," writes Byung Mu Ahn.[41] The missionaries of colonial Europe brought a Jesus who was set in concrete and unable to adapt to the cultural realities. Yet as C. S. Song states, "The ready-made Jesus encased in a statue, enshrined in a cathedral, endorsed by church traditions and doctrines, is not the real Jesus."[42] The play seeks to demonstrate that the real Jesus can live only when set free from the concrete captivity.

The play also makes the point that it is the Minjung (Korean poor) who set Jesus free from the concrete. In the same way that the woman who touched the hem of Jesus' garment (Mark 5:25-34; Luke 8:43-48) released the power of his healing, "the cries of the Minjung . . . took off the crown of Jesus."

Byung Mu Ahn declares, "So we, for the first time, came to hear his voice and see his tears. That is to say, we experienced that Jesus, confined in the cement, could only be liberated by the Minjung."[43] The biblical understanding of Jesus as good news to the poor is held captive in many cultures and nations and must be set free. Jesus is released from concrete dogma when he is linked up with the life of the vast numbers of people in this world who are desperate for hope.[44]

The Galilean Jibaro Jesus

After Jesus is set free by the Minjung, he joins the poor in solidarity as a Galilean jibaro (a Puerto Rican peasant). According to Orlando Costas, Latinas and Latinos in the United States can think of Jesus "as the promised son of God who became a Galilean jibaro and lived the Hispanic experience of poverty and ignorance, of being 'slighted for his . . . manner of speech,' of rejection, loneliness, exile, suffering, and death."[45] The Galilean Jibaro Jesus lives the experience of people who are marginalized by poverty and prejudice. Jesus was raised as a Jew in Galilee. As a Galilean, he was "a borderland reject."[46] He lived in a culturally diverse setting and was disenfranchised by both colonial Rome and religious Jerusalem.

The experience of feeling cut off from one's culture of origin and unaccepted by the dominant culture is one that many people today can understand. Our world is teeming with people who have become refugees, immigrants, or displaced persons, as well as others who are caught in a cultural limbo. They often do not feel fully accepted in either culture. Also they find themselves pulled in opposite directions by old loyalties and new demands as they face uncertain cultural understandings. As a Galilean jibaro, Jesus understood this predicament. As a person from Galilee, Jesus lived in the midst of the struggle between two worlds: Rome and Jerusalem. Each world placed expectations on him, and often he was an outcast in both worlds.

Jesus chose to be in solidarity with the masses of people, the jibaros. This solidarity, which began at his birth, creates a sense of trust for a majority of the world's population who live in similar circumstances today. Justo Gonzalez writes: "We are comforted when we read the genealogy of Jesus, and find there, not only a Gentile like ourselves, but also incest, and what amounts to David's rape of Bathsheba. The Gospel writer did not hide the skeletons in Jesus' closet, but listed them, so that we may know that the Savior has really come to be one of us—not just one of the high and mighty, the aristocratic with impeccable blood lines, but one of us."[47]

Jesus demonstrated his solidarity with the jibaros of his day by "being born one of them, learning from them, going to their homes, and eating with them."[48] Once the gold crown is removed, setting Jesus free from the concrete image, he becomes a Galilean jibaro and lives with the people as one of them. Elizondo declares, "It is in the face and person of Jesus the poor Galilean that the face of God is manifested."[49]

Jesus, the One Crowned with Thorns

The Burakumin people of Japan have added an emphasis on liberation to the images of the Gold-Crowned Jesus and the Galilean Jibaro Jesus. The Burakumin—the indigenous people of the island of Japan—have been treated poorly by the larger society. Out of their experience they have come to identify Jesus as "the one crowned with thorns."[50] They view Jesus as both a cosufferer and a liberator. As Kuribayashi Teruo says: "The crown of thorns has become a symbol of the solidarity of God with the marginalized, the oppressed, and the exploited. It has come to signify the person of Jesus, who makes the groaning of the despised his own cry for liberation. The symbol reveals that God is also suffering with them, while promising their freedom from that oppression."[51]

The crown of thorns was meant to humiliate Jesus as a criminal (Matthew 27:27-31). It was a mockery of the claim made by the people a few days earlier when they proclaimed Jesus as the King of the Jews. Jesus was further humiliated when Pilate displayed him in front of the crowds in Jerusalem wearing the crown of thorns and asked the people to vote on whether or not he should die (John 19:5-6). The crown of thorns was placed on his head to signify that Jesus was powerless at the hands of the Roman authorities. Yet through the resurrection, the crown of thorns became a symbol of Jesus overcoming suffering.[52] The crown of thorns says that "weeping may linger for the night, but joy comes with the morning" (Psalm 30:5). The Burakumin look to Jesus the One Crowned with Thorns as a reminder that morning will come even as they struggle through the night of suffering.

It is interesting to note that the Burakumin were not church attendees when they embraced Jesus as the One Crowned with Thorns. In a country where Christians make up a small percentage of the population, "they simply took the Bible and read in it their daily experience."[53] Through their study of the Bible, they "came to relate their own experience to the biblical symbol of Jesus' passion."[54] All around the world people have started reading the Bible for themselves. Rigoberta Menchu calls the Bible the "main weapon" for empowering the indigenous people in Guatemala to struggle for freedom.[55] The Bible has become a critical tool for empowerment. "If Jesus is to have any meaning for Asian peoples, he must take off the gold crown as Kim alludes to in the play. He must regain a simple crown of thorns and join the oppressed in their suffering and joy," writes Teruo. "If Jesus is a savior merely for the powerful, he has nothing to do with the wretched in Asia."[56] Jesus the One Crowned with Thorns intimately understands the pain of oppressed people, yet at the same time leads the way in the hope for liberation.

Jesus the Great Healer

An understanding of Jesus as a liberator who lives in solidarity with people who are hurting naturally leads to the conclusion that his healing role must not be overlooked. In many cultures in Africa, the role of the healer is highly significant. Anselme T. Sanon states, "To see the face of Christ, to recognize his African face, is to find an African name for him."[57] One of the names Jesus is called in various parts of Africa is "the Great Healer." This should come as no surprise because "in his programmatic discourse, borrowed from the prophet Isaiah, Jesus presents himself primarily as a healer."[58] In Luke 4:18-19 Jesus proclaimed his agenda for ministry: "The Spirit of the Lord is upon me, because he has anointed me to bring good news to the poor. He has sent me to proclaim release to the captives and recovery of sight to the blind, to let the oppressed go free, to proclaim the year of the Lord's favor." According to Anne Nasimiyu-Wasike, Jesus' ministry "inaugurated the restoration of individuals and societies to wholeness."[59]

With the great amount of suffering occurring in several countries on the continent of Africa, it makes sense that Jesus needs to come as "the Great Healer." Yet as Cece Kolie writes, "To proclaim Jesus as the Great Healer calls for a great deal of explaining to the millions who starve [and] to victims of injustice and corruption."[60] In the midst of terrible tragedy, one often questions how God could let this happen. The message of healing must be declared in the larger context of society. Those who are suffering physically and psychologically are not the only ones in need of healing. Those in power who perpetuate suffering also need to be healed from their greed, ambition, and callousness. Kolie writes that "Jesus' therapy is articulated upon acts and deeds calculated to alter social relationships. Jesus is aware that it is never on the physical level alone that one is deaf or blind, and that consequently neither can healing or salvation remain on that level."[61] "Jesus the Great Healer" addresses the ills of social systems that produce suffering and ultimately heals the souls of suffering humanity.

Once set free from the concrete and living in solidarity with the masses, Jesus emerges as a liberator who is a healer, a therapeutic force. Kolie sums up the message: "We proclaim a crucified Messiah, a scandal to the Jews, madness to the Greeks and sickness to the Africans. For the person of black Africa . . . the presence of someone ill in the family is a scandal."[62] Jesus the Great Healer provides a holistic therapy that addresses the need for physical, psychological, and spiritual healing at both the individual and institutional level. Both the powerless and the powerful are invited to come to Jesus the Great Healer and receive a life-transforming touch.

A White Jesus for Today: Jesus the Truth Teller

Many people of color are creatively seeking fresh reflections of Jesus, while white people remain captive to a defective image of Jesus. Although white people need to accept that Jesus of Nazareth was Afro-Asiatic, Jesus as the Christ can appear in culturally appropriate images to address their current issues. I would like to suggest that such a culturally appropriate image would allow Jesus to come to white people as a truth teller. Jesus had this relationship with his own people. He told the truth to his people who were in power, as well as those out of power. Jesus was sometimes harsh in his honesty. He called some among the religious leaders "whitewashed tombs," "snakes," and a "brood of vipers." He challenged their "hypocrisy" because they had neglected justice, mercy, and faith and had developed a religion based on vanity, legalism, greed, and self-indulgence (Matthew 23:1-39). Jesus was truthful with other power brokers as well. He confronted a rich young ruler who was held captive by his wealth and told him he could be set free by selling all that he had and giving it to the poor among his people (Matthew 19:16-22; Mark 10:17-22; Luke 18:18-25). Jesus visited the home of Zacchaeus, a corrupt tax collector who was oppressing his own people. Whatever it was that Jesus said to him caused Zacchaeus to admit that he had defrauded his own people and commit to making restitution (Luke 19:1-10).

A white Jesus for today would be found living in solidarity with poor and working-class whites. He would offer them a faith that lifted their spirits and empowered them in their daily efforts to satisfy life's basic needs. This Jesus would also stay in the homes of middle-class whites and talk with them about their spiritual needs (as he did with Mary and Martha of Bethany in Luke 10:38-42). Jesus would warn of the trap of materialism and remind them that one's identity must be found in God, not possessions (or the desire for material things). At length, Jesus would listen to poor and middle-class white people as they voiced their concerns and fears regarding employment, adequate health care, education for their children, safe neighborhoods, and the like. These interests, Jesus would say, are the shared concerns of all people in the human family. He would tell them not to let their need to take care of their own family divide them from their other sisters and brothers in the human family. They should resist the temptation to blame or scapegoat people of color as white supremacist groups do. The real problem is a system that needs to be fixed.

This white Jesus would go to the offices and homes of rich and powerful white people and listen to them describe the stresses of their lives. He would then challenge them to use their wealth and influence to create a more just society. As Jesus said in the first century and would say today, "From everyone to whom much has been given, much will be required; and from the one to whom much has been entrusted, even more will be demanded" (Luke 12:48). In other words, while the responsibility is considerable, the opportunity to serve God is even more far-reaching. Jesus would ask those with wealth to use their financial resources to underwrite ministries of compassion, reconciliation, and social justice, just as people of means supported the ministry of Jesus in the Bible (Matthew 27:57; Luke 8:3).

A truth-telling Christ would be honest about the history of systems based on theories of white superiority. He would describe how a group made up primarily of elite and powerful white males created a system of oppression that has brutalized people of color around the world and exploited the

COMING TOGETHER IN THE 21ST CENTURY

masses of white people. The system has been called by different names—colonialism, slavery, apartheid, segregation, genocide, racism—but regardless of what it is called, it has had the same effect. A white Jesus would honestly admit that institutional forms of Christianity were often used to support this system, causing a spiritual illness that still affects the church today.[63]

A white Jesus would also celebrate the lives of those dedicated whites who have stood for justice and not bought the dominant lie. He would say to those with power that they should follow the example of the apostle Paul, who used the "power" of his Roman citizenship to gain access to Caesar (Acts 22:25–28:31). He would invite others to join in the struggle against unjust systems around the world.

An Inclusive Christ

Jesus entered history in the first century as an Afro-Asiatic Jewish male from Galilee. He came into the world at a time when ethnic tensions were simmering just below the surface and communities were isolated from each other. Jesus of Nazareth came with a prophetic word, calling for a just society based on individuals and institutions reconciling themselves with God and each other. In the course of history, the image of a white Western Jesus was used to dominate people of color around the world for economic gain. The effects on people of color and whites have been devastating. We must regain the postresurrection understanding of Jesus as the Christ who is free to be incarnated in all cultural settings in order to proclaim the good news that leads to a relationship with an all-inclusive God.

4

READING THE APOSTLE PAUL THROUGH GALATIANS 3:28

Mimi Haddad

Gender segregation that excludes women from sharing authority with men in church leadership and marriage has been advanced by biblical and rhetorical arguments. The writings of the apostle Paul are frequently cited to subordinate women to male authority in the church and also in marriage.[1] A common rhetorical device used to exclude women from leadership suggests that while men and women are created equal by God, God has designed different "roles" for men and women. By "gender roles" they do not mean that men shovel snow, install household appliances, and balance the checkbook while women oversee the housework and child care. Rather, the argument that men and women are equal but created for different "roles" centers largely on one issue—authority. Men, it is suggested, hold final authority in the church and in the home.[2] The logic in such a statement is clearly strained. How can you be equal to someone yet without equal authority? To hold this view renders the word *equal* meaningless.

The notion of "separate but equal" was used years ago to segregate schools, restaurants, restrooms, hotels, and even churches according to skin color. "Separate but equal" was pressed on the poorest in our nation and furthered educational and economic inequities. Ultimately a cry for justice went to the Supreme Court, where it was determined that separate was never equal. In a world of sin, domination, and greed separate *is* inherently unequal.

While Scripture has been used to segregate and oppress people based on superficial issues such as skin color, gender, and class, the Bible is filled with examples that regard gender, class, and ethnicity as irrelevant to one's service in God's covenant community. For instance, the apostle Paul told *all* Christians to submit to one another (Ephesians 5:21). Wives have authority over their husbands' bodies, just as husbands have authority over their wives' bodies (1 Corinthians 7:4). Paul exalted the leadership of women and enslaved persons throughout his epistles. He commends female deacons (Romans 16:1), prophets (1 Corinthians 11:4-5; 14:31; Acts 2:17-18; 21:9), house church leaders (Acts 16:13-15, 40; Romans 16:3-5), a female apostle (Romans 16:7), teachers of the gospel (Acts 18:26), evangelists (Philippians 4:3; Romans 16:3), and those who did the very heaviest of gospel labor (Romans 16:12). Paul asked Christians in Corinth to submit to Stephanas's household—a household that included enslaved persons and women (1 Corinthians 16:15-16). Persons who were enslaved or free, Greeks or Jews, men or women, educated or illiterate together shared spiritual authority—just as they shared in the risen life of Christ (Galatians 3:27-29). Ultimately their oneness in Christ would overturn slavery and the subjugation of women.

Yet, when the topic of women's authority in the church is raised, individuals often turn to the writings of the apostle Paul, to passages such as the following:

> Women should remain silent in the churches. They are not allowed to speak, but must be in submission, as the law says. If

they want to inquire about something, they should ask their own husbands at home; for it is disgraceful for a woman to speak in the church. (1 Corinthians 14:34-35)

Wives, submit yourselves to your own husbands as you do to the Lord. (Ephesians 5:22)

A woman should learn in quietness and full submission. I do not permit a woman to teach or to assume authority over a man; she must be quiet. For Adam was formed first, then Eve. And Adam was not the one deceived; it was the woman who was deceived and became a sinner. But women will be saved through childbearing—if they continue in faith, love and holiness with propriety. (1 Timothy 2:11-15)

These passages are frequently considered the final biblical voice extending authority to men over women, even while overlooking the main corpus of Paul's theology of gender—of shared authority and service between women and men—noted in his shared ministry beside women such as Priscilla, Junia, Phoebe, Chloe, and Nympha. Sadly, throughout history, a selective reading of Paul has led to the exclusion of women from teaching and leadership positions. This is tragic not only because it overlooks the way Paul built the church beside women, but also because such an approach engages a superficial reading of one the most difficult passages in the New Testament to interpret—1 Timothy 2:11-15.

To prohibit women from exercising their God-given gifts not only impoverishes the church, but also denies women shared authority in marriage and within the body of Christ. This does violence to the cause of Christ—namely, the reconciliation of humanity to God and to one another. This chapter will therefore redress a selective reading of Paul by examining the apostle himself, his life as a Pharisee, his radical conversion, and his theological foundations for the shared service of women. These factors will provide the basis by which to assess passages that have been used to prevent women from holding positions of authority with men in the church and family.

The Apostle Paul

The conversion of the apostle Paul is one of the most astonishing events in history. Paul's inner transformation as a Christian so altered his worldview that it compelled him to promote one of the most redemptive social policies in all of human history. Paul's encounter with the cross was so powerful that he abandoned and opposed the ethnic and gender segregation of the Jewish priesthood, promoting in its place the priesthood of all believers, developing a social structure of spiritual leadership that would ultimately undermine slavery and the subjugation of women. If ever there was evidence of God's redemptive power opposing the patriarchy of biblical culture, it is keenly noted in the life of Paul.

Prior to his conversion, Paul (at that time Saul), was a great biblical scholar rooted in a Jewish cultural and religious identity. He was highly trained in interpreting the Torah—the Jewish Scriptures—and as a leading Pharisee, he vigorously persecuted Jews who became Christians. In this effort, Saul received permission from the high priest to travel to Damascus and imprison Jews, both men and women who had come to faith in Christ (Acts 9:1-2). While on the Damascus road, Saul encountered Christ, as "suddenly a light from heaven flashed around him. He fell to the ground and heard a voice say to him, 'Saul Saul, why do you persecute me?' 'Who are you, Lord?' Saul asked. 'I am Jesus, whom you are persecuting,' he replied" (Acts 9:4-5).

Though Saul was instructed to visit the house of Judas (Acts 9:11), the Christians living in Damascus were reluctant to welcome him because Saul had persecuted the church as a Pharisee. Suffering rejection by Christians after his conversion, Saul retreated to the desert outside Damascus where his faith in Christ and his calling as an apostle to the Gentiles was forged. Saul, now Paul, emerged from this extended period of retreat to become one of the greatest theological architects of the church.

While in Arabia, Paul very likely reconciled his training as a Pharisee with his new faith in Jesus Christ. He worked through his understanding of the Jewish law in relation to grace through faith in Christ. He came to terms with his training in the Torah and his encounter with the living Word—Christ Jesus. Paul came to understand the contrast between the narrow requirements of the Jewish priesthood (the first-born, of a specific lineage and learning, a male without blemish, and so on) with the priesthood of all believers, which included Jews and Greeks, enslaved and free, males and females.

Let us explore why, apart from the empty tomb, the conversion of Saul of Tarsus and the life he lived as the apostle Paul are perhaps the most astonishing events in all of history. For a Pharisee such as Paul, holiness was an arduous human task. The fragility of holiness required constant work, and it also demanded separation from all that was viewed as unholy.[3] As a Pharisee, Paul excelled as an elite among elites. He wrote:

> If others think they have reasons to put confidence in the flesh, I have more: circumcised on the eighth day, of the people of Israel, of the tribe of Benjamin, a Hebrew of Hebrews; in regard to the law, a Pharisee; as for zeal, persecuting the church; as for righteousness based on the law, faultless.
>
> But whatever were gains to me I now consider loss for the sake of Christ. What is more, I consider everything a loss because of the surpassing worth of knowing Christ Jesus my Lord, for whose sake I have lost all things. I consider them garbage, that I may gain Christ and be found in him, not having a righteousness of my own that comes from the law, but that which is through faith in Christ—the righteousness that comes from God on the basis of faith. (Philippians 3:4-9)

Paul's life of service, like his conversion, rested on God's grace, attained not because of human effort or because of birthright or gender, but acquired through faith in Christ. Paul, as the apostle of grace, now worked beside women, enslaved persons, and Romans, and this fact alone was such a great offense to the Pharisees that they attempted to kill Paul, and his life was constantly in danger.

In the Spirit of Jesus and Pentecost

Like Jesus' life, Paul's life proved shattering to the social system of the Pharisees. Jesus' call to holiness embraced those whom society viewed as unholy;[4] he ate with sinners and prostitutes. Jesus engaged women theologically and expected women to respond not as a distinct class but as people, as disciples. Jesus broke holiness taboos, and Paul did the same. Women were among Paul's closest coworkers—those who labored beside him in the gospel. Jesus treated female disciples as he did his male disciples, by allowing them to learn at his feet rather than insisting they return to their gendered work. Jesus' holiness was not about separation. Holiness in the new covenant was about access.[5] It was inclusive.[6] It was the new wine that bursts the old wineskins.

Social inclusion was also keenly evident at Pentecost. Access to God was no longer attained through an elite group of Jewish males, but through God's Spirit, who drew three thousand to faith from many tribes and nations.

> "Parthians, Medes and Elamites; residents of Mesopotamia, Judea and Cappadocia, Pontus and Asia, Phrygia and Pamphylia, Egypt and the parts of Libya near Cyrene; visitors from Rome (both Jews and converts to Judaism); Cretans and Arabs—we hear them declaring the wonders of God in our own tongues! . . .
>
> "This is what was spoken by the prophet Joel: 'In the last days, God says, I will pour out my Spirit on all people. Your sons and daughters will prophesy, your young men will see visions, your

old men will dream dreams. Even on my servants, both men and women, I will pour out my Spirit in those days, and they will prophesy.'" (Acts 2:9-11, 16-18)

As the fulfillment of Joel's prophecy, the Holy Spirit gifts all Christians for service, without regard to ethnicity, class, or gender. Unlike the tradition of the Jewish priesthood, which was based on gender and birth into a specific tribe, in the body of Christ priesthood was the birthright of all those born of the Spirit. Moreover, the Pharisees did not allow women to learn Torah. They were silenced and excluded from priestly roles. Yet Paul realized that in the same fashion as women, Parthians, Medes, and Elamites, he too was grafted into Christ and was therefore part of the new covenant where he, like all believers, received power and gifts for service.

Paul established the theological foundations of the new covenant throughout his epistles, particularly in Romans 6, where we learn that the basis for our new life in Christ comes through a baptism into Christ's death and resurrection (6:1-10). Through baptism each sinner dies to sin with Christ on the cross. United to Christ's death spiritually, we also rise from the grave with Christ in newness of life and as heirs of God's kingdom.[7]

> In Christ Jesus you are all children of God through faith, for all of you who were baptized into Christ have clothed yourselves with Christ. There is neither Jew nor Gentile, neither slave nor free, neither male nor female, for you are all one in Christ Jesus. If you belong to Christ, then you are Abraham's seed, and heirs according to the promise. (Galatians 3:26-29)

What was true for Jews was also true for Greeks; what was true for free persons was also true for enslaved persons; and what was true for men was also true for women.[8] Paul did not suggest that in Christ there were no males or females. "What is obliterated is the significance of these distinctions and the (basically divisive) values—ethnic-racial (Jew/Gentile), socioeconomic (slave/free), and sexual-gender (male/female)— based on them."[9]

Baptism and the Cross

Life in the new covenant community was expressed publicly through Christian baptism. In the old covenant, circumcision was the outer expression of one's covenantal relationship with God, and only men were circumcised. In the new covenant, baptism replaced circumcision. Baptism was open to any person: males, females, Jews, Greeks, enslaved persons, and free persons. The inclusivity of Christian baptism, which Paul rehearsed in Galatians 3:28, was inscribed on early Christian baptismal fonts—making Paul's emphasis clear. To be united with Christ not only realigns our identity and status with respect to God, but also redefines our status with respect to one another. In the same way that Christ establishes peace and justice between sinners and God, so Christ also establishes peace and harmony between the members of his body—the church. Theologians put it this way: our soteriology (what we understand about the work of Christ on the cross) directs our ecclesiology (what we understand about the work of the church in the world).[10] To be in Christ is never simply a statement about one's redemptive status. Our redemption directly influences our relationships with one another as members of Christ's body.

Paul states boldly in Galatians 3:28 that Jew and Greek, enslaved and free, male and female are all one in Christ. He wrote these words to individuals who had already come to faith in Christ! Therefore we must assume that this passage addresses social relations within the church. Moreover, Paul offered these words to a world in which enslaved persons and women were more than half of the population. In a profound way, Galatians 3:28 is one of the most radical statements ever made, certainly in the first century. Why? Because in Paul's culture, a person's identity, dignity, and sphere of influence were determined by ethnicity, gender, and class.[11] To such a world Paul courageously declared that a person's significance and influence were no longer established by his or her earthly parents. Believers are ultimately heirs of their heavenly Parent because of Calvary. And they are also given God's Spirit to oppose and resist sins that divide and oppress people because of gender, ethnicity, or class.

Paul did not overturn slavery or release women from cultural bondage during his lifetime. Yet through his writings, in his dealings with the enslaved Onesimus, and because of the women beside whom he labored, Paul revealed that the power of Christ's kingdom triumphed over culture. This is what makes Paul so extraordinary! The power of the cross overcomes what philosophers call ascriptivism—ascribing value and influence according to ethnicity, gender, or class. Christ's completed work on Calvary was the basis of the new covenant and established Christian unity and mutuality. This is acknowledged in Christian baptism (a practice that was open to all women and men) and celebrated in the sharing of the bread and the cup (or the agape meals). These events were open to all people. The first-century followers of Jesus Christ lived out this unity each day in the Spirit in mutual deference to one another, regardless of gender, class, or ethnicity.

The transforming power of the cross so renewed Paul's life that it enabled him to place the realities of Christ's kingdom above the ethnic, class, and gender prejudices of his day. Paul was certain that God was building a new people, with Jesus as head and with all the redeemed serving beside each other equally as joint members of Christ's body. Paul's unshakable confidence in the power of the cross compelled him to live out the ideals he expressed in Galatians 3:28. Thus we find enslaved persons, Gentiles, and women spreading the gospel and serving beside Paul. Paul did not hesitate to ask slave owners to live as brothers and sisters with persons who were held as slaves (Ephesians 6:5-9; Colossians 3:22–4:1). Paul told

Philemon that Onesimus was better than a slave because he was Philemon's brother in Christ (Philemon 16). By asking Philemon to receive Onesimus as a brother, Paul's Christian faith took precedence over cultural expectations (1 Corinthians 2:6; 7:31). According to tradition, Philemon released Onesimus, who went on to become bishop of Ephesus. Galatians 3:28 became the cornerstone or the heartbeat of Paul's teachings, both theologically and in terms of practice. Unless we understand the full impact of Galatians 3:28, we cannot grasp the rest of what Paul wrote. Using Galatians 3:28 as Paul's theological and social foundation, we will observe the work of Paul as he labored beside women.

Women as Coworkers with Paul

In Acts we find the story of the first church in Philippi, also the first church in Europe (16:13-14, 40). Paul encountered a group of women praying. Here Paul met Lydia, a wealthy merchant of purple and a woman of faith. The Lord opened her heart to respond to Paul's message, and her entire household was baptized (16:14-15). Her home became a house church, and the Scriptures suggest she was the leader of this house church. In Paul's letter to the Philippians, we find the great affirmation and love he had for this church. We are told that the church in Philippi was the only church that regularly contributed to Paul's support (Philippians 4:10, 14-19).

The realities of Galatians 3:28 are evident in the start of the church at Philippi, which grew out of the conversions of three diverse individuals, including the Jewish businesswoman—Lydia (Acts 16:13 15), an enslaved Macedonian girl (Acts 16:16 18);[12] and a Roman jailer (Acts 16:19-34). Paul mentions two women from this church who functioned as his coworkers, Euodia and Syntyche (Philippians 4:3). Euodia and Syntyche struggled beside Paul in the work of ministry. He affirmed these women as his coworkers, a term Paul used to identify leaders such as Mark, Timothy, Titus, Philemon,

Apollos, and Luke. Rather than silencing women, Paul supports the evangelism of the first church in Europe, begun by Lydia, an enslaved Macedonian girl,[13] Euodia, and Syntyche. Lydia was not the only female leader of a house church. Nor was she the only woman who colabored with Paul in the gospel. Paul mentioned Nympha and the church that met in her house (Colossians 4:15), Chloe (1 Corinthians 1:11), Apphia—a leader in the church in Colossae (Philemon 1:2),[14] and Priscilla (1 Corinthians 16:19).

Paul cited Priscilla and Aquila more often than anyone else except Timothy. Priscilla and Aquila were living examples of Galatians 3:28. Priscilla was a Roman gentile and was possibly well established financially (Acts 18:2). She was married to a Jew named Aquila. Aquila was most likely set free from slavery, given his name, which means "eagle's feather." When Jews were banished from Rome by decree of Claudius, Priscilla and Aquila left Italy in AD 51, reaching Corinth before Paul. The apostle Paul visited this couple in Corinth because, like him, they were tent makers. Priscilla and Aquila invited Paul to live with them. Paul does not mention leading them to faith, so they likely were Christians at the time of Paul's visit. All three relocated to Ephesus eighteen months later.

While in Ephesus, Priscilla and Aquila gained prominence not only through the church they established in their home (1 Corinthians 16:19), but also by risking their lives for Paul (perhaps during the riots mentioned in Acts 19:23-41), a deed for which all the Gentile churches gave thanks (Romans 16:4). Paul noted Priscilla's prominence in his greetings to the couple at the close of his letters to the church in Rome, where he sent his greetings to the church that met not in Aquila's house, but in "their" house (Romans 16:5).

Luke recognized Priscilla and Aquila as skilled teachers for having instructed Apollos, who was himself well versed in the Scriptures, though he lacked some theological insight, which Priscilla and Aquila provided. Apollos received Priscilla's instruction without reservation. Far from condemning her for having taught a man, both Luke and Paul acknowledged Priscilla. Her authority in the early church is highlighted by Paul, who called Priscilla his "coworker." Moreover, her name is mentioned first in four of the six references to the couple, suggesting she was the more distinguished. Both Luke and Paul honored her in this way.

Paul named Phoebe as a deacon in the church in Cenchrea (Romans 16:1). She may have been responsible for carrying Paul's letters between Greece and Rome. Once in Rome she remained there offering commentary on Paul's letter. Paul also referred to Phoebe as a *prostatis*, which literally meant one who was in authority or who presided. This is the only place in the New Testament where this noun appears. Paul used the verb form of *prostatis* in 1 Thessalonians 5:12, where it means exercising leadership.[15]

In Romans 16:7 we learn of the female apostle Junia. Not only was she an apostle, but she was prominent among the apostles because she served Christ prior to Paul's conversion, a fact he honors. Junia and Paul suffered imprisonment together, most likely for missionary activity. Church leaders such as Jerome, Origen, and John Chrysostom were familiar with the oral tradition of the church, and they cited Junia as a female apostle.[16]

The Spiritual Gifts and Women

If Paul intended to limit service or authority because of gender, ethnicity, or class, the most obvious place to make this known would be Paul's teachings on the spiritual gifts. Yet, in all three passages where Paul discussed spiritual gifts (Romans 12:6-8; 1 Corinthians 12:7ff.; and Ephesians 4:11), he never suggested or stated that the gifts were given along gender lines. Rather, spiritual gifts were open to all people to build up and edify the church. The Spirit equips Christians to serve as evangelists, prophets, pastors, teachers, and apostles. Scripture cites women who served as evangelists and house church leaders/pastors (Acts 16:40, Romans 16:3, 1 Corinthians 1:11, 16:19, Colossians 4:15, Philemon 1-2), prophets (Acts 2:17, 21:9, 1 Corinthians 11:5, 14:31), teachers (Acts 18:26), and one as an apostle (Romans 16:7).

The gift of prophecy is mentioned in all three passages that address the spiritual gifts. As in the Old Testament, prophets in the New Testament publicly corrected and encouraged believers, and the moral and spiritual health of the church depended upon the challenge from those with prophetic gifts (Acts 13:3-4; 21:10-11; Romans 12:6-8; 1 Corinthians 12:8-10; 28-31; 14:1, 24, 29-31; Ephesians 2:20; 4:11). Luke identified leaders as prophets and teachers (Acts 13:1), and Paul suggested that prophets and apostles made known the mysteries of Christ, (Ephesians 3:4-5). Women were prominent as prophets in the Old Testament (Numbers 12:1-16; Judges 4:4-5, 5:7, 2 Kings 22:14). In the New Testament, female prophets were active. In Acts 2:15 Peter explains the events of Pentecost by citing Joel 2:28-32 where Joel predicts the prophesying of women, suggesting that women prophesied at Pentecost. Philip the evangelist had four prophesying daughters (Acts 21:9). Paul also mentioned female prophets in a letter to the church in Corinth (1 Corinthians 11:5) and exhorted all Christians in Corinth to seek the gift of prophecy (14:1).

Does Paul Silence Women?

Given the patriarchal and ethnic prejudice of the ancient world, there were an astonishing number of biblical women who exercised spiritual authority and leadership, building the church beside Paul. Yet three biblical passages appear to oppose women's leadership, a leadership Paul affirmed elsewhere. Was Paul calling women to be silent in the churches at all times? Or was he asking specific women, in specific churches to be silent due to a specific problem? The first passage reads: "Women should remain silent in the churches. They are not allowed to speak, but must be in submission, as the law says. If they want to inquire about something, they should ask their own husbands at home; for it is disgraceful for a woman to speak in the church" (1 Corinthians 14:34-36).

Paul's letter to the church in Corinth reveals a troubled and struggling church. Corinth was a wealthy and decadent city. It was the location of the temple of Aphrodite—a temple that boasted of a thousand prostitutes. Corinthians was written about AD 55 and was directed to address a set of difficulties in the church in Corinth. Writing from Ephesus, Paul was made aware of those specific problems and addressed them in his letter. These included divided loyalties and dissensions (1:10-17; 3:4-9; 6:1-11), sexual immorality (5:1-5, 9-11; 6:12-20; 10:7-11), drunkenness (11:21), and food sacrificed to idols (8:4-13; 10:14-22). In addition, there was disorder and confusion during teaching and worship (14:23-33). In response, Paul asked the women in the Corinthian church to cover their heads and refrain from asking their husbands questions during worship (11:5-6, 10, 13-15; 14:34-35) and to be silent in the church (14:34). But three chapters earlier he told women how to dress when speaking: "Every woman who prays or prophesies with her head uncovered dishonors her head" (11:5). It is hard to prophesy when silence is required.

Paul's instruction to silence women appeared at the end of his exhortation to teach the gospel in an orderly way so others might hear and understand (1 Corinthians 14:1-36). Paul's primary concern was evangelism. The gospel was best taught in an orderly, educational atmosphere. To maximize the learning of all people, Paul insisted on order in worship. Women and men sat in separate places as they had in the synagogue, so women could not ask their husbands anything without disrupting the assembly. The trouble was not that women spoke in general, but that they chose to speak during worship, which made their speaking disruptive. For this reason, married women should ask questions of their husbands at home. When three chapters earlier Paul told women how to dress when speaking in public (with covered heads), he was addressing a specific problem in Corinth regarding women's disruptive speech during worship. Thus this passage should not be viewed as universal in application. We observe the same priority given to prophecy over speaking in tongues (14:5, 9, 18-19, 32-33). While Paul celebrated the gift of tongues, exhorting others to speak in tongues as he did, he limited the expression when it disrupted worship.

A second passage found in 1 Timothy is perhaps the passage used most often to prohibit women from using their leadership and teaching gifts.

> A woman should learn in quietness and full submission. I do not permit a woman to teach or to assume authority over a man; she must be quiet. For Adam was formed first, then Eve. And Adam was not the one deceived; it was the woman who was deceived and became a sinner. But women will be saved through childbearing—if they continue in faith, love and holiness with propriety. (1 Timothy 2:11-15)

In this passage Paul raised three issues that may be summarized by three questions: (1) Does Paul suggest that women should never exercise authority or speak in the church? (2) What is the significance of Eve in the above passage? (3) Why would Paul argue that women are saved by childbirth? To answer these questions, we must consider the historic background of Paul's letter to the church in Ephesus.

Paul's letter was addressed to Timothy rather than to the church as a whole. Its purpose was to advise Timothy as he served a troubled church in Ephesus. The temple of Artemis— a fertility goddess—was located in Ephesus and was considered one of the seven wonders of the ancient world. Artemis had many worshipers throughout Asia, especially in Ephesus. In Acts 19:24-35 we learn that the artisans associated with Artemis resented the encroachment of the gospel, and in protest they began shouting, "'Great is Artemis of the Ephesians!' Soon the whole city was in an uproar" (Acts 19:28).

The woman-centric goddess Artemis promised her worshipers fertility of land and livestock. She also promised women safety in childbirth. Unlike most goddesses, Artemis was without a male partner. She was independent of men because her powers of fertility did not require male assistance. As represented in her statues prominent throughout Ephesus, Artemis was covered with testicles; this was how Artemis had reproductive capabilities independent of men. Artemis was considered superior to and independent of men. The women who worshiped her hoped for the same status. Because so many women died in childbirth in the ancient world, women were drawn to the worship of Artemis who promised them safety in childbirth.

Paul's letter to Timothy addressed false teachers who were influenced by the worship of Artemis. Paul suggested that myths and endless genealogies were destroying the faith of the Ephesian church (1 Timothy 1:3-7, 19-20). These false teachers (some of whom may have been women) were forbidding marriage (4:3) and ursurping authority or domineering over men (2:12b), while also insisting upon food rituals (4:3). In the context of false teaching, the first interpretive question this passage asks is, can women teach or have authority over men? If women were advancing myths regarding Artemis, they were unschooled in the truths of Christ. Paul prefaced his silence of women in the Ephesian church with a call for women to "learn in quietness." Rabbis were said to "learn in silence." Learning correct theology is the antidote to heresy. To suggest that women should learn was radical! To focus on Paul's injunction to silence women while overlooking his eagerness that women should learn is inconsistent.

In 1 Timothy 2:12 Paul forbade women both to teach and to hold authority over men. However, what is not obvious to non-Greek readers is that Paul selected a rare Greek word for "authority." Rather than using the most common Greek terms for authority or oversight (*exuosia* or *proistemo*) Paul used the term *authentein* a word that would have caught the attention of first-century readers. For the word *authentein* was used in Paul's day for domineering, misappropriated, or usurped authority. The word can also mean to behave in violent ways. It can even mean murder! *Authentein* appears only once in Scripture (1 Timothy 2:12), and it was used by Paul to connote authority that was destructive. For this reason, various translations of Scripture rendered the specific meaning of this word as follows:

- Vulgate (fourth-fifth century AD): "I permit not a woman to teach, neither to domineer over a man."
- The Geneva Bible (1560 edition): "I permit not a woman to teach, neither to usurp authority over the man."
- King James Version (1611): "I suffer not a woman to teach, nor usurp authority over a man."
- The New English Bible (1961): "I do not permit a woman to be a teacher, nor must woman domineer over man."[17]

This unusual Greek word makes it clear that what Paul was objecting to in 1 Timothy 2:11-12 was an ungodly authority. Were the Ephesian women domineering over men because they had been deceived by false teachers? Is this why Paul asked them to learn in silence—or studiously—in the preceding verse? Did Paul insist upon their continued education, because like Eve they had been led astray by deception? Possibly Paul was asking women to learn in silence, as the rabbis learned, so that when they did teach, they would teach truth, not error. Undoubtedly, Paul was hoping they would become able teachers just as Priscilla was a skilled teacher who instructed Apollos (Acts 18:24-26).

We should not underestimate the influence of Artemis in this passage, who was widely worshiped, especially in Ephesus (Acts 19:27). According to the myth, Artemis helped women in childbirth. So Paul may have been insisting that women would be saved through the childbearing process—not by putting faith in Artemis, but by putting faith in Christ, evidenced by "faith, love and holiness with propriety" (1 Timothy 2:15). Paul was calling these women to live godly lives, not as though men were unnecessary, or by domineering over men, but in marriage. In 1 Timothy 5:14-15 Paul wrote, "I counsel younger widows to marry, to have children, to manage their homes and to give the enemy no opportunity for slander. Some have in fact already turned away to follow Satan." As Eve did? Paul asked these women, who were likely widows, to marry and have children and live holy and faithful lives as wives and mothers.[18]

The women referred to in 1 Timothy 2:12 were involved in false teaching and exercising abusive authority over men. Paul called them to learn, to live respectable lives that did not abuse authority, to serve Christ, and to value marriage and family. Ultimately, Paul sent Priscilla and Aquila back to Ephesus to work with Timothy (4:19). Priscilla could use her gifts of teaching to assist those who were deceived in Ephesus, as she had done elsewhere, to which neither Paul nor Luke expressed any objection.

A third passage has been used to place husbands in positions of authority over wives, because the passage asks women to submit to their spouses, and also because husbands are said to be "head" of their wives as Christ is head of the church.

> Submit to one another out of reverence for Christ.
> Wives, submit yourselves to your own husbands as you do to the Lord. For the husband is head of the wife as Christ is head of the church, his body, of which he is the Savior. Now as the church submits to Christ, so also wives should submit to their husbands in everything (Ephesians 5:21-24).

Though many Bibles (including the TNIV) start a new paragraph with verse 22, this verse in Greek lacks a verb ("to submit"). Paul's thought began in verse 21, where the verb "submit" appears. Most translators insert the verb "submit" into verse 22. However, it is clear that Paul's thought regarding submission began with verse 21, where he instructed all Christians to submit to one another out of reverence for Christ. Hence, Paul's call to submission is mutual—something he asked of all Christians. In verse 22 he reminded wives to submit themselves to their husbands just as husbands as believers also submit to their wives! Christians were to be known by their mutual submission. Paul asked wives to submit voluntarily to the loving sacrifice of their husbands. The verb used here is *submit*, not *obey*. Submission is the call for voluntary deference.

In verse 23 Paul said that the husband was head of the wife, just as Christ was head of the church. This verse has been interpreted to suggest that husbands hold absolute authority over their wives. But "head" (Gk., *kephale*) can also mean "source." To render *kephale* as source maintains the centrality of love, intimacy, and oneness embedded in Ephesians 5 where Paul clearly referred to the one-flesh relationship of Adam and Eve (described in Genesis 2:24). In this Ephesians text, Paul's emphasis was love.

> Husbands, *love* your wives, just as Christ *loved* the church and *gave himself up for her.* . . . In this same way, husbands ought to *love* their wives as their own bodies. He who *loves* his wife *loves* himself. After all, people have never *hated* their own bodies, but they *feed* and *care* for them, just as Christ *does* the church—for we are members of his body. "For this reason a man will leave his father and mother and be united to his wife, and the two will become *one flesh*." This is a profound mystery—but I am talking about Christ and the church. However, each one of you also must love his wife as he loves himself, and the wife must respect her husband. (5:25-32, emphasis mine)

Just as the man's body was the source of the woman's body in Genesis 2:21-22, so Christ is the origin or source of the church. Christ died to bring others to life. In the same way, husbands are to love their wives sacrificially—as their own flesh. This underscores the idea of oneness and intimacy in marriage. The one-flesh relationship of marriage is an image of the communion, mutuality, and sacrificial love that prompt us to submit to Christ and also to one another (Ephesians 5:21). All Christians are to be characterized by their mutual deference, for that is how the church and marriage work best. It is the same intimacy and mutuality that operate within the Godhead, between members of the Trinity (1 Corinthians 11:3).

Notice how Paul placed the ethos of the new covenant above the gender and cultural norms of his day. Paul asked husbands and wives to share authority in marriage (1 Corinthians 7:3-4). In fact, all Christians were to submit to one another (Ephesians 5:21). In the same breath, Paul also placed additional responsibility on husbands, asking them to love their wives as they loved their own bodies—a new request for first-century men! Taking it one step further, Paul required husbands to love their wives as Christ loved the church, denying even their own lives if needed. How radical this must have seemed to first-century people! Remember, husbands held ultimate authority over their households. As such, husbands could require the sacrifice (even the very lives) of their slaves and also their wives. Paul now asked husbands to give *their* own lives as sacrifices for their wives—a complete reframing of gender, class, and authority. A new culture based on Christian values was forming! Paul even wrote that the free were now enslaved and the enslaved were now free (1 Corinthians 7:21-22). The burden of sacrificial love was placed squarely on the shoulders of those who held cultural authority—men. Husbands were those whom Paul primarily addressed, reminding them not to be deceived by temporal authority, for the world in its present shape was passing away (1 Corinthians 2:6; 7:31). The gospel was radical medicine for a world divided by ethnicity, gender, and class, a world that, like ours today, emphasized these differences in order to maintain divisions and inequities.

Reading Paul through Galatians 3:28

If we are to read the Bible with understanding, we must read it consistently, through the mainstream of Paul's thought, which is most clearly articulated for us in Galatians 3:28. The main thrust of Paul's teaching was that women are equally gifted by God and equally called to service in building the church according to their spiritual gifts. Paul prohibited the public ministry of specific women in Ephesus and Corinth because they were exercising abusive authority and teaching false doctrine in Ephesus and because of their disruptive behavior in Corinth. However, Paul made it clear that women should learn correct theology (1 Timothy 2:11), so that their behavior might be consistent with correct doctrine. Finally, Paul called all Christians to submit to one another in Ephesians 5:21. He also asked husbands to love their wives sacrificially, just as Christ loved the church. To ask first-century husbands to love their wives, and to love them as they loved their own bodies was most radical indeed.

I have tried to show that in the writings and teachings of the apostle Paul, union with Christ, through Christian baptism, was the foundation of life in the church, as best summarized in Galatians 3:28. What was true for one member of Christ's body was also true for the others. All Christians do not possess the same spiritual gifts, but to be born of the Spirit is to have the potential for teaching and leadership, if so called by God. Paul worked alongside an impressive group of female leaders, and like Jesus, Paul viewed their service through the empowering of the Holy Spirit, not as gender-based, but as gift-based.

Paul managed many challenges in his ministry, including dealing with heresy, disruption, and false teachers. At times this meant a short-term limit on the expression of women's freedom in Christ in a particular location. Ultimately, women and men, from all tribes and socioeconomic groups, exhibited the transformative power of the gospel, as members of Christ's body, in which there is no Jew or Greek, enslaved or free, male or female.

5

ADDRESSING INJUSTICE

A popular chant in protest marches has been "No justice, no peace." This phrase is often meant as a threat. If the group making the demands does not receive the "justice" it wants, then it will make sure that there is no peace for those who are committing the injustice. Yet the phrase also can be understood as a sober reminder of a fundamental truth: if we do not address the injustices in our world, there is no realistic possibility of developing long-term peace. As the prophets have said, we must not cry "peace" when there is no peace (see Jeremiah 6:14; Ezekiel 13:10; Micah 3:5; see also Luke 19:41-44). It is irresponsible to create false hopes for peace. Peace is not the lack of violence; it is the absence of injustice and oppression. More than that, though, peace comes when we take redemptive and strategic action against injustice. Peace results when a society is built on just and equal relationships among its people. This vision caused the prophet Amos to cry out, "Let justice roll down like waters, and righteousness like an everflowing stream" (5:24). He knew that justice was Israel's only hope for peace. Isaiah said that only when "a spirit from on high is poured out on us" can we find justice. He went on to make the connection between justice and peace: "Then justice will dwell in the wilderness, and righteousness abide in the fruitful field. The effect of righteousness will be peace, and the result of righteousness, quietness and trust forever" (32:15-17). Jesus blessed "the peacemakers" (Matthew 5:9) and considered justice among the "weightier matters of the law" (Matthew 23:23).

In the Bible, peace and justice walk hand in hand as complimentary components of God's desire for this world. Since peace requires justice, we must strive to create a just society. I will give attention to biblical strategies for responding to three forms of injustice in contemporary society: racism, sexism, and classism. All forms of injustice are interrelated and require urgent and comprehensive analysis by biblical activists in an age of diversity. Injustice exists both in the society and in the church. Therefore, biblical strategies for eliminating racism, sexism, and classism have both an inward focus toward the community of God and an outward focus toward society. As Justo Gonzalez writes, "Injustice thrives on the myth that the present order is somehow the result of pure intentions and a guiltless history."[1] Let us break the power of this myth by examining afresh the biblical resources that may inspire us to be people empowered by God. We must take action against injustice if we are ever to discover peace and reconciliation.

Racism

The pages of this book repeatedly speak of the effects of colonialism, slavery, genocide, and other injustices that have been perpetrated based on theories of racial superiority. There is hardly a place or a people in the past few centuries that has not been affected by racial injustice. Steve Charleston describes how racism has affected Native Americans: "The most virulent form of the disease of racism has been used against Native America. Like other oppressed people, we have known slavery, poverty, and political conquest. We have also known something else—genocide. . . . Western colonialism may speak of an American history. Native People speak of an American holocaust."[2] People from other cultures and races could add their stories to his. Many people, particularly among the dominant group, would like to believe that racism should be spoken of in the past tense. Yet this plague on humanity still exists. Individuals are racist when they believe in the superiority of their own racial group and the inferiority of others. An institution or a society's culture is racist when power is exercised to enforce the myth of racial superiority and inferiority in ways that negatively affect those defined as inferior and privilege those seen as superior.

The life of the church has been affected by racism. Oneness in Christ has been compromised by congregations and denominations that are segregated by race. The greatest barrier to effective multicultural ministry is racism. Numerous individuals have rejected the Christian faith because of the racial prejudice of church people. E. Stanley Jones, speaking in reference to Mahatma Gandhi, wrote, "Racialism has many sins to bear, but perhaps its worst sin was the obscuring of Christ in an hour when one of the greatest souls born of woman was making his decision."[3]

People of all cultures and races are included in God's salvation story. Jesus himself was a racially mixed Afro-Asiatic Jew from Galilee. There were no social or economic systems based on race or skin-color designations in the biblical era. The Bible was composed in a time before racism and theories of racial types.[4] Racism is a postbiblical aberration of God's creative design. It is an attempt to mutilate the image of God imprinted onto humanity. Racism is nothing less than a denial of the God of the Bible and therefore is apostasy. Infants are not born to be racists. It is a learned prejudice, an acquired taste. Racism is sin and, like all sin, requires repentance. The racism found in institutions, put in place intentionally for economic gain or power needs, affects whole groups of people in a society.

Racism becomes ingrained in a culture as individuals and institutions instruct the next generation regarding their biases. Once it has become a part of the culture, racism is very difficult to root out and reproduces itself automatically. Racism becomes "normal." Followers of God are compelled to fight racial injustice in all of its forms: individual, institutional, and cultural.[5] Even though the Bible was written in a time before racism per se, there is a wealth of information available for use in addressing it. People in biblical times were just as prejudiced as we are today. The way God addressed human bigotry in the Bible gives us insights as to how we should respond to prejudice's modern-day cousin, racism.

Samaritans had been effectively marginalized in the first-century society of Jesus' upbringing. Many of Jesus' peers avoided any contact with Samaria and Samaritans because they were considered "unclean," ritually impure. Jesus addressed the prejudice perpetuated by this "unclean" theology. He infused the culture with new and positive images of Samaritans that accurately declared their full humanity. Jesus began by refusing to permit any derogatory images of Samaritans. On one occasion, the people of a Samaritan village would not let Jesus and his disciples stay overnight in their village because they were traveling to Jerusalem for the Passover (Luke 9:51-56). This was due to the Samaritan belief that religious festivals should be held on Mount Gerizim (see Deuteronomy 11:26-30; John 4:20-24). The people in this village chose not to support Jesus as he traveled to what they considered to be a false religious event. The disciples wanted him to call down fire on the village. Jesus refused to use this village's act of religious bigotry as an excuse to act in a way that reinforced existing negative stereotypes of Samaritans.

Another example of Jesus' refusal to buy into this "unclean" theology was when the religious leaders attempted to insult Jesus by saying he had a demon and calling him a Samaritan (John 8:48-49). The term *Samaritan* was meant as a derogatory ethnic slur. Jesus directly challenged their assertion that he had a demon. He informed the religious leaders that they had dishonored him. However, he did not respond at all to the "Samaritan slur." It seems that Jesus did not consider being called a Samaritan an insult or a sign of disrespect.

Jesus also challenged the prevailing cultural perceptions by publicly associating with Samaritans. He spent the night in Samaritan villages, conversed with both Samaritan men and women, and reached out to Samaritans in ministry and healing (Luke 17:11-19; John 4:4-26, 39-42). After the resurrection, Jesus sent forth his disciples to do the same (Acts 1:8), a commission they followed (Acts 8:5-25).

The most powerful way that Jesus addressed the prejudice against Samaritans that permeated the culture of first-century Palestine was the inclusion of positive images of Samaritans in his sermons and parables. In the story of the Good Samaritan, it was the Samaritan who demonstrated the neighborly compassion that was commanded of the Jews (Luke 10:29-37). The Samaritan was the hero of the story, helping someone who probably would have refused his help if he were not unconscious. It is interesting to note that while Samaritans were considered inferior in the first century, this story has made the name "Samaritan" a title of honor in our day. Jesus' story successfully changed the cultural image of the Samaritan from "unclean" to "good."

The God of the Bible calls us to address the racism of individuals, institutions, and culture. When racism is entrenched in the culture, it not only appears to be a normal part of society, it also replicates itself without any effort. In the case of the "unclean" Samaritans in first-century Palestine or the "cursed" people of color of this modern age, the implication of inferiority is passed down from generation to generation as though it is the truth. Our challenge is to extricate racism from the entanglement of culture's web and then reintroduce into society the truth that God's loving regard is applied equally to all women, men, and children in the human family.

Sexism

Although racism based on skin color was not a part of the biblical world, sexism was deeply woven into the fabric of the times. Women in this period had very few rights. They generally were considered the property of men. They began as the property of their fathers and at the time of marriage became the property of their husbands.[6] The Bible was written by men in a male-dominated and male-oriented society. This has no doubt affected the interpretation of God down through the centuries.[7] The effect has not gone unnoticed. A new generation of women scholars is speaking the hard, yet honest, truth about this biblical legacy.[8] Renita J. Weems writes that "specific texts are unalterably hostile to the dignity and welfare of women."[9] Elsa Tamez adds that "women find clear, explicit cases of the marginalization or segregation of women in several passages of both the Old and the New Testaments."[10] Elisabeth Moltmann-Wendel simply concludes that the Bible "contains a number of sexist remarks."[11] The sexism of the times influenced and was often unchallenged by the authors of the Bible, as has been well documented by these and other scholars.

For many women, the experience of Christianity has been disappointing and devastating. Renita Weems describes the experience of many: "Dutifully, we have sat through sermons, lectures, and Bible study lessons, nodding when appropriate, copiously taking notes when expected, and, when called upon, obediently recapitulating what we have been told. All the while our souls have starved for a new revelation on the role of women in salvation history. Surely, God did not mean for us to be a footnote to redemption."[12] Sexist interpretations of the Bible have created a church that "mirrors the blasphemous duplicity of a society that proclaims that all are created equal, but excludes certain groups from access to justice and opportunity."[13] Cheryl Sanders writes, "This state of affairs is blasphemous insofar as it is grounded in the belief that God favors the white male, who alone bears God's image."[14] Because much of the church has accepted uncritically the sexism of society, we must seriously consider how biblical interpretation has been affected.

In the midst of ethnocentrism among God's people, the oneness of the human family kept emerging in the Bible. The same is true in regard to women. Despite the sexism of the time and the fact that the authors of the Bible were presumably all male, God kept calling and empowering women as equals and as sources of God's power. In chapter 4 Mimi Haddad demonstrated this powerfully in the ministry of the apostle Paul and the first-century church. I will add more about the witness of the Hebrew Bible and the ministry of Jesus.

When one opens the Bible and encounters the first reference to humanity, the reader finds that both men and women were created equally in the image of God. Here the image of God includes both the feminine and the masculine: "So God created humankind in his image, in the image of God he created them; male and female he created them" (Genesis 1:27). There is no suggestion of the subordination of women. Even though the man was created first, according to Genesis 2, the creation order was not meant to convey the message that men should dominate. That would invalidate the image of equality presented in Genesis 1. One could easily argue that the woman should hold the upper hand, because usually the prototype has flaws that are corrected in a second phase of the creative process.[15]

Throughout the Hebrew Bible there are examples of women who heard the call of God and served in the same ways that men did. The prophet Joel acknowledged this equality: "I will pour out my spirit on all flesh; your sons and your daughters shall prophesy. . . . Even on the male and female slaves, in those days, I will pour out my spirit" (Joel 2:28-29, see Acts 2:17-18). According to biblical scholar Marie Strong, it was "very radical" for Joel to suggest that sons would prophesy, because nothing happened without the permission of the oldest male in the family. It was "radical in the extreme" for women to prophesy. Even the female slaves were included.[16]

Although Joel appears to be speaking of a future event, God was already speaking through female prophets in the male-oriented Israelite society. Miriam, who was often overshadowed by her brother Moses, was a prophet (Exodus 15:20-21). Two chapters of the Bible are devoted to the work of Deborah, a prophet and a judge (Judges 4–5). Huldah prophesied the word of the Lord to the king of Judah (2 Kings 22:14-20; 2 Chronicles 34:19-28). Noadiah was among the prophets that Nehemiah feared (Nehemiah 6:14). Isaiah's wife was a "prophetess" (Isaiah 8:3). Then there was Anna, an eighty-four-year-old prophetess in the tradition of the Hebrew Bible. When she saw the infant Jesus in the temple, she "began to praise God and to speak about the child to all who were looking for the redemption of Jerusalem" (Luke 2:36-38).

Parallel to the prophetic tradition of Israel, the Hebrew Bible includes the stories of strong women like Hagar (Genesis 21:14-21); Naomi and Ruth (Ruth 1:1–4:17); Hannah (1 Samuel 1:2–2:10); Abigail (1 Samuel 25:2-42); the queen of Sheba (1 Kings 10:1-10, 13; 2 Chronicles 9:1-9, 12); the Shunammite woman (2 Kings 4:8-37); Esther (Esther 2:5–9:32) and others. One woman, Athaliah, ruled Judah (2 Kings 11:1-3). The ideal wife, according to Proverbs 31:10-31, is a strong and self-sufficient woman. The woman in the Song of Solomon is presented as an equal to the man in understanding and initiating the intimacies of love.

In addition to illustrating the leadership abilities of women, the Hebrew Bible contains feminine images of God.[17] The prophet Isaiah, speaking for God, said, "As a mother comforts her child, so I will comfort you; you shall be comforted in Jerusalem" (Isaiah 66:13). Some other examples of feminine images include presentations of God as pregnant and giving birth (Numbers 11:12; Deuteronomy 32:18; Isaiah 42:14; 46:3-4; 49:15; 66:9), nursing (Numbers 11:12; Isaiah 49:15), and serving in the role of the traditional Israelite mother (Hosea 11:1, 3-4).

Perhaps the most powerful commentary found in the Hebrew Bible regarding sexism is the story of David and Bathsheba (2 Samuel 11:1–12:13). The author described how King David ordered Bathsheba to have sexual intercourse with him. His behavior was sexist as well as adulterous. Also, as the king, David was in effect ordering Bathsheba to have sexual relations with her husband's employer, for Uriah, Bathsheba's husband, was a soldier in David's army. If she refused, it could affect her husband's job. By today's Western standards, this would be tantamount to sexual harassment. It could also be considered an act of rape. Had Bathsheba refused, the king could have ordered her death. David had abused his power and violated Bathsheba's marriage. In the face of such blatant sexism, God sent the prophet Nathan to confront King David powerfully with his sin: "You are the man! . . . Why have you despised the word of the LORD, to do what is evil in his sight?" (2 Samuel 12:7, 9).

The life and ministry of Jesus significantly influence how we understand God's view of women and how men are to relate to women. Anne Nasimiyu-Wasike writes, "The original relationship between women and men first established by God at creation was restored in Jesus Christ."[18] Jesus related to women as equals. "The fact that this impression has been transmitted through the writings of men who shared the assumptions of their culture indicates how strong this feature was in the ministry of Jesus," states Barbara J. MacHaffie.[19]

Jesus affirmed women in many ways. In a society that strictly segregated the relationships of men and women, he was very comfortable in the presence of women. Jesus was not afraid to touch women physically. He offered a healing touch to a woman who had been bent over for eighteen years (Luke 13:10-17). Then he called her a "daughter of Abraham," and her dignity was given new life. Men were called sons of Abraham, but it was unheard of to call a woman a "daughter of Abraham." Women also touched Jesus, and he was neither embarrassed nor dismayed by this action. A woman with an issue of blood touched his garment, hoping to be healed (Matthew 9:20-22; Mark 5:25-34; Luke 8:43-48). Jesus did not scold her for touching a rabbi. He celebrated her faith. Once a "sinful" woman bathed Jesus' feet with her tears, dried them with her hair, kissed them, and anointed them with ointment. When others questioned her intimate actions, Jesus accepted this act of love as born out of her gratitude for God's forgiveness (Luke 7:36-50).

Jesus often talked with women about matters of faith. Most men considered this to be inappropriate and a waste of time. Jesus considered these discussions about faith to be at the center of his ministry—a ministry that was directed equally to women and to men. So he conversed about godly matters with a woman from Samaria (John 4:7 26), a Canaanite woman (Matthew 15:21-28; Mark 7:24-30), Martha of Bethany (John 11:21-27), Mary of Bethany (Luke 10:38-42), Mary Magdalene (John 20:17), and others. Among those who followed Jesus in his ministry were women (Matthew 27:55-56; Mark 15:40-41; Luke 8:2-3). There was Mary Magdalene, Mary the mother of James and Joseph, the mother of the sons of Zebedee, Salome, Susanna, Joanna (the wife of Herod's steward), and many others who were left unnamed. Biblical scholar Joachim Jeremias called this "an unprecedented happening in the history of that time."[20] Barbara MacHaffie has said that "these women broke with Jewish custom in order to leave their homes and travel openly with Jesus."[21] Female followers funded Jesus' itinerant ministry (Mark 15:40-41; Luke 8:2-3). Jesus often stayed as a guest at the home of two sisters, Mary and Martha of Bethany, who were also among the women who followed Jesus (Luke 10:38-42; John 11:1-45).

The call to follow Jesus was very demanding and required great sacrifice. It meant leaving behind family members. Among the sacrifices of discipleship, Jesus included leaving behind sisters (Matthew 19:29; Mark 10:29-30). In male-oriented Palestine, leaving behind a brother, a father, and perhaps a mother brought a sense of loss. Leaving behind your sister was not worth comment or consideration.[22] Yet Jesus thought it was significant.

Women played some of the most important roles in the life and ministry of Jesus. The first person to receive the knowledge that Jesus was the Messiah was a woman in Samaria (John 4:25-26). While Peter is best known for his declaration that Jesus was the Christ (Matthew 16:16), Martha of Bethany also professed that Jesus was the Messiah (John 11:27). The first evangelist of the Christian era was a woman (John 4:28-30, 39-42). A woman, Mary of Bethany, was the first to be aware that Jesus was going to die (Matthew 26:6-13; Mark 14:3-9; John 12:3-8). Those who stayed with Jesus through the crucifixion were all women, except for "the disciple whom [Jesus] loved" (Matthew 26:56; Mark 14:50; John 19:25-27). Women were the first to discover the empty tomb (Matthew 28:1; Mark 16:1-2; Luke 24:1-12; John 20:1-10). The first people to see Jesus resurrected were women (Matthew 28:8-10; Mark 16:9-11; John 20:11-18). In fact, as Elisabeth Moltmann-Wendel reminds us, "The most important traditions, i.e., those of the death, burial and resurrection of Jesus, go back to women, because they were the only followers of Jesus who were there at the time."[23]

The equality of women can also be observed in how Jesus balanced his teachings and illustrations between the life experiences of both men and women.[24] Jesus said that the kingdom of heaven was like a mustard seed planted by a man and the yeast used by a woman in baking (Matthew 13:31-33). He compared the kingdom of heaven to ten bridesmaids and to a man and his servants (Matthew 25:1-30). He likened the joy in heaven when a sinner repents to a shepherd who left behind ninety-nine sheep to find the one that was lost and to a woman who swept her house looking for the coin she lost (Luke 15:3-10). When talking about prayer, Jesus equated the act to a widow who constantly demanded justice from a judge and to the attitude of two men, a Pharisee and a tax collector (Luke 18:1-14). In a sermon about the end of times, Jesus said that two people would be together with one being taken and the other left behind. He first illustrated this with two men in a field and then with two women grinding meal (Matthew 24:41-42). Jesus also used feminine imagery in his teaching. When Jesus spoke to the theologian Nicodemus about his spiritual need, he used the image of giving birth to describe the spiritual transformation that Nicodemus needed in his life (John 3:3-7). On another occasion, Jesus compared his own mission to a hen gathering her chicks under her wings (Matthew 23:37; Luke 13:34).

Jesus addressed the various forms of sexism of his day. The laws on divorce were biased in favor of men; only men could divorce their wives. This was because the wife was essentially the property of the man.[25] While Jesus did not endorse divorce, he allowed that a woman had the same right as a man to initiate a divorce (Mark 10:11-12). In another setting, Jesus challenged the perception that only women could commit adultery (John 8:3-11). The religious leaders were ready to stone a woman they had caught in the very act, yet they showed little interest in identifying the man. Jesus disarmed their sexism at the point of their own sin. He also confronted the sexism of the culture in first-century Palestine, where women were seen as objects of lust (Matthew 5:27-29).

The fact that the Jesus of history was born a male causes concern for some who seek to hear the feminine voice of God. Yet, considering the male-dominated society of the first century, sending Jesus as a man could be perceived as a stroke of genius. Jesus could respond to sexism by modeling how men (and society in general) should relate to women. Virginia

Fabella writes, "By being male, Jesus could repudiate more effectively the male definition of humanity and show the way to a right and just male-female relationship, challenging both men and women to change their life patterns."[26] Kelly Brown Douglas adds that Jesus "was able to reject the privileges of being male in a patriarchal world."[27] Ultimately, Jacquelyn Grant is correct when she states that "the significance of Christ is not his maleness, but his humanity."[28]

In the act of creation, God presented to the world a man and woman both equally possessing the image of the Almighty. Even in the midst of a highly sexist society, God just kept calling, liberating, and empowering women, as demonstrated by the extensive involvement of women as leaders in the biblical narratives. The actions of Jesus, as the incarnation of God, speak forcefully in favor of the equality of women and men. Given the evidence, it is hard to believe that anyone can doubt this. The biblical texts that reflect the sexist attitudes of earlier times and undergird sexist tendencies in the church today seem contrary to the reality of the biblical record we just perused. Yet, as Carolyn Osiek writes, "A headache for biblical conservatives and an embarrassment for biblical liberals, the problem of oppressive texts will not soon go away."[29] But to say that women are less than equal to men is to demean the image of a just and righteous God.

How can we deal with the incongruity of the Bible on the issue of women? We must be willing to struggle with the seeming discrepancies in the Scriptures, which really point out the evolution of different ancient traditions, without losing sight of the fact that God created women as equal partners to men in the human endeavor. The men who wrote the Bible were attempting to recount the story of God's salvation, while often at a human level they were wearing the blinders of a sexist culture. Much of the time they captured the truth, as in the passages delineated above. Sometimes they were caught in their human limitations. Both men and women need to embrace the approach to the Bible suggested by Osiek, when she states, "To read the Bible as women is to participate in a long and rich tradition, to be ready to critique the parts of that tradition that no longer serve, and to celebrate our belonging in a way that will make our contribution to generations to come."[30]

Classism

Like racism and sexism, classism inhibits the world's ability to be just. We live in a society that values people based on their status, power, appearance, celebrity, and wealth. In the class-conscious United States, people are ranked as upper class, upper middle class, middle class, lower middle class, working class, lower class, and under class. Other countries have their own class distinctions or caste systems. Unfortunately, many churches reflect this class division. The first-century followers of Jesus—fishermen, tax collectors, militant activists, prostitutes, tent makers, and other poor and working people— would not feel comfortable in some congregations today. In fact, the carpenter turned-preacher Jesus would not be welcome in some churches.

The Bible has much to say about the issue of social class.[31] Ronald Sider says that "the sheer volume of biblical material that pertains to questions of hunger, justice and the poor is astonishing."[32] The Scriptures lift up those who are oppressed (the poor, widows, orphans, sojourners, the sick, women, Samaritans, and others) and challenge the powerful and the rich to practice justice and equality. It is hard to believe that the Bible has been used to support economic domination when it has so much to say about God's concern for the poor in its more than 250 references to them.[33] "The variety of the terms used to describe the poor in the Bible and the frequency of their occurrence is striking, and gives a unique flavour to the religiosity of the Bible," writes George M. Soares-Prabhu. "No other religious tradition I know of gives such importance to the poor or assigns to them so significant a role."[34] Soares-Prabhu defines the poor in the Bible as "all those who are in any way, and not just economically, deprived of the means or the dignity they need to lead a fully human existence; or who are in a situation of powerlessness which exposes them to such deprivation. . . . But whatever its form, poverty in the Bible is experienced not as a natural phenomenon. . . . It is always identified as the avoidable and undesirable consequences of injustice and exploitation."[35]

The Hebrew people served a God who had liberated them from the oppression of slavery and "low" social status. God expected them to treat others who were vulnerable with the same compassion. As the author of Exodus wrote, "You shall not wrong or oppress a resident alien, for you were aliens in the land of Egypt. You shall not abuse any widow or orphan" (22:21-22). The liberation of the Hebrew people was vitally important to their understanding of how Israelite society should operate. John R. Donahue writes that for Israel, their treatment of "the marginal groups in society—the poor, the widows, the orphans, the aliens—become[s] the scale on which the justice of the whole society is weighed."[36] The author of Deuteronomy summed up the promise of Israel's social legislation: "There will, however, be no one in need among you, because the LORD is sure to bless you" (15:4).

In the midst of oppression and poverty, God does not forget those who cry out in their misery. The psalmists and the prophets spoke of God's love for the poor. The following two verses capture these sentiments:

> "Because the poor are despoiled, because the needy groan, I will now rise up," says the LORD; "I will place them in the safety for which they long." (Psalm 12:5; see 35:10)

> When the poor and needy seek water, and there is none, and their tongue is parched with thirst, I the LORD will answer them, I the God of Israel will not forsake them. (Isaiah 41:17)

A lack of social justice in ancient Israel and the concern of God for the vulnerable gave rise to the prophets and their mission. It was the prophets in the Hebrew Bible who challenged Israel to live up to their calling to be a model of justice. The prophetic books speak at length regarding the issue of classism. The prophets warned Israel's leaders of the dire consequences of their disobedience. These words of Isaiah, Ezekiel, and Amos represent the concern expressed by many of the prophets:

> Ah, you who make iniquitous decrees, who write oppressive statutes, to turn aside the needy from justice and to rob the poor of my people of their right, that widows may be your spoil, and that you may make the orphans your prey! What will you do on the day of punishment, in the calamity that will come from far away? To whom will you flee for help? (Isaiah 10:1-3; see 3:15)

> This was the guilt of your sister Sodom: she and her daughters had pride, excess of food, and prosperous ease, but did not aid the poor and needy. (Ezekiel 16:49; see 22:29)

> I will not revoke the punishment; because they sell the righteous for silver, and the needy for a pair of sandals—they who trample the head of the poor into the dust of the earth, and push the afflicted out of the way. (Amos 2:6-7; see 8:4-7)

Not only did the prophets shout loudly the warning of God to those who were acting unjustly; they also called forth to the people of Israel, inviting them to return to a right relationship with God. Any relationship with God that was judged righteous had the practice of justice as its prime component. Isaiah, Jeremiah, and Micah summed up the perspective of these voices crying out in the wilderness:

> Is not this the fast I choose: to loose the bonds of injustice, to undo the thongs of the yoke, to let the oppressed go free, and to break every yoke? Is it not to share your bread with the

hungry, and bring the homeless poor into your house; when you see the naked, to cover them, and not to hide yourself from your own kin? . . . Then you shall call, and the LORD will answer; you shall cry for help, and he will say, Here I am. (Isaiah 58:6-7, 9)

For if you truly amend your ways and your doings, if you truly act justly one with another, if you do not oppress the alien, the orphan, and the widow . . . then I will dwell with you in this place. (Jeremiah 7:5-7; see 22:15-16)

He has told you, O mortal, what is good; and what does the LORD require of you but to do justice, and to love kindness, and to walk humbly with your God? (Micah 6:8)

Jesus came as the incarnation of God's love for the poor and despised. As James H. Cone has stated, "To understand the historical Jesus without seeing his identification with the poor as decisive is to misunderstand him and thus distort his historical person."[37] The message of justice for the poor and oppressed was prophesied over Jesus even while he was still in the womb of his mother, Mary. It was she who proclaimed, "He has brought down the powerful from their thrones, and lifted up the lowly; he has filled the hungry with good things, and sent the rich away empty" (Luke 1:52-53). Jesus was reared in a "working-class" home. His first sermon spoke of "good news" for the poor and oppressed (Luke 4:18-19). He chose his disciples from among the powerless and despised of society, in effect lifting up the lowly.[38] Jesus echoed the words of his mother's prophecy in his Sermon on the Plain when he proclaimed blessings on the poor and woes on the rich (Luke 6:20-26). He lived a life of solidarity with those who were considered outcasts. He often slept outside because he had "nowhere to lay his head" (Matthew 8:20; Luke 9:58).

Jesus had little patience for classism. He challenged individuals whose egos were intertwined with class-based needs for wealth and status. Two such individuals were a rich young ruler (Matthew 19:16-30; Mark 10:17-31; Luke 18:18-30) and Zacchaeus (Luke 19:2-10). Jesus invited them to let go of worldly wealth and become "spiritually rich." Jesus also addressed institutional classism. His most dramatic effort was the clearing of the money changers from the temple (Matthew 21:12-17; Mark 11:15-19; Luke 19:45-48; John 2:13-17). Jesus confronted the classism of the culture by exalting people like the widow who contributed all she had to the temple offering (Mark 12:41-44; Luke 21:1-4). He also told parables like that of the rich fool (Luke 12:13-21) and the rich man and Lazarus (Luke 16:19-31) to address class issues. When Jesus washed the feet of his disciples, he powerfully exalted the role of the servant (John 13:1-20).

Every aspect of Jesus' life and ministry contradicted the nature of class structures. He reached out to those pressed down by social class and confronted those benefiting from class at the expense of others. Jesus lived and taught the ethic of the intrinsic equality of all people and the creation of all in the image of God. In the final judgment, according to Jesus, salvation is directly equated with one's concern for the vulnerable (Matthew 25:31-46). According to Jesus, the classist will find herself or himself responding in the following manner: "'Lord, when was it that we saw you hungry or thirsty or a stranger or naked or sick or in prison, and did not take care of you?' Then he will answer them, 'Truly I tell you, just as you did not do it to one of the least of these, you did not do it to me.' And these will go away into eternal punishment, but the righteous into eternal life" (Matthew 25:44-46).

The early church included many who were poor or marginalized by society because it was initiated by those who followed Jesus during his ministry. When some congregations began to prosper economically, there remained a commitment to serve the poor. This was illustrated by Paul's effort to collect money from a number of congregations to help the poor believers in Jerusalem (Acts 11:29-30; 24:17; Romans 15:25-27; 1 Corinthians 16:1-3; 2 Corinthians 8–9; Galatians 2:10). Also, Paul regularly reminded the churches that in Christ there were to be no class distinctions (1 Corinthians 12:13; Galatians 3:28, Colossians 3:11).

The letter of James in the New Testament provides the strongest rebuke of classist behavior (2:1-13) and perhaps the most stringent statement directed at the rich (5:1-6). James challenged the faith of his readers in this area:

> My brothers and sisters, do you with your acts of favoritism really believe in our glorious Lord Jesus Christ? For if a person with gold rings and in fine clothes comes into your assembly, and if a poor person in dirty clothes also comes in, and if you take notice of the one wearing the fine clothes and say, "Have a seat here, please," while to the one who is poor you say, "Stand there," or "Sit at my feet," have you not made distinctions among yourselves, and become judges with evil thoughts? (2:1-4)

James questioned whether one can truly be a Christian if one exhibits such classist behavior. His question should cause many of us in our time to reexamine our attitudes and how our faith is lived. James continued his commentary on the classism that was seeping into the church:

> Has not God chosen the poor in the world to be rich in faith and to be heirs of the kingdom that he has promised to those who love him? But you have dishonored the poor. Is it not the rich who oppress you? Is it not they who drag you into court? Is it not they who blaspheme the excellent name that was invoked over you?
> You do well if you really fulfill the royal law according to the scripture, "You shall love your neighbor as yourself." (2:5-8)

James challenged his readers to observe the rich faith of the people they were treating with such disregard. Then he reminded these believers that they were favoring the very people who had oppressed them.

So often we seek acceptance from the people who are hurting us. The systems of our world are often in direct contradiction to the faith we claim. Both the Hebrew Bible and the New Testament inform us that poor and needy people will always live among us (Deuteronomy 15:11; Matthew 26:11; Mark 14:7; John 12:8). This is simply an honest recognition of the fact that evil pervades our world through the practices of unjust individuals and oppressive systems that keep people poor. For this reason, throughout the Hebrew Scriptures there is a constant refrain condemning classism and expressing God's love for the poor. This theme remained a priority in the ministry of Jesus and the early church. The book of Revelation also speaks of the future judgment of those who lived in luxury at the expense of the poor and downtrodden (chaps. 18–19). While the biblical record on sexism seems at times to be incongruent, Scripture makes it very clear that classism is contrary to the will and the nature of God.

No Justice, No Peace

Racism, sexism, and classism intersect. All injustice is intertwined. The woman Jesus conversed with at Jacob's well in Samaria was affected by racism, sexism, and classism (John 4:4-18). She experienced prejudice as a Samaritan, sexism as a woman, and classism because of her lifestyle. This woman had been married five times and was living with a man who was not her husband. So intense was her shame and rejection that rather than getting water in the cool of the morning or evening, she drew water from the well in the heat of the day. The Samaritan community experienced life as outcasts. This woman from Samaria had been cast out of a community of outcasts. Jesus reached out in compassion and empowered her in the presence of his disciples and her community.

Jesus broke nearly every social taboo of first-century society by liberating the victims of injustice and by challenging the individual, institutional, and cultural forms of injustice.

Our biblical faith calls us to follow his example. Let our sentiments be like those of Mercy Amba Oduyoye: "I have arrived at a point where I no longer wish to be patient with sexism, racism, and injustices against the dignity that rightly belongs to beings made in the image of God. These labels are losing their force, but the realities they point to, the burden and the evil we are naming, continue."[39] We must not cry, "Peace, peace," when there is no peace. And there will be no peace until we take seriously the biblical mandate to work for social justice.

6

THE SOURCE OF LIBERATION AND EMPOWERMENT

In this age of diversity—when a majority of the world's people are poor, feel oppressed, and experience prejudice based on nationality, race, culture, gender, skin color, social status, or religion—we must ask a most urgent question, "Is faith in God liberating?" Most of the people in our world do not have the time or the luxury to embrace a faith that does not help set them free. Those of us who believe in the God of Abraham, Hager, Sarah, Jacob, Rachel, Moses, Jesus, Mary, Peter, Apollos, Phoebe, Paul, and Priscilla must ask ourselves afresh if our biblical faith is truly liberating. Will this faith empower us personally to survive life's daily struggles? Can this faith lead to liberation and justice at a societal and structural level? Is the Bible a source of liberation and empowerment for people, cultures, and societies? If we cannot answer these questions with a strong and resounding yes, then the Bible, and our faith, has little to offer our world in this age of diversity.

The Bible has been used as a tool for oppression. Colonial expansion, slavery, crusades, holocaust, segregation, sexism, apartheid, classism, cultural genocide, racial prejudice, and a host of other forms of injustice have been supported by a selective use of Bible verses. "The gospel was not liberating for Indian people but was a form of bondage," says George Tinker. "It's not the gospel that's not liberating, though; it's the proclamation of the gospel that puts Indians in bondage."[1] Misuse of the Bible to endorse the domination of one group over another has caused many to see Christianity as the religion of the rich and powerful and the Bible as the cornerstone undergirding systems of exploitation.

Yet concurrently, throughout history, people have been empowered by a liberating biblical faith that instilled in them the resolve to survive poverty, sexism, racism, and many other injustices. Still today, people who feel that they do not have a voice cry out in many different languages for a faith that liberates. These cries for freedom are being expressed by Christians in as many ways as there are places of oppression: Latin American liberation theology, black liberation theology, feminist theology, womanist theology, *minjung* theology, Caribbean emancipation theology, American Indian theology of place, *mujerista* theology, Asian liberation of theology, aboriginal liberation theology, and on and on. In this context of struggle, biblical interpretation becomes "both a response to the call of the gospel and the cry of the people, which are both really the same."[2]

Elsa Tamez describes liberation as "an equitable distribution of possessions and power and, with it, the elimination of poverty; the presence of God; just government; humanization; peace; life; freedom; truth; joy."[3] A liberated life is one in which we stand before God and each other free to experience the fullness of all that God created us to be. All around the world, in various cultural settings, people are seeking a faith that will set them free from the external circumstances and the internal responses that keep them from experiencing life as God meant it to be. Whether it is from government repression or personal depression, people are crying out for liberation. Many are discovering in the Bible the source for experiencing liberation and empowerment in all realms of their lives— political, economic, social, and spiritual.

Liberation is a central message in the biblical proclamation. Two foundational understandings of God in the Bible speak to the centrality of liberation—the God "who led Israel out of Egypt and who raised Jesus Christ from the dead."[4] As we shall see, in the exodus event and in the life, death, and resurrection of Jesus, the God of the Bible is indeed, fundamentally, the God of freedom and empowerment.

The Exodus Event

Central to the faith understanding of the Hebrews was the Exodus event, when God led them out of the bondage of slavery in Egypt (Exodus 1–15). The author of Exodus told the story in great detail: the Hebrews suffered and cried out for help; Moses was called by God to take leadership in negotiating for the Hebrews' freedom; Pharaoh remained stubborn; God intervened in miraculous ways to liberate the Hebrews from slavery. Each generation retold the story, and it is recorded in various forms throughout the Hebrew Bible. The exodus story became Israel's creed and was stated in capsulized form: "We were Pharaoh's slaves in Egypt, but the LORD brought us out of Egypt with a mighty hand" (Deuteronomy 6:21).

At the very core of the faith of the Hebrew people and their understanding of this God they followed was an act of liberation. Even God's name was revealed in the context of the liberation story of the Hebrew people. The name Yahweh, "I AM WHO I AM," was revealed to Moses as a confirmation that God was going to liberate the Hebrews from slavery (Exodus 3:13-15).[5] The Hebrew view was that God desired freedom not slavery, liberation not oppression, hope not despair. This God would respond to cries for help and provide a way of escape. The story of the exodus was the foundational faith story of the Hebrews, who later became the ancient nation of Israel. It informed them of who they were and who this God was they followed. The exodus story was "the clue to who God is" and the example for how God's "people should seek justice in society as the only appropriate response to the liberation they had experienced."[6] The retelling of the exodus story later became a part of the liturgy of ancient Israel and took on the role of a national epic. This liturgy reached its climax every year in the Feast of the Passover.

The liberative spirit of the exodus event found concrete form in the year of jubilee (Leviticus 25; see also Luke 4:16-20). It was to be a time when all debts were forgiven and everyone could have a fresh start. The author of Leviticus described the jubilee year:

> You shall count off seven weeks of years, seven times seven years, so that the period of seven weeks of years gives forty-nine years. Then you shall have the trumpet sounded loud; on the tenth day of the seventh month—on the day of atonement—you shall have the trumpet sounded throughout all your land. And you shall hallow the fiftieth year and you shall proclaim liberty throughout the land to all its inhabitants. It shall be a jubilee for you: you shall return, every one of you, to your property and everyone of you to your family. (25:8-10)

The twenty-fifth chapter of Leviticus ends with a reminder from God that the Hebrews "are my servants whom I brought out from the land of Egypt" (v. 55).

Although it seems that the jubilee year was never practiced as outlined, the intent was to make liberation a vital part of Israel's system of government. Freedom was to be more than rhetoric. It needed an action component. It needed to be integrated into the political system and the culture.[7] The jubilee year informs us that not only is it God's will that we create a society where freedom is guaranteed, but that it is humanly possible to do so. Unfortunately, the ancient Israelite governments decided to relegate the exodus experience to a theological statement without any practical applications. They wanted to worship the God of their liberation but not develop a society that followed the liberating principles of God.[8] This pattern has been repeated in many nations throughout history.

The proclamation of God as liberator, the God of the exodus and the jubilee, found renewed vigor with many of the prophets in the Bible. Isaiah is a prime example:

> The Spirit of the LORD GOD is upon me, because the LORD has anointed me; he has sent me to bring good news to the oppressed, to bind up the brokenhearted, to proclaim liberty to the captives, and release to the prisoners; to proclaim the year of the LORD's favor, and the day of vengeance of our God; to comfort all who mourn. (61:1-2)

Isaiah was speaking as a visionary at a time when the Israelites were seeking to rebuild their community.[9] He was reminding them that their hope for community was rooted in this God of liberation who was going to set them free and then call on them to set others free. Isaiah firmly believed in "God's commitment to justice and concern for the poor and suffering" and the need to empower the people to "confess their faith in God by showing that same commitment and concern."[10]

The God of the Hebrews was a God of liberation and empowerment. The act of God's self-revelation in the exodus event demonstrated and later symbolized this truth. The jubilee year was placed in the law of the new nation as a constitutional guarantee that the Hebrew people would live according to this understanding of the God they worshiped and followed. When the Hebrews (or the ancient nation of Israel) chose not to follow the way of the God of the exodus, the prophets challenged them to return to the foundation of their faith.

The exodus remains a powerful story today for those seeking freedom from bondage. It is a reminder that God works in human history through people. Moses was sent by God to the Hebrew people to convince them that they needed to leave Egypt to be free. Although they were crying out "on account of their taskmasters" (Exodus 3:7), they had not organized an escape. Perhaps after generations of slavery, "the Hebrews had developed the mentality of slaves."[11] Cyris H. S. Moon believes that the exodus story instructs us that God is not "the sole actor in the movement for liberation. Rather, humanity is invited to act as a partner with God." He adds that "if oppressed people are to obtain liberation, they must—with God's aid—confront the pharaohs of the world."[12] The exodus story and the jubilee laws have inspired people to believe that God desires their freedom and that a just society is possible. A belief in this God of liberation has motivated countless people to stand up to the pharaohs of their societies. Many have become the Moseses of their time and place in history, saying, "Let my people go!"

Jesus as the Incarnation of the Jubilee

Jesus was raised in the tradition of the exodus and the prophets. The ministry and message of Jesus extended "the experience of Exodus to the whole world. In Jesus, God is revealed as the liberator not only of Israel, but of all humankind."[13] His opening sermon text comes from the section of Isaiah 61 that is intended to inspire readers with the spirit of the exodus and the jubilee. The words of Jesus, in his inaugural sermon at Nazareth, spoke of his understanding that the good news of God was liberation. He indicated that he was intent on implementing this in his ministry:

> "The Spirit of the Lord is upon me, because he has anointed me to bring good news to the poor. He has sent me to proclaim release to the captives and recovery of sight to the blind, to let the oppressed go free, to proclaim the year of the Lord's favor. . . . Today this scripture has been fulfilled in your hearing." (Luke 4:18-19, 21)

By quoting Isaiah 61, Jesus declared in his inaugural sermon at Nazareth that his ministry was seeking to reintroduce the spirit of the jubilee year. The reign of God (that is, the kingdom of God) that Jesus proclaimed throughout his ministry would dawn when the spirit of the jubilee year was written on people's hearts. This God of Jesus was a God of freedom who desired that all people live a liberated life.

Jesus understood the need for liberation firsthand in his human experience. God took on flesh in an environment of oppression—Jesus was a Jew living under the domination of colonial Rome. Because Jesus was not a Roman citizen, "if a Roman soldier pushed Jesus into a ditch, he could not appeal to Caesar; he would be just another Jew in the ditch."[14] Jesus had to live daily in a setting that did not value or understand his cultural background. In addition to the daily burden of being a Jew in colonial Rome, Jesus was born under unusual circumstances, and many considered his birth illegitimate. Shortly after his birth, Jesus and his family fled to Egypt as Palestinian refugees. He grew up in a working-class family and during his ministry often slept outside with "nowhere to lay his head" (Matthew 8:20). Jesus experienced the unrestrained brutality of Pilate's law enforcement officers when he was arrested and they "spit on him, and took the staff and struck him on the head again and again" (Matthew 27:30 TNIV). Jesus' social experience was that of one who needed liberation. The life of Jesus of Nazareth parallels that of many people of color and others who experience life as cultural or social outsiders today.

In the midst of these circumstances, Jesus reached out in solidarity to others and demonstrated that the God he preached about and prayed to was a liberator. Jesus did not just proclaim a theological statement on liberation; he lived it. When John the Baptist sent his followers to discover if Jesus was the one they were looking for, Jesus told the messengers, "Go and tell John what you have seen and heard: the blind receive their sight, the lame walk, the lepers are cleansed, the deaf hear, the dead are raised, the poor have good news brought to them" (Luke 7:22; see also Matthew 11:4-5). For Jesus, liberation was active. It was experienced in dramatic ways. It could be observed. People who were enslaved physically, emotionally, economically, spiritually, and politically were set free by Jesus in the name of this God of the exodus and the jubilee. Jesus was the incarnation, the fulfillment, of the jubilee (Luke 4:21). As Virginia Fabella writes, "He showed us that we cannot work toward our true humanity, our true liberation, unless we seek the true humanity, the true liberation, of all."[15]

The act of the exodus from Egypt was a defining moment for the Hebrews, revealing the identity of the God they served. It was during the Passover celebration of the exodus that the death and resurrection of Jesus became, for his followers, the moment that defined the identity of the God that Jesus had been telling them about. The resurrection was the ultimate act of liberation and empowerment. It symbolized God's victory over death, sin, and oppression. The resurrection of Jesus demonstrated that God's power to liberate was stronger than any power of oppression, even crucifixion. The resurrection validated Jesus' message that God is a liberator.

In reference to the exodus, Elsa Tamez stated that God's revelation comes in concrete ways. She reaffirmed this fact when writing about Jesus: "The Good News takes a very concrete form. The central message is this: the situation cannot continue as it is; impoverishment and exploitation are not God's will; but now there is hope, resurrection, life, change. The reign of God, which is the reign of justice, is at hand."[16] The exodus, the jubilee, the prophets, the message and life of Jesus, and the resurrection all point to the preeminent position that liberation and empowerment take in the Bible's description of God.

When the "Liberated" Become the Oppressors

The attempt to portray the God of the Bible as a liberator is challenged by some who are seeking liberation. Robert Allen

Warrior believes "that the story of the Exodus is an inappropriate way for Native Americans to think about liberation,"[17] because God employed "the same power used against the enslaving Egyptians to defeat the indigenous inhabitants of Canaan. Yahweh the deliverer became Yahweh the conqueror. The obvious characters in the story for Native Americans to identify with are the Canaanites, the people who already lived in the promised land." Warrior continues, "As a member of the Osage Nation of American Indians who stands in solidarity with other tribal people around the world, I read the Exodus stories with Canaanite eyes."[18] We cannot simply disregard the hard questions of new voices in the dialogue on biblical interpretation. In an age of diversity, we must be willing to accept such challenges and examine new perspectives. Warrior's statement is critical for exploring our assumption that the Bible can be a source of liberation given the diversity of peoples in our world.

The book of Joshua describes in great detail the move of the Hebrew people, now called the Israelites, into Palestine ("the Promised Land"). It is a story of the conquest of the indigenous peoples of Palestine, the Canaanites and others, at God's initiative and with God's blessing. In the portrayal of the procurement of "the Promised Land" and in other passages in the Hebrew Bible, God is presented as ordering and even delighting in the oppression or killing of whole societies. This has been described by some as necessary for God's plan of redemption.[19] It certainly is a portrayal of God that is in contrast with the God of the exodus and the God of Jesus.

It is very important to remember that the faith of the Hebrews was a faith formed in the experience of the exodus and that the God they worshiped was a God of liberation. This central understanding of God is essential for dealing with other episodes recorded in the Bible in which the Israelites claim that God was in favor of their oppressive acts. The Israelites' declarations about God must be viewed through the lens of the revelation of God in the exodus event, the core of their faith understanding. A God who, by definition, sets people free does not turn around and become an oppressor. The Bible even makes reference to God's acts of liberation on behalf other nations: "Did I not bring Israel up from the land of Egypt, and the Philistines from Caphtor and the Arameans from Kir?" (Amos 9:7).

We must be willing to struggle with these inconsistencies and not be swayed from the essence of the Bible's proclamation that God is a liberator, even if, as the apostle Paul said to the believers at Galatia, "an angel from heaven should proclaim to you a gospel contrary to what we proclaimed to you" (Galatians 1:8). The conflict seems to lie with God's self-revelation through the exodus event and an ancient Israelite cultural interpretation of a God that endorsed everything ancient Israel did. The Hebrew Bible served as both Holy Scripture and a people's history. The history writers in the Bible wrote with the purpose of placing ancient Israel as the centerpiece of God's will for humanity. Many of the prophets (and later Jesus), on the other hand, were much more willing to see God as the God of all people in the world. As in Amos 9:7, God speaks of liberating the Philistines and the Arameans as well as Israel.

Throughout history many have used "God's will" to build support for objectives that have much more to do with power, control, economic gain, and empire building than the will of God. The biblical story of Israel's conquest of Canaan has provided a framework for such attempts at exploitation. Some have claimed to be the chosen people of God entering their promised land and have declared that the indigenous peoples were the Canaanites waiting to be conquered. The history of the United States, South Africa, and other countries resound with these themes. The Bible itself must be liberated from such use. This is critical so that "people who seek to be shaped and molded by reading the text [Exodus] will differentiate between the liberating god and the god of conquest."[20]

What happened after the exodus also provides "an example of what can happen when powerless people come to power."[21]

How could the Hebrews, who had just been set free from oppression in Egypt, oppress the Canaanites? One of the greatest tragedies in history is when people who have been set free from oppression turn around and oppress someone else. Unfortunately, history is full of such examples. Some claim their freedom in the name of God and then in the name of God dominate and subordinate another group of people. The "liberated" often use the Bible to support their oppressive actions.

For previously oppressed, now liberated, people to avoid becoming oppressors themselves, there must be a "revolution of images."[22] Too often the newly liberated have learned well the ways of power that have been used against them. Rather than creating new ways for ordering relationships in society, such as the jubilee year, the old ways are simply adapted and reshaped by the formerly oppressed. Soon they become the oppressors, another group of people cries out for liberation, and the cycle continues. Liberation must, as Amos Niven Wilder writes, "operate at a deeper level where the wrestling is with the loyalties, banners, and spells that rule a way of life and its institutions."[23] Liberation involves more than just changing one's social or economic circumstances. True liberation means being set free from the need for control and being empowered to create an equitable society. Without the personal healing of the souls of people who have been damaged by oppression, the liberation and empowerment of hurting people will lead to the next generation of oppressors. Oppressive ways are learned and passed on from one generation to the next. They are passed on in both the cultures of the powerful and the powerless (who want to be powerful). Liberation must be followed by healing before empowerment takes place. This is true for individuals, cultures, and societies.[24]

Such a therapeutic process of healing was in place for the Hebrew people. God sent a healer and a liberator in the person of Moses. Although born a Hebrew slave, Moses was raised in Pharaoh's household. He did not personally experience the damage to his psyche and his spirit that comes from the dehumanization of enslavement. Moses did not inherit the feeling of powerlessness inbred in the culture after nearly four hundred years of bondage. He had not been indoctrinated with the belief that he was by nature a slave and therefore less than human. Yet because he had significant contact with his Hebrew family and his spiritual roots, Moses did not accept uncritically the benefits of power he enjoyed as Pharaoh's adopted grandson. So when Moses was sent by God to lead the Hebrews to freedom after centuries of bondage, he carried neither the emotional nor the cultural scars of slavery (Exodus 1–4).

The subsequent forty years that the Hebrews wandered in the wilderness after the exodus from slavery provided enough time to complete the healing process. In fact, nearly a whole generation of Hebrews died during this period, allowing for fresh leadership to emerge that had limited experience with the pain of slavery. They even had in place a plan for a new society based on the jubilee year regulations. Unfortunately, it seems that the necessary healing did not take place during the forty years of roaming the wilderness. When Moses died, Joshua became the next leader. Joshua was one of the few remaining Hebrews still alive who had lived as a slave under Pharaoh. It was Joshua who led the Hebrews, now called the Israelites, into battle against the indigenous people of Palestine. Warrior offers a note of hope for those following the God of the Bible: "Perhaps, if they are true to their struggle, people will be able to achieve what Yahweh's chosen people in the past have not: a society of people delivered from oppression who are not so afraid of becoming victims again that they become oppressors themselves."[25]

The Power of Personal Liberation

One of the reasons for so much injustice in our world is that people need to be set free on a personal level— emotionally, psychologically, and spiritually. Liberating the social and economic aspects of life is apparently not enough. An important question then becomes, in an age of diversity, is the Bible a source of personal liberation? Vine Deloria Jr. directly challenged the power of biblical faith to liberate the personal when he wrote about the difference between Native American tribal religions and Christianity: "There is no question which tradition is capable of speaking meaningfully to the diversity of peoples. A Sweat Lodge, a Vision Quest, or a Sing performed in a sacred place with the proper medicine man provides more to its practitioners than a well-performed Mass, a well-turned sermon argument, or a well-organized retreat. Christian rituals simply have no experiential powers."[26]

Deloria would have us believe that biblical faith, particularly in its rituals, has little value for personal liberation or healing. What must be kept in mind is that faith in God, as presented in the Bible, does not focus on rituals as the prime source of experiential power. The emphasis in the Scriptures is on a direct relationship with a personal God. The Bible does speak of the experiential side of liberation, but in a relational mode rather than a ritualistic one. Many can witness to the experiential power of a personal relationship with God.

One such witness was Martin Luther King Jr. He provides us with an example of an individual who was committed to social liberation yet needed and experienced moments of personal liberation as well. Late one night during the 1950s bus boycott in Montgomery, Alabama, a phone caller threatened King's life, saying, "Nigger, we are tired of you and your mess now. And if you aren't out of this town in three days, we're going to blow your brains out and blow up your house." Unable to sleep, King went to the kitchen to drink some coffee and found himself overwhelmed by the pressures of leadership. King recounted his prayer that night: "Lord, I'm down here trying to do what's right. I think I'm right. I think the cause we represent is right. But, Lord, I must confess that I'm weak now. I'm faltering. I'm losing my courage." Then, in the midst of his prayer, he felt as if he could hear an inner voice speaking to him: "Martin Luther, stand up for righteousness. Stand up for justice. Stand up for truth. And, lo, I will be with you, even until the end of the world." When later reflecting on this event of personal liberation and empowerment in a sermon, King said, "I heard the voice of Jesus saying still to fight on. He promised never to leave me, never to leave me alone." He said that the mystical experience had an immediate affect: "Almost at once my fears began to go. My uncertainty disappeared."[27]

This God that King preached about as the source of liberation for African Americans in racially segregated Montgomery became a source of personal empowerment in a time of real fear for King. The words of encouragement that King heard in his mystical experience were from biblical themes. "And, lo, I will be with you, even until the end of the world" is from Matthew 28:20.[28] These words and themes from King's biblically nurtured faith provided him with a personally transforming experience.

Three days later an elderly woman, known to everyone as Mother Pollard, rose to her feet after King finished preaching and walked to the front of the church.[29]

> "Something is wrong with you," said Pollard. "You didn't talk strong tonight."
>
> "Oh, no, Mother Pollard," King replied. "Nothing is wrong. I am feeling as fine as ever."
>
> "Now you can't fool me," she said. "I knows something is wrong. Is it that we ain't doing things to please you? Or is it that the white folks is bothering you?"
>
> . . . Before he could say anything, she moved her face close to his and said loudly, "I done told you we is with you all the way. But even if we ain't with you, God's gonna take care of you." . . .
>
> Later, King said that with her consoling words fearlessness had come over him in the form of raw energy.[30]

A few minutes later, King was informed that his house had indeed been bombed as the caller had threatened three days earlier. He went home and found an angry crowd ready for revenge. King stepped to the front of the house and said: "We must meet hate with love. . . . I want it to be known the length and breadth of this land that if I am stopped, this movement will not stop. . . . For what we are doing is right. What we are doing is just. And God is with us." The crowd eventually dispersed peacefully into the night.[31]

Mother Pollard echoed the words that King had heard in his mystical experience three days earlier: God would always be there for him. King, now empowered, offered the same encouragement to the angry crowd. The same God who spoke to Moses in a burning bush and to Saul on the Damascus road spoke to King in his inner consciousness. This God prompted Mother Pollard to approach King three days later as his house was being bombed, reaffirming God's message that everything was going to be all right. This is but one example of a countless number that could be shared. The God proclaimed in the Bible is both a social and personal liberator with experiential powers who will meet the needs of people in this age of diversity.

We must not disregard Deloria's challenge. His comments are no doubt grounded in his observations of the faith experience for too many Christians. Many people call themselves Christians but have a faith devoid of any transforming power. Some who embrace the social dimension of biblical liberation fail to allow for the personal renewal that must accompany it for one to remain empowered in the struggle. Deloria's comments remind us that people need to be personally liberated and empowered in their lives. Martin Luther King Jr.'s kitchen experience reminds us that a faith rooted in the God revealed in the Bible does have extraordinary experiential powers.

Merging Personal and Social Liberation

For many Christians, the problem is not one of too much emphasis on the social aspects of a liberating biblical faith but an exclusive focus on the personal aspects of faith in Jesus Christ. Many people consider faith a personal matter without implications for one's society. While this belief is held by some who are powerless in society, it is more pervasive among the powerful. People who face some form of injustice are more apt to seek out the Scriptures that speak of social liberation because of their individual circumstances. The sense of comfort experienced by those in power often blinds them to this message of the Bible because they have no felt need. Japanese American Lloyd K. Wake recounts an example of this: "Our Mennonite Brethren friends visited us while we were in the concentration camps in the Arizona desert during World War II. It was a compassionate act for which we were very grateful. But their religious faith never led them to speak against that injustice."[32] As we have demonstrated, a faith in God divorced from social concerns is not biblical.

The merger of a zeal for personal salvation with a commitment to social salvation could be found among many evangelical Christians during the 1800s in the United States. The revival meetings that called people to a personal conversion experience also called for the end of slavery, the right of women to vote, the need to address poverty, and in some cases, the end of war.[33] Charles G. Finney was an outstanding example of this integration of personal and social liberation. He thought of himself as an evangelist inviting people to experience personal conversion, but he preached that conversion leads to new ways of acting regarding social issues. Speaking of what he believed was an ineffective Christian faith, Finney said, "Many churches have taken the wrong side on the subject of slavery, have suffered prejudice to prevail over principle, and have feared to call this abomination by its true name."[34]

There were hopes for resurrecting this Finney-style evangelism in the 1950s. Martin Luther King Jr. envisioned the possibility of joint crusades with Billy Graham with Graham preaching for personal conversion and King for social action. King's organization, the Southern Christian Leadership Conference, already had as its motto "To redeem the soul of America." These two great Baptist orators could have preached to interracial audiences about the need for personal and social salvation, as well as called for repentance from racism as a personal and structural sin. King's counterpart was not ready.[35]

The challenge to bring together the personal and social dimensions of liberation, as well as the Hebrew Bible and the New Testament, is given impetus by the suggestion of Kosuke Koyama to merge the messages of these two biblical texts:[36]

> What does the LORD require of you but to do justice, and to love kindness, and to walk humbly with your God? (Micah 6:8)
>
> "Here is the Lamb of God who takes away the sin of the world!" (John 1:29)

For Koyama, these two texts capture the essence of what it means to be a follower of the God of liberation. The work of social liberation, "doing justice," needs a personal experience of liberation with "the Lamb of God who takes away the sin of the world," and vice versa. As Koyama writes, "Redemption cannot be complete without justice, nor justice without redemption."[37] Biblical liberation is both personal and social.

In this time of increasing diversity, the search is for a faith that liberates. This quest cuts across racial, cultural, economic, and gender lines. People who feel powerless want to be empowered. Some cry out for liberation at a systemic level. Others cry out for liberation from the daily grind of life. Even many of the powerful seek personal liberation from a life that is without ultimate meaning. The Bible is a source for discovering the God of liberation who desires to set people free. We must embrace the Bible's emphasis on liberation and empowerment if our Christian faith is to be relevant for this generation. As James Cone writes: "Many people think that religion has everything to do with an individual's personal relationship with God and nothing to do with society and one's fight for justice in it. . . . I contend that the depth of any religious commitment should be judged by one's commitment to justice for humanity, using the liberation activity of human beings as the lens through which one sees God."[38]

7

A ROUNDTABLE ON THE BIBLE, LIBERATION, AND RECONCILIATION

Brenda Salter McNeil, Richard Twiss, Jean Zaru, and Allan Aubrey Boesak

The biblical cry for liberation and social justice can seem to be in tension with the biblical call to be ambassadors of reconciliation. Four scholar activists speak to this dilemma in their own communities: African America, Native America, the Occupied Palestinian Territories, and South Africa. They speak with candor regarding these tensions, as well as about the hope that is found when reconciliation and liberation intersect with each other.

Seizing *Kairos* Time in Our Generation— Brenda Salter McNeil

In 1986 I discovered that the world was changing. That year my husband and I traveled to England to lecture at the Oxford Centre for Mission Studies on the history of the black church in the United States of America. The Church of England was facing unprecedented institutional challenges and numerical decline. Beautiful gothic church buildings were closing their doors as places of worship and being used as office spaces, being turned into libraries, or simply being left vacant. Convinced that these changes were occurring in part because of urbanization, the staff of the Oxford Centre wanted to learn from churches that thrived in these conditions. They had discovered that the black church in the United States excelled at dealing with the challenges of the urban environment, growing strong vibrant churches in the midst of the city. So they invited us to come and teach on everything we knew about the African American church. The students took copious notes. It was the first time in my life someone had expressed a sincere interest in understanding my experience as an African American Christian. I had no idea that my life as a black Pentecostal female had any relevance to anyone else. No one had ever asked.

I left that trip convinced that God was getting ready to do something extraordinary, and that this "new thing" was going to unite people from all over the world who didn't look like one another. I began to sense that this "new thing" was going to uniquely and strategically include people of color. People who had previously been marginalized and minimized would now be used by God to provide prophetic leadership as agents of reconciliation and renewal around the world. When I returned home, I was introduced to a document from South Africa called The *Kairos* Document, which was a sociopolitical and theological mandate calling for the end of apartheid.[1] The concept of kairos was unfamiliar to me. I studied the Bible to better understand the term. I learned that *kairos* is a Greek word that means the right time, the set time, the opportune time, the strategic time, or the decisive time. Kairos is the "pregnant" time. When a man and woman conceive a child, they wait for months in anticipation of their child's birth. Even in the age of ultrasound, when parents can learn the gender of the child and cherish grainy photos from the womb (they can only guess at what their child will look like), they wait, hope, and pray in

133

eager expectation. Then one night, usually when she least expects it, the woman starts to feel something different in her
body. She turns to her husband, nudges him gently but firmly,
and says, "Honey, wake up. It's time!" She doesn't want him
to tell her the time on his watch. She wants him to get up and
spring into action, because kairos time is a decisive time that
demands a response.

In the New Testament, Jesus used the word *kairos* when he
talked about the kingdom of God being close at hand. There
are times in history when people must accurately recognize
and respond to the reign of God in their midst. These times are
not determined or controlled by human beings, and to miss
them is to risk serious consequences. Jesus spoke of kairos
time in Jerusalem.

> As he came near and saw the city, he wept over it, saying, "If you,
> even you, had only recognized on this day the things that make
> for peace! But now they are hidden from your eyes. Indeed, the
> days will come upon you, when your enemies will set up ram-
> parts around you and surround you, and hem you in on every
> side. They will crush you to the ground, you and your children
> within you, and they will not leave within you one stone upon
> another, because you did not recognize the time of your visita-
> tion from God." (Luke 19:41-44)

Jesus was grief stricken for the people he loved because of
their inability to discern their kairos moment. He had just pro-
cessed through the city streets and had been greeted by people
praising him, waving palm branches, and cheering, "Hosanna!
Hosanna! Blessed is he who comes in the name of the Lord!"
But instead of being overjoyed by this reception, he was weeping outside Jerusalem because they did not recognize their
kairos moment.

I believe that we, too, are faced with a kairos moment in
history—a time when God is moving and radical change is
approaching. Like the signs that accompany a birth, they can

134

prompt anxiety or nurture anticipation, but they demand a response. This kairos moment is seen in the election of Barack Obama as the first African American president of the United States of America. Although some said he was unprepared, Obama discerned a growing collective need among U.S. citizens for hope and real change. As a result, he seized the day and captured the collective imagination of people from different ethnic, racial, cultural, socioeconomic, religious, and geographic backgrounds. Barack Obama inspired ordinary citizens to unite beyond obvious differences to make a radical change in the political process and in the world. I believe that African Americans are uniquely positioned to provide this type leadership all around the world. The tragedy of our past has uniquely qualified us to speak on issues of liberation and reconciliation with an authority that is born out of experience.

To seize this moment in history, we must expand our models of liberation and reconciliation beyond those of the civil rights era to include new global paradigms. We must find new ways to have old conversations if we are to remain relevant in the midst of changing demographic, economic, and global concerns. This is how the biblical call for liberation and reconciliation must be heard and responded to by the African American community. This is our kairos moment. Nelson Mandela reportedly said, when asked how he became the president of South Africa, "I suffered my way into leadership." African Americans must also understand that our liberation from racial injustice, prejudice, and discrimination has positioned us to be reconcilers with global significance and a calling to give prophetic leadership. Wherever racial, ethnic, and tribal hostilities exist around the world, there are people who are waiting for African Americans to come and share our unique perspective, talents, and gifts.

I experienced the reconciling power of this during our trip to Oxford, England. My husband, Derek, found himself saying candidly that after centuries of trying to be included in the white church, black people had developed their own vibrant church life and no longer wanted or needed to be accepted by white Christians. While he was expounding forcefully on this topic, a white Anglican priest named John Mockford interrupted. "Wait a minute, lad. Your church is young and agile. Our church has become old and arthritic. We need you to wait up for us." A single tear fell from his eye. He turned to a man sitting next to him and said, "This is embarrassing, eh?" There was a moment of total silence. Then Derek said, with a new level of empathy in his voice, "By asking me to wait up for you, you have just empowered me to be in relationship with you." That day we experienced an authentic moment of racial reconciliation—because one man had the courage to acknowledge his need for someone who was racially and ethnically different from him. This is an example of the reconciling work God is doing in the earth through the power of African American prophetic leadership. This is our kairos moment. And if we seize it, we have the potential to unite people from every tribe, language, culture, ethnic group, and nation.

Liberation and the Land—Richard Twiss

God came to earth as a "two-legged." Jesus was a member of the tribe of Judah, a people with an ancient history of connection to the land. Land was a sacred place of identity, belonging, provision, and fellowship with Creator. It was not a commodity or an untamed wilderness to be overcome, conquered, and developed. Land was a place of belonging. Jesus was a man of the land. I want to suggest that authentic biblical dialogue about reconciliation requires we address the issue of land from a Native American perspective.

In the *Cobell v. Norton* case, U.S. district judge Royce C. Lamberth reminds us that our pursuit for biblical reconciliation and liberation in the United States is far more than a call for theological reflection; it is a call to action. Injustice is not a thing of the past but a living reality for native people today.

For those harboring hope that the stories of murder, dispossession, forced marches, assimilationist policy programs, and other incidents of cultural genocide against Indians are merely the echoes of a horrible, bigoted government-past that has been sanitized by the good deeds of more recent history . . . this case tells the dreary story of [the Department of the] Interior's degenerate tenure as Trustee-Delegate for the Indian trust—a story shot through with bureaucratic blunders, flubs, goofs and foul-ups, and peppered with scandals, deception, dirty tricks and outright villainy—the end of which is nowhere in sight.[2]

Land and identity are inseparable realities for indigenous populations. In today's modern world, our peoples struggle to live in harmony within the continuum of life, land, and identity. As native followers of Jesus, it is only the dualism of modernity or Western thought that compartmentalizes these realities—one labeled "geopolitical" and the other "sociocultural." It is the Creator's breath that brought the world to life and sustains it as one living reality; the earth is the Lord's in all it fullness.

"When I shut up the heavens so that there is no rain, or command the locust to devour the land, or send pestilence among my people, if my people who are called by my name humble themselves, pray, seek my face, and turn from their wicked ways, then I will hear from heaven, and will forgive their sin and heal their land." (2 Chronicles 7:13-14)

God speaks of the interconnection between people's heart condition (sin), natural disaster, land, spirituality, and blessing.

Many in the church have made this prayer a kind of mantra for returning the United States to its "Christian foundation." However, what does it mean if we as First Nations followers of Jesus pray this prayer? Does the question, "Whose land is it?" have any implications for how God responds to this prayer? Does land have value or meaning only if it has a legal definition or is owned (by a nation state)? What does God want to heal, and for us, does that mean the United States of America or the sovereign Nations of Native North America? When we pray that prayer, what does the answer look like?

Liberation from a Native American perspective requires that we deconstruct the pseudo-theological framework of Manifest Destiny that justified, moralized, and invoked God's blessing on the obscene and immoral acquisition of native land and brought genocide to America's original inhabitants. In February 1887 the Dawes Act caused tribes to lose 90 million acres of reservation land. Today federally recognized tribes, such as the Rosebud Sioux tribe, Navajo Nation, White Mountain Apache, and others govern their affairs on reservation land allotted to them by the Dawes Act but do not legally own their own land. It is in fact held in trust for them by the Department of the Interior (DOI), Bureau of Indian Affairs (BIA) Office. Technically, native people are still wards of the government. Since then, the revenues generated by various agricultural, ranching, or mining operations that occurred on reservation "trust lands" for tribes and their members (or lessees) have been held in trust by the Bureau of Indian Affairs. The use of the word *trust* in the management of native land remains a national travesty.

In 1996 Elouise Cobell of the Blackfeet Nation and her co-plaintiffs filed a class action lawsuit against the secretary of the Interior, assistant secretary of the Interior, and secretary of the treasury on behalf of more than three hundred thousand Native Americans.[3] It is estimated that more than eight billion dollars including interest cannot be accounted for and, with no paper trail, is lost in the quagmire of BIA bureaucracy. Judge Lamberth wrote of this travesty, "The idea that Interior would either instruct or allow BIA to withhold trust payments, and then to stonewall the Indians who dared to ask why, is an obscenity that harkens back to the darkest days of United States-Indian relations."[4]

As native people, our identity is connected to where we come from. The Navajo bury the umbilical of newborns so they will always know where their home is. Land is a place of life and mystery, a "sacred space" where Creator and humans connect. Notions of biblical liberty for today's Native American peoples must take into account the fundamental need for tribal sovereignty and self-governance. Whether on the reservation or in the city, we are seeking how to reconnect to our earthen roots buried under a few centuries of the asphalt myth of divine chosenness and civilization in the United States. A Eurocentric Christianity, with its Western theological assumptions, has sought to remove us and relocate us to a theological reservation called modernity.

With such injustice, is it possible to have biblical reconciliation without restitution? In the 1980s I ran a business that sold 1970s muscle cars. One day someone stole my sweet 1970 Pontiac Firebird. The car was never found. Suppose that twenty-five years later a man came to me and confessed he was the one who stole my Firebird. He remarked that he had become a Christian and was making amends for past sins and needed to come and ask forgiveness for the grief and pain his thievery had cost me. As I offered him my forgiveness, I asked if he could return my stolen car. Taken aback, he responded that many years ago he had the title changed to register him as the legal owner. After all these years, he considered the car his and did not intend to give it back. He said he would consider selling it to me at a fair price though.

In contrast to this story, Hollywood made a movie about Robert Kearns, the man who invented the intermittent windshield wiper for the automobile. His invention was purloined by major auto manufacturers. He later won lawsuits against the Ford and Chrysler motor companies. The court verdict could have simply required Ford and Chrysler to apologize and ask Mr. Smith for his forgiveness and be done with it. Instead, appropriate compensation had to be made in order for justice to occur. Does reconciliation possess a compensatory dimension?

I have thought of reconciliation as a process rather than a one-time event. First, a person acknowledges a wrong done and takes responsibility for it; this leads to remorse and repentance; then forgiveness is sought for the wrong done; forgiveness then results in some form of restitution, compensation, or retribution as an outward expression of genuine repentance. Only then does reconciliation happen. Reconciliation occurs at the end of the process.

The land called America is rapidly changing before our eyes. In one hundred years it will have reinvented itself as a land of rich diversity and multiplicity of culture and ethnicity. Our sovereign native nations and people will be alive and growing. If we pray and hope that God will bless that future land, what or whose land will God be blessing? What should a biblically informed response to issues of the land be for us today? What awaits our children's children?

What are we doing and how are we living to help prepare our children and children's children to successfully move reconciliation and biblical liberation to a more comprehensive and deeper level in their generation?

Sulha, Reconciliation—Jean Zaru

Finger pointing and blame are the fuel of the cycle of conflict.[5] But the prophet Isaiah gives hope to those who would find another way.

> If you remove the yoke from among you, the pointing of the finger, the speaking of evil, if you offer your food to the hungry and satisfy the needs of the afflicted, then your light shall rise in the darkness and your gloom be like the noonday. The LORD will guide you continually, and satisfy your needs in parched places, and make your bones strong; and you shall be like a watered

garden, like a spring of water, whose waters never fail. Your ancient ruins shall be rebuilt; you shall raise up the foundations of
many generations; you shall be called the repairer of the breach,
the restorer of streets to live in. (Isaiah 58:9-12)

How do we take away the yoke and the pointing of the finger? What are the demands of reconciliation? I cannot reconcile myself to structures of domination and oppression, covered over with words of peace and reconciliation. To me, it
is hypocrisy when words of peace and healing are preached
without regard to any genuine change in the oppressive situation created by the powerful over the weak. Too often in our
talk about peace and reconciliation, the victimized are called
to forgive and reconcile in a way that perpetuates rather than
rectifies the root causes of injustice, alienation, and division.
Reconciliation can mean a collapse into acceptance of the status quo because of the belief that nothing can be done.

Real reconciliation involves a fundamental repair to human
lives, especially to those who have suffered. It requires restoring the dignity of the victims of violence. Reconciliation contains four dimensions: political, economic, psycho-social, and
spiritual. Christ did not merely announce the good news that
the sick can be healed. He healed and in that act proclaimed
the kingdom. Word and deed are one. They are inseparable.
Reconciliation is central to the gospel and those of us who
are Christians must be active in reconciling—in repairing lives
and proclaiming the good news. Reconciliation as a way of
transformation challenges us to resist the temptation simply to
rearrange the furniture, whether that rearrangement is in the
structures of our psyche or those of our planet.

But the fact remains that many Israelis do not feel guilt for
what they did; they do not feel that they have done anything
wrong because of their Zionist ideology. Therefore, reconciliation is not an issue for them. Many talk to us about reconciliation by suggesting a hasty peace. They speak of reconciliation
instead of liberation or reconciliation as a managed process.

These calls want us, the victims of violence, to let bygones be bygones and exercise a Christian forgiveness. In trivializing and ignoring the history of suffering, the victims are forgotten and the causes of suffering are never uncovered and confronted. Reconciliation is not a hasty peace that tries to escape the examination of the causes of suffering. If the causes are not addressed, suffering is likely to continue. The wheel of violence keeps turning and more and more people get crushed.

Let me share with you our Palestinian and Arab way of making peace and granting forgiveness. If my neighbor or any member of the community has violated my dignity in any way or even has taken my land or injured any of my family members, the first step in this nonviolent form of peacemaking is for the person who wronged me to choose a mediator, someone who is well respected in the society for his or her values of justice and reconciliation. Then we proceed in the following way:

- A date is set to visit me in my home in the presence of my extended family members. Reconciliation involves community participation.
- The person who wronged me will come with the mediator and his/her extended family members. Reconciliation involves this expression of humility.
- The person who has wronged me recognizes the hurt that was done. Then a commitment is made to repair the damage and forgiveness is asked for. Reconciliation involves the heartfelt expression of truth and a commitment to repair.
- The mediator takes the responsibility of executing the repairing of the damage. There is a trusted third party to see to it that reparations are followed through.
- Then forgiveness is given (*"ahli samah imnah"*) by saying, "You are in our home. You are one of us and we take it upon ourselves to help and protect the person who has done us wrong." It is then proclaimed, "Forgiveness is a

gift from God" (*"samah min Allah"*). Forgiveness is essential for real reconciliation.

- Finally, all share in eating together, breaking bread together, which is a commitment of friendship and sharing rather than enmity and exploitation.

This way of making peace and reconciliation, called *sulha*, respects and restores the dignity of both parties. Rather than continue a cycle of humiliation and violence, sulha takes steps toward a new relationship of equity and respect. In my humble experience, I have found that peculiar strength of nonviolence comes from the dual nature of its approach: offering respect and concern on the one hand while meeting injustice with noncooperation and defiance on the other. Let us nurture the growth of a breakthrough community of friends that crosses boundaries, deconstructs the dominant ideology that normalizes sin and injustice, and shapes an alternative praxis of mutuality.

And Zacchaeus Remained Sitting in the Tree—
Allan Aubrey Boesak

More than most Truth Commissions working during the 1980s and 1990s, South Africa's Truth and Reconciliation Commission (TRC) seems to have made an impact on politics around the world. There are two reasons for that, I think. First, South Africa quite deliberately forged the link between "truth" and "reconciliation," which was even more remarkable because of the long and hard struggle for liberation that led to our democratization. Second, we were looking for more than just the truth about human rights abuses. The TRC was meant to be a platform to break the silence on all those unspeakable things that happened during the reign of apartheid, giving the victims of apartheid crimes the opportunity to bare their souls to the nation, to listen to the perpetrators and hear the truth. But the ultimate goal was to effect reconciliation between victim and perpetrator, and in the process enable South Africans to confront their past, learn from that past, and move on together as a reconciled people. Our reconciliation process was meant to be the crowning glory of our liberation struggle.

The South African government itself set reconciliation, reconstruction, and development as the goals of this process. It was not just to achieve "socioeconomic justice" but also the "restoration of the moral order in our society," according to the deputy minister of justice, Johnny de Lange. It was aimed at "nation building, restorative justice, and reconciliation."[6] With the majority of ordinary South Africans steeped in the language and ideals of the liberation struggle and firmly rooted in the Christian tradition that emphasis resonated deeply. For them it meant that the struggle for liberation would not be over until we reached the goal of a "reconciled nation," and it gave the process the seal of biblical sanction. As Christians we knew that reconciliation lies at the very heart of the gospel. There was no dispute, "for the love of Christ urges us on" and we were a "new creation." "All this is from God, who reconciled us to himself through Christ, and has given us the ministry of reconciliation. . . . So we are ambassadors for Christ" (2 Corinthians 5:14, 17, 18-20). This is the Christ whose lordship we have sought in every area of life, also in our struggle for liberation; on whose name we called in suffering and hope. Because of his steadfast love and justice, we knew that our struggle would not be in vain and that our freedom was secure. How shall we now say "nay" when in that name we are called to forgive and build our new nation on the solid rock of reconciliation?

Even as we mention this, a question arises. Was this link between truth, justice, liberation, and reconciliation a genuinely serious matter for South African politicians, or was it pure political deception to garner much needed support at a crucial time for a process both difficult and fraught with danger? In other words, were our leaders really driven by the biblical demand for reconciliation without which they knew our dream of liberation would not survive. Or was it a ploy to sanctify unseemly political compromises in the eyes of the eighty percent of South Africans who profess to be Christian, especially black people whose faith stood so much at the heart of the struggle?

I believe the answer is the latter: it was a ploy. In a painful inversion of the apartheid ploy to use the Bible to justify apartheid and our subjugation, the new political elite deliberately used the Bible to deceive South Africa's Christian faithful into believing that our reconciliation process was to be real, biblically grounded, just, and liberative. It is true that the addition of "reconciliation" to "truth" was proposed by former president F. W. De Klerk, but the African National Congress (ANC) was quick to see its benefits. In the end, much of the truth was never heard, perpetrators of injustice literally got away with murder, and there was little sign of genuine remorse, penance, and responsibility. Accountability was haphazard; no, worse: it was selective. Justice, as the restoration of human integrity, dignity, and fulfillment of meaningful relationships has still not materialized.

Our disdain for the rights of the poor and the marginalized, our failure to recognize and resist racism, our unwillingness to embrace and celebrate our diversity as a nation, our lack of sensitivity for the establishment of justice, our outrageous flirtation with the language and the tools of violence, and our debonair attitude toward genuine transformation—all these things cripple our reconciliation process as a paradigm for righteous politics and make a mockery of liberation.

As a result, all across our nation, from the streets to the halls of academia, from the pulpit to the lectern, there is a serious reevaluation of our reconciliation process. More and more South Africans now speak, in the words of Dr. Mamphela Ramphele, of "the miracle that never was."[7]

Despite the legal framework and intentions, our TRC was a very Christian affair. The authoritative presence of Archbishop Desmond Tutu as chairperson almost guaranteed that, but so did that deliberate addition of "reconciliation" to "truth." What the politicians thought should be a tool for domestication in fact was a revolutionary standard that would expose more truth than anyone was ready for. When Christians in South Africa think of reconciliation, they think of Jesus and Paul. But they also think of Zacchaeus. When they speak of the TRC now, they wonder why the name of Jesus was called upon, why Paul seemed to be always present, but why Zacchaeus was never called to testify. This wonderful multilayered story from Luke's gospel about Jericho's rich, notorious tax collector who built his wealth on clever manipulation of the Roman tax system, exploitation, and sheer greed, has radical consequences for reconciliation. It is logical that it might have been the rich who resented him, but it was the poor who suffered most from the corruption of Zacchaeus and his subcontractors. There are no prizes for guessing at the tensions between the community and this man "of short stature" whose name means "innocent."

Zacchaeus hid in the tree. Jesus stopped right underneath and looked up. The whole crowd faded into fuzzy irrelevance as the focus was entirely on the little man in the sycamore tree—his conversation with Jesus, his conversion, and his reaction. Zacchaeus drew radical conclusions from his conversion and the act of being reconciled with God. He knew this reconciliation needed to be effected with the community in order for it to be genuine. He understood that reconciliation has to mean transformation if it is to mean anything: of his life and lifestyle, his relationships with the community, and especially with those he had wronged. Zacchaeus knew that reconciliation means the restoration of justice, relationships, dignity, integrity, and human fulfillment.

So Zacchaeus set out to do just that. He had no excuses, no half measures. He spared neither his possessions nor himself. For him reconciliation is not cheap: "Look, half of my possessions, Lord, I will give to the poor; and if I have defrauded anyone of anything, I will pay back four times as much" (Luke 19:8). Zacchaeus did not believe in reconciliation that cost him nothing. And because Jesus, the incarnation of the reconciliation and compassionate love and justice of God, understood how crucial Zacchaeus's actions were, he did not enter into some meaningless moralizing about the relative worth or worthlessness of money, or how just love is enough. Jesus was just as radical, linking Zacchaeus's response immediately to his salvation. "Today salvation has come to this house" (19:9). Not just to the man, but to his *house*. And because crucial lessons are to be drawn from this, the crowd is brought back into the conversation: "because he too is a son of Abraham" (19:9).

The intriguing thing here is the radical consequences of reconciliation: transformation, restoration, and justice, which Jesus sums up as salvation. That is the fulfillment of liberation. Herein was the greatest challenge for the TRC, and here is where it stumbled. Zacchaeus was never called to testify. As far as the TRC was concerned, Zacchaeus, with his radical understanding of reconciliation, was too political, too uncomfortable, and too demanding. He remained sitting in that tree.

But as South Africans are discovering once again, the Bible is not about domestication, subjugation, or justification. The Bible is about genuine liberation and reconciliation, the purpose of which is forgiveness and conversion, personal and societal transformation, restitution, and restoration, and conviction and compassionate justice. Zacchaeus might have been ignored, but one cannot call upon Jesus without recalling Zacchaeus, and he may be left in that tree, but his testimony will remain a ringing indictment of all efforts at reconciliation and liberation that do not take the story of Zacchaeus as their yardstick.

Response by Curtiss Paul DeYoung

Brenda Salter McNeil says that we are in a historic kairos moment for reconciliation, and we must open our eyes and not miss the visitation of God. Richard Twiss declares that there will be no reconciliation for Native Americans unless there is restitution related to land. Jean Zaru cries out for a restoration of respect and dignity for Palestinian people, the repair of historical memory, and a return to the land. Allan Boesak preaches that Zacchaeus is still sitting in the tree waiting to be called into the commission hearing on reconciliation and liberation. What emerges from these diverse contexts and voices is a strong statement that reconciliation cannot proceed without liberation, and in particular restitution or reparation. Something of great value has been taken through acts of injustice. The relationship cannot find health unless there is a restoration that brings the injured party back to wholeness. Yet there is a sense as one hears these voices that liberation or freedom by itself is not enough. Liberated people need healing from the scars of their oppression. People who have been held captive by the oppressive tendencies of their nation or ethnic group also need healing. Our four twenty-first-century prophets cry out for an authentic process of reconciliation. We need to heal the land. We need to practice sulha. We need to invite Zacchaeus out of the tree to participate in our reconciliation journey. It is kairos time! The pronouncements of Salter McNeil, Twiss, Zaru, and Boesak are clarion calls for a biblical reconciliation rooted in social and economic justice that leads to shalom.[8]

8

COMMUNITY IN THE MIDST OF DIVERSITY

Throughout this book we have examined the ways in which cultural perspectives enrich our understanding of the Scriptures. God, as revealed in the Bible, is a God of liberation who calls us to confront injustice. Racism, sexism, and classism are barriers to peace and reconciliation. Our biblical faith invites us to follow an Afro-Asiatic Jesus of history who was, by the resurrection, transformed into the universal Christ. As such, Christ embraces, critiques, and transcends all cultures. We have consistently lifted up the biblical passages and themes that proclaim the oneness of the human family, as well as those that celebrate the rich mosaic of our cultural expressions.

Although we may be one family, it is easy to demonstrate that "community" is a rare experience in society. In many parts of the world, we find people isolated by the unique aspects of their humanity. Men and women, even in marriage, can find themselves lonely for someone who truly understands their journey. Parents and children under the same roof often live in worlds with dramatically different value systems. The opportunities of the rich versus those of the poor, the experiences of whites versus those of people of color, the perspectives of East versus those of the West, and the histories of indigenous peoples versus those of immigrants—all contribute to a multitude of differing cultural worldviews. Our lifestyles are often barely comprehensible to each other. These different, and sometimes conflicting, ways of understanding human existence have led to an experiential separation by race, culture, nationality, gender, age, economic status, and the like. The breakup of the human family leads to using the "other" as a scapegoat for all the world's problems. This fragmentation has brought us ethnic cleansing, holocaust, genocide, and a host of other ills. Discovering a humane and beloved community in the midst of human diversity is indeed an imposing proposition.

Even among people who are "alike" we discover very little real community. In the so-called advanced societies in our world, modern technology has made direct human interaction nearly unnecessary. We can now work exclusively through computers and fax machines, communicate through text messages and Facebook, eat food delivered to our doorstep, shop for material needs online, relate intimately with images of people created by virtual reality, seek counseling by phone, and get religion through television. Too many people's lives are structured by a daily existence that isolates them from others.

Even though bona fide community is an unusual occurrence in our world, people still long for a sense of belonging and togetherness. We need community, a place to call home, and a relational web built on trust and support.[1] Howard Thurman has mused, "Every person is at long last concerned with community. There is a persistent strain in the human spirit that rejects the experience of isolation as being alien to its genius . . . community is the native climate of the human spirit."[2] Without the experience of community, our life is deprived of meaning.

The Bible and Community

The Bible has much to say about community. In the very act of creating humanity, God initiated community. When God created humanity, the spiritual aspect of community began (God and human forging a relationship). In creating Adam and Eve, God initiated human community. From the beginning, God determined that community is indeed "the native climate of the human experience." In general, the book of Genesis views the extended family as community. It began with the union of Adam and Eve and continued through the families of Noah, Abraham and Sarah, Isaac and Rebecca, and Jacob, Leah, and Rachel. The biblical concept of community expanded during the days of enslavement in Egypt from consisting of the extended family of Jacob to including a community of people, the Hebrews. After the exodus from Africa, community came to be understood as encompassing the whole nation of ancient Israel. In the Hebrew Scriptures, community proceeded from the relationship of a man and a woman and their immediate family, to an extended family, to a cultural understanding (the Hebrews), to an ethnic understanding (the ancient nation of Israel). Finally, some of the prophets began to tentatively speak of a more universal understanding that was inclusive of people from all nations (Isaiah 2:2-4; 19:24-25; Hosea 2:23; Amos 9:7; Zephaniah 3:9-10).

Jesus' ministry, and that of his disciples, was concerned with redefining and expanding the notion of community based on the prophetic understanding of God's love for all of humanity. One way of looking at Jesus and his followers is to view them as a community of women and men who had been cast aside by society. This fact, combined with the understanding of the prophets, greatly influenced the shape of the Jesus community. The early church understood community as those persons who had a relationship with a resurrected and living Jesus Christ.

Probably the most commonly used word by Christians for the community of God's people has been "church" (*ekklesia*), those who were "called out." In Matthew 16:18, Jesus declared that he would build his church on the faith of the disciples. The early disciples thought of themselves as the people of Jesus, the church.[3] For some, the image of "the church" has become a stumbling block to faith. It describes a state or civic church that has lost its relevance. This understanding of church does not have the vibrancy necessary to motivate people to come together in community. In today's world the term *church* evokes differing images and therefore sends mixed signals.

Another image used by the apostle Paul to describe the community of faith was "body of Christ" (*soma Christou*). Paul's image revealed that every member of the community had something to give, and all gifts were valued (1 Corinthians 12:12-27). Paul Minear saw in the image of the body of Christ "a way of describing a social revolution." He wrote, "The image of the head and its body was thus used to attack at its deepest cosmic and psychic roots the perennial human habit of accepting as ultimate the world's way of dividing mankind into competing societies, whether religious, racial, cultural, or economic."[4] Unfortunately, in our day, the concept of the head and its body has been used to support domination: husbands over wives, men over women, pastors over congregations, and so on. The image of the "body of Christ" no longer communicates the biblical vision of community in some circles.

There are a number of images of community in the Bible. We will peruse four such images that have great potential and particular relevance in our time for portraying what God's community should be like. They are: ancient Israel as a contrast community, the household of God, the *koinonia* fellowship, and the table fellowship of Jesus.

Contrast Community

The Hebrew people were set free from slavery in Egypt by God for the express purpose of creating a community that would be a model to the other peoples in the region. This is the contention of George M. Soares-Prabhu when he calls ancient Israel a "contrast community."[5] He writes, "Biblical history thus begins with the liberation of the poor. A group of utterly powerless bonded labourers rescued by Yahweh are summoned to be the nucleus of his contrast community."[6] Israel was to offer an alternative, a contrast, to the ways of other nations. Soares-Prabhu supports his assertion, saying: "The Sinai covenant spells out the new social order which Israel is to adopt in order to become Yahweh's people, that is, to form the free, just, non-exploitative community that will serve as a 'contrast community' to the oppressive, violent and power-hungry city states among which Israel lives."[7] The laws given in Exodus, Leviticus, and Deuteronomy emphasized social justice and human relations.[8] The jubilee year was an exemplary ideal of placing just relationships at the core of ancient Israel's community life. The contrast community implies that for community to flourish, it must integrate equality and justice into the formation of its organizational principles and ways of daily living.

This image of the contrast community is exemplified well by Steve Charleston's understanding of the tribe, which he calls "a metaphor for community."[9] Charleston maintains:

> Native civilization in North America represented a political, social, and economic system that radiated out from a religious center through the communal network of extended family and kinship. . . . Native People do not share the assumptions and mythologies of their oppressors. They do not simply want a higher place on the pyramid of capitalism; they do not want a bigger piece of the action for themselves; they do not aspire to joining the middle class. They do not want more. As the tribe they want enough for all to share equally.[10]

This exemplifies what the Hebrew people, as a contrast community, were to model for their neighbors. They were to be a community that emphasized liberation, social justice, equality, and human dignity by refusing to assimilate to the ways of governing found in Pharaoh's court.

The experimental use of ancient Israel as a model of God's justice and liberty did not last long. Soares-Prabhu believes that it ended when Israel asked for a king.[11] I would suggest that the contrast community was never implemented. The underlying concepts for this contrast community were developed in the wilderness years during the charismatic leadership of Moses. But when Joshua led the Hebrew people into the "Promised Land" of their new communal home, the children of Israel did not model this sense of justice when relating to their new neighbors. Soares-Prabhu concludes that "the dream of one day realizing this 'contrast community' remains an inalienable part of Israel's hope."[12]

Had the contrast community been actualized, it would have revolutionized biblical—indeed, world—history. It would have been much like Charleston's vision of the tribe. He issues the following invitation:

> The tribe as a metaphor for community is dangerous. It is dangerous to colonial capitalism. It is dangerous to racism. It is dangerous because it is a symbol for the strength of the oppressed. It is an inclusive symbol for all women and men who want to wake up from the dream. It says to people of all colors and cultures: There is a better way. Let go of the myths and the images and the empty promises. Join hands in the strong bond of kinship. Become a tribe.[13]

Charleston's challenge to people of faith to become a tribe resonates with the understanding that Jesus and the early church had of community, as we shall see in the following images of God's community.

Household of God

The vision of a contrast community expressed the need for people to be organized in nonoppressive ways. The biblical community of God was not only called to offer a contrast to the way society was organized; it proclaimed that relationships needed to be reordered. The household of God (*oiheioi tou Theou*) is an image that conveys powerfully these new ways of understanding relationships that are needed for a sense of community to thrive. In the New Testament, the image of the household of God was used to depict the followers of Jesus Christ in the Petrine literature (1 Peter 4:17) and the Pauline literature (Galatians 6:10; Ephesians 2:19). The apostle Paul captured the essence of the household:

> So then you are no longer strangers and aliens, but you are citizens with the saints and also members of the household of God, built upon the foundation of the apostles and prophets, with Christ Jesus himself as the cornerstone. In him the whole structure is joined together into a holy temple in the Lord; in whom you also are built together spiritually into a dwelling place for God. (Ephesians 2:19-22)

In the household of faith, our relationship with God takes priority over our relatedness to family, race, culture, nation, gender, or any other group we belong to. This reordering also transforms how we relate to each other. The concept of family was reconstrued in the household of God. The terms *sister*, *brother*, *mother*, *father*, *friend*, and *neighbor* were all reinterpreted and redefined by Jesus. As Jesus said, "For whoever does the will of my Father in heaven is my brother and sister and mother" (Matthew 12:50).

In the story of the prodigal son (Luke 15:11-32), Cain Hope Felder suggests that the "householder epitomizes the work of Jesus, who—unlike many other ancient Jews—forgives and shows extraordinary compassion for all who languish in the margins of ancient Jewish society: women, children, slaves, outcasts, tax collectors, prostitutes, paralytics, the blind, epileptics, the mentally ill, and even Gentiles."[14] The household of God includes people from diverse cultures and life experiences. According to Felder, "Because of Christ's blood, all believers are supposed to be transported into a new household of reconciliation and solidarity."[15]

The household of God calls us back to our oneness. African theologian Anselme T. Sanon illustrates this concept:

> In the tradition of a region of my tribe, a new village is always founded on the banks of two currents of water, so that, at their confluence, the root, or place of rooting, of the village is found. In the new community of Christ, which must be founded on all shores of the world, a junction must be struck, under penalty of treason, at a confluence—to drain the rich alluvions of all peoples of all lands of the great river, to the shore of shores, the face of Christ.[16]

The household of God is an image that beckons the community of Jesus Christ to be a place of convergence for the great rivers of humanity. People of all cultures, races, languages, nations, tribes, and clans reside in the household of faith.

Koinonia

God's community is meant to be a model of justice. Its household includes a rich mosaic of people who are invited by God. The people of God are also summoned to be a fellowship based on equal sharing. The biblical image of koinonia epitomizes a quality of fellowship that encourages participation and togetherness linked by a common cause. The use of koinonia as an image of the community of God was modeled in the communal life of the believers after Pentecost. Luke described their way of life:

> All who believed were together and had all things in common; they would sell their possessions and goods and distribute the proceeds to all, as any had need. Day by day, as they spent much

time together in the temple, they broke bread at home and ate their food with glad and generous hearts, praising God and having the goodwill of all the people. And day by day the Lord added to their number those who were being saved. . . .

Now the whole group of those who believed were of one heart and soul, and no one claimed private ownership of any possessions, but everything they owned was held in common. With great power the apostles gave their testimony to the resurrection of the Lord Jesus, and great grace was upon them all. There was not a needy person among them, for as many as owned lands or houses sold them and brought the proceeds of what was sold. They laid it at the apostles' feet, and it was distributed to each as any had need. (Acts 2:44-47; 4:32-35)

This passage informs us that true community is possible only when there is sacrifice and substantial sharing. Perhaps because we live in a time of selfishness, we can hardly conceive of economic sharing as the will of God for the Christian community. We have heard too many sermons claiming that the evidence of God's blessing is financial prosperity. Consumerism has become a form of spirituality for some. A spirit of koinonia brings great freedom. Individuals can be set free from the emptiness of material prosperity or the desperation of poverty by meeting at the common ground of koinonia.

The koinonia community is embodied in the Native American understanding of the circle. The symbol of the "circle is self-defining; it defines the limits of the people."[17] George Tinker writes:

The fundamental symbol of Plains Indians' existence is the circle, a symbol signifying the family, the clan, the tribe, and eventually all of creation. Because it has no beginning and no end, all in the circle are of equal value. . . . Native American egalitarian tendencies are worked out in this spatial symbol in ways that go far beyond the classless egalitarianism of socialism.[18]

God's koinonia invites us to a radical sharing of all of our resources: finances, education, skills, gifts, wisdom, time, and the like. As the circle has no end, so our sharing is to be measureless. We are all equal in the koinonia community, needing both to give and to receive.

Table Fellowship

Community emerges in the midst of diversity when all are invited, embraced, accepted, and included. The most provocative image of community that Jesus modeled in his life was his fellowship around the table with people who were considered sinners and outcasts in society.

> As he sat at dinner in Levi's house, many tax collectors and sinners were also sitting with Jesus and his disciples—for there were many who followed him. When the scribes of the Pharisees saw that he was eating with sinners and tax collectors, they said to his disciples, "Why does he eat with tax collectors and sinners?" (Mark 2:15-16)

Sharing a meal in first-century Palestine indicated the acceptance of those around the table. As Albert Nolan explains:

> In societies where there are barriers between classes, races or other status groups, the separation is maintained by means of a taboo on social mixing. . . . The scandal Jesus caused in that society by mixing socially with sinners can hardly be imagined by most people today. It meant that he accepted them and approved of them and that he actually wanted to be "a friend of tax collectors and sinners" (Matthew 11:19). The effect upon the poor and the oppressed themselves was miraculous.[19]

Jesus intentionally shattered the boundaries instituted by society and fashioned a new understanding of community rooted in the grace of God. He boldly reached out to those who were shunned by society and brought them to his table.

Jesus publicly ate meals with individuals like Zacchaeus, "a chief tax collector" (Luke 19:2-10), and others who had been ostracized and isolated by society and religion. The personal implications for the people around the table were significant. As Marcus J. Borg writes, "It must have been an extraordinary experience for an outcast to be invited to share a meal with a man who was rumored to be a prophet. . . . and therefore his acceptance of them would have been perceived as a claim that they were accepted by God."[20] The table of God's community was open to everyone!

Jesus was called "a glutton and a drunkard, a friend of tax collectors and sinners" because of the people he invited to join him around the table (Matthew 11:19; Luke 7:34). Religious leaders denounced Jesus by exclaiming, "This fellow welcomes sinners and eats with them" (Luke 15:2). As Nolan reminds us, "All the men of religion, even John the Baptist, were scandalised by the way he mixed socially with sinners, by the way he seemed to enjoy their company. . . . In terms of group solidarity his friendship with sinners would classify him as a sinner."[21] Jesus taught about community by living in the presence of those who hungered for it most. No one was excluded from the table. Jesus even shared a table with Judas, who was preparing to betray him in a few hours (John 13:25). The concerns of the religious leaders did not intimidate Jesus. In fact, he allowed a woman who was considered a "sinner" to anoint his feet with tears and kiss them right at the table of a Pharisee (Luke 7:36-39). Again Nolan indicates the significance of such acts:

> It would be impossible to overestimate the impact these meals must have had upon the poor and the sinners. By accepting them as friends and equals, Jesus had taken away their shame, humiliation and guilt. . . . The physical contact which he must have had with them when reclining at table and which he obviously never dreamed of disallowing must have made them feel clean and acceptable.[22]

Jesus' table fellowship also had implications for the broader society. Jesus' meals "became a vehicle of cultural protest, challenging the ethos and politics of holiness, even as it also painted a different picture of what Israel was to be, an inclusive community reflecting the compassion of God."[23] The table fellowship of Jesus gave birth to the contrast community for which the Hebrew Scriptures had expressed hope. Jesus' parable of the great banquet described this revolutionary reordering of community by inviting the oppressed to the table (Luke 14:15-24). In the story of the rich man and Lazarus (Luke 16:19-31), Jesus made it clear that excluding the poor from one's table of fellowship could lead to one's exclusion from God's table in the life after death. (The reordering of community was evident in the fact that Lazarus was at the heavenly table.)

It is clear that Jesus' table fellowship turned first-century society upside down. It has been said that "Jesus was killed because of the way he ate."[24] It would be hard to dispute that as a partial truth. Jon Sobrino summarizes the importance of the table fellowship of Jesus as an image for God's community when he writes:

> Jesus states that solidarity does not exist in his society, and then moves toward those whom that society has ostracized. He defends prostitutes, he speaks with lepers and the ritually impure, he praises Samaritans, he permits ostracized women to follow him. These are positive actions of his, calculated to create a new collective awareness of what solidarity is, that it actually exists, and the partisan way in which it ought to develop. . . . Correspondence with a kingdom of God "at hand" is had when human beings feel solidarity with one another around a common table. Jesus approaches the ostracized not only individually, but in their community, re-creating them as a social group through the materiality of the dining table.[25]

Among the modern tables of fellowship are barbershops and beauty salons. The former Classy Cuts in Minneapolis captured some of the nuances of Jesus' table. Classy Cuts was operated by Becky and Hop. Hop is from Vietnam, and Becky is from Mexico. Who ever would have imagined that a woman of Mexican heritage and a woman of Vietnamese heritage would start a business together in the cold climate of Minnesota? This small, storefront operation attracted a wide diversity of customers. It was common to hear Vietnamese, Spanish, Hmong, Lao, English, and other languages spoken in the course of a few hours at the salon. Every day Hop and Becky attracted people across the boundaries of language, race, culture, gender, denomination, and economic status for the common purpose of getting a haircut. The household of God is called to cross similar boundaries to build a visible representation of Jesus' table fellowship.

A Fresh Vision of Community

The biblical images just presented can inspire and ignite a process of envisioning new ways to think about community. It is time to join Jesus at the table, where, as Ivone Gebara states, "Men and women will eat the same bread, drink the same wine, and dance together in the brightly lit square, celebrating the bonds uniting all humanity."[26] A fresh vision of community requires that ineffective and oppressive systems be removed so that brand-new approaches can originate. Often it is the old and barren structures that are blocking novel and innovative designs. Vincent Harding has said that this is the problem in the United States where "for years white America was busy building this house, and then had people from different cultural groups living in the yards or shanties around the house. The liberal contribution since the civil rights activity of the '60s has been to say, 'We have to open our house and invite these people to come in and stay.' But the problem . . . is [it's]

161

still their house. We're still guests."[27] The systems on which we build our society need to be evaluated. If the systems are unjust, then something needs to change. Often the problems we struggle with in our world are the result of a faulty foundation for our life together.

The biblical images we examined offer a blueprint for the house of faith where the foundation is the justice of God and all are invited to share in the development of God's community. As George Tinker says, "We need to think about building a new house where everybody gets equal say in its design and has equal ownership. Then we need to tear that old house down."[28] Naomi P. F. Southard, using an image from an essay by Audre Lorde, says, "In order to build a new kind of house, one in which we will be truly at home, we must not only dismantle the master's house, but design new tools to create our dreams."[29] Jesus' parable about the new wineskins, in which he said: "No one puts new wine into old wineskins; otherwise the new wine will burst the skins and will be spilled, and the skins will be destroyed. But new wine must be put into fresh wineskins. And no one after drinking old wine desires new wine, but says, 'The old is good'" (Luke 5:37-39; see also Matthew 9:17). Jesus told his followers that new understandings cannot be contained by old structures. Southard's statement about designing new tools for creating our dream of community is critical. The old tools were developed for the purpose of building the old structure. A fresh approach to community entails new methods and skills, that is, new tools. Some of the new tools that are needed are outlined in the rest of this chapter.

Spiritual Transformation

The community ideal begins with God's initiative in reaching out to humanity for a particular kind of relationship. Centering our communal relationships in God produces a spirit that Howard Thurman said "knows no country and its allies are to be found wherever the heart is kind and the collective will and the private endeavor seek to make justice where injustice abounds, to make peace where chaos is rampant, and to make the voice heard on behalf of the helpless and the weak."[30] The spirit that produces community is the Spirit of God. Each individual's relationship with God prepares her or him for the experience of building a sense of community. God awakens the desire for community through spiritual transformation.

In the early 1980s, I was a member of the Covenant House Faith Community[31] in New York City. We lived a communal life that embraced prayer as central to our life together. Our work was with youth and children who were homeless. So our prayers often focused on the young people we served. One evening a teenage girl who had run away from home and had become trapped in prostitution came to our shelter badly beaten by her pimp. (She had been in and out of the shelter up to this point.) After spending a few days there attempting to heal from the physical and emotional scars of her ordeal, she asked me if I still prayed. She was aware that I lived in the faith community. I responded to her query by assuring her that I did. She asked me to pray that she could go home. (Her parents were not receptive to her return, believing that she would be a bad influence on a younger sister.) Due to persistent prayer and the fine work of social workers, she went home in a few months. I learned a few years later that she had turned her life around and was in nursing school.

This encounter took on greater meaning upon reflection. I believe that what the young woman ultimately wanted was the unconditional love of God and a place to belong. As she was asking me if I still prayed, she was kneeling down before me tying a piece of ribbon on the lace of one of my sneakers. It frightened me a bit, for I could not help viewing her actions as an act symbolically reminiscent of the woman who kissed and anointed Jesus' feet (Luke 7:36-39). It was a gesture of profound gratitude for possible grace. It was a cry for God. It was a plea for community.

Experience of Community

In addition to the need for spiritual transformation, one of the greatest barriers to the formation of community is that many do not understand community experientially. When Howard Thurman reflected on his experience of developing a multi-cultural congregation, the Church for the Fellowship of All Peoples, he wrote that "one basic discovery was constantly surfacing—meaningful experiences of unity among peoples were more compelling than all that divided and separated."[32] The experience of togetherness, even if brief, awakens a desire for and inspires hope in the possibility of community.

Local congregations should be places where the kind of community described in the biblical images exists. Yet there are people who have attended church all of their lives who have never experienced a sense of togetherness. Experiences of community exhibit themselves in unusual ways and at un-expected times. The experience may be a brief moment in a worship service or a meeting when the Spirit of God brings reconciliation. It may also occur when an unlikely group of people finds themselves thrown together by circumstances. Those who hunger for community need to seek opportunities for experiencing togetherness by taking the second step, after acknowledging God's initiative, to go to where community exists. If we are open to the unfamiliar and to others, God will lead us to experiences of community.

Everyone Has a Voice

For community to have the equality that God expects, every-one must have a voice. This means that those who have power in society (or the church), and thereby already have a voice, will need to listen more. Those who have been voiceless in society will have to become emboldened by the Spirit to speak, because very likely "the answer for a more livable society rests with those whose voices are too often unheard and rarely sought."[33] The challenge is to find ways to hear from everyone. Sadly, many among the ranks of the voiceless, crushed, and alienated will not speak unless invited.

For everyone to have a voice, a koinonia spirit of sharing is necessary. Those of us who have a strong psychological need for receiving credit for our ideas and contributions will want to learn how to place the need for community above our own egos. A focus on individual accomplishments should be replaced by a community-centered agenda. This will be a challenge for persons trained in settings where individualism is highly valued. Southard states that "in the Asian context, decision making and discussion is a community enterprise, not the task of one person to layout and the rest react to."[34] Justo Gonzalez adds, "In most traditional cultures, an idea belongs to the community, not to the individual who somehow was the channel employed by the spiritual powers to communicate the idea to the community."[35] When ideas are considered community property and no one needs to claim ownership of what they share, we are closer to realizing koinonia. In such a community; roles are based on gifts with individuals leading in the areas of their giftedness. Everyone has a voice, and all the glory goes to the householder, Jesus Christ.

The Discipline of Dialogue

To create an environment where everybody's voice is heard, we will need to become skilled at what James Earl Massey calls "the discipline of dialogue."[36]

> Dialogue is the way of community. It is the personal dimension of sharing. Dialogue concretizes the will to be in relation with another person. It is the self-conscious response of an individual with another self. It is the form of the personal; it is the way of the willed encounter, a means of grace, a celebration of shared meaning. Dialogue is the way of explored intention, the way of God who is always seeking to share himself with others.[37]

For a community that values equality to develop, we believe that every person is created in the image of God and therefore has dignity, worth, and something of value to share. So we must develop the art of listening. This will be particularly challenging as we try to listen to those whose experience in life is very different from ours. As we dialogue with people from different cultural perspectives, we will need to "learn how to listen to voices and melodies that are unfamiliar to us."[38] These voices may hold the keys to unlocking the doors that open our minds to the essential components for creating our desired unity.

The more inclusive the dialogue, the richer the content and the stronger the outcome. Delores S. Williams says that womanist theologians use a "multidialogical" approach where one participates "in dialogue and action with many diverse social, political, and religious communities concerned about human survival and a productive quality of life for the oppressed." She continues, "Multidialogical activity may, like a jazz symphony, communicate some of its most important messages in what the harmony-driven conventional ear hears as discord, as disruption of the harmony."[39] This womanist approach can be embraced by all of us in our efforts to build truly inclusive collaborations.

There are bound to be differences and disagreements when people dialogue. When everyone is given a voice, a greater number of outlooks are laid out on the table. These are the moments that reveal whether our respect for the other person is genuine. For unity to be maintained, we must sincerely believe that people can disagree and still love God. One of the most damaging things in the Christian community is the spirit of judgmentalism. This spirit creeps in when one professed believer doubts the faith of another professed believer because of a difference of opinion or belief on a particular issue. A spirit of community requires that we accept that each one is doing her or his best to understand and apply his or her faith in this complex world (and we leave the judging to God).

Worship has the potential to be an exceptionally powerful form of dialogue in the Christian community. In worship we are invited to interact with God and each other in ways that are reflective, emotive, and mystical. Therefore, our worship also needs to reflect a "multidialogical" intent. Some years ago I visited the Cathedral of St. John the Divine in New York City. It was a weekday, and the organist was there rehearsing for the Sunday Mass. I was unfamiliar with the order of service, but the organist must have progressed to the point where Holy Communion would be served. All at once the antiphonal trumpets sounded forth with a majestic melody of praise to God. It was a glorious moment of worship! I also spent many Sundays at the Congregational Church of God, north of the cathedral in Harlem, listening as the choir would exuberantly sing the refrain "There is no power like the power of the risen Lord," and again I would feel caught up in a moment of praise to God.

I believe that anyone who focuses her or his attention on God can worship in any setting where the intent is to bring glory to the Almighty. We can worship God in a noisy celebration and in a silent meditation. We can worship God in the singing of gospel music and in the chanting of the Psalms. We can worship God in the quiet shedding of a tear and the loud shout of "Hallelujah!" We can worship God when the preacher reads the sermon with little emotion while standing in the pulpit and when the preacher speaks extemporaneously in a voice filled with emotion as he or she walks back and forth on the platform. If we blend our various worship traditions into a beautiful harmony, the multicultural community can produce unique symphonies of praise to God.

Multicultural Fluency

If we are to practice the discipline of dialogue in this diverse world, we must become fluent in cultures other than our own. This was the genius of the apostle Paul, who wrote: "To the

Jews I became as a Jew, in order to win Jews. . . . To those outside the law I became as one outside the law . . . so that I might win those outside of the law. To the weak I became weak, so that I might win the weak. I have become all things to all people, that I might by all means save some" (1 Corinthians 9:20-22). Paul developed the ability to understand and communicate with people from different cultures and experiences. The widespread effects of racism require us to work through stereotypes and develop a sensitivity to cultural differences. This is particularly true for those who are isolated in culturally exclusive ghettos, suburbs, or rural areas. They may understand only their own cultural experience because they have no felt need to do otherwise. It is imperative that all of us become adept at understanding different cultures. We will never become "experts" on the lives of others, but we can become "fluent" in a variety of cultures. Some may choose to immerse themselves exclusively in another culture and become bicultural. But the mandate for most of us is to gain some expertise in the broad diversity of cultural experiences in our world. We must become "multicultural."

Dietrich Bonhoeffer, a German Christian martyr during the Nazi regime, developed a way of seeing the world through the eyes of others he called "the view from below." He described it as follows: "There remains an experience of incomparable value. We have for once learnt to see the great events of world history from below, from the perspective of the outcast, the suspects, the maltreated, the powerless, the oppressed, the reviled in short, from the perspective of those who suffer."[40] Bonhoeffer's commitment to work for reconciliation and social justice led him to understand the importance of solidarity with the oppressed. For Bonhoeffer, solidarity was not merely living with the oppressed; it was comprehending life from the perspective of the person who suffered. The "view from below" meant having the ability to see the world through the eyes of one who was being oppressed. Bonhoeffer allowed his life experience to mold his way of perceiving and thinking.

The concept of viewing the world from the vantage point of people who are suffering can be broadened to include the ability to understand life from the perspective of many other human beings. Not only do the powerful need to understand the experience of the oppressed, the powerless need to fathom empowerment. It is also important for the person who comes from a life of oppression to understand those who face injustice of a different sort (such as a person experiencing sexism seeking to become familiar with the suffering of racism). To live in community we need to develop the skill of comprehending the life experience of our brothers and sisters in the human family.

We can only fully value and comprehend what it means to be human when we are at home with the perspectives of another's culture. A part of us becomes African when we live in community with persons of African descent. We better understand what it means to be indigenous when we sit with Native Americans. When we commune with Latinas and Latinos we become more familiar with Latin experience. We resonate with that part of us that is European when we engage with people of European heritage. When we are with Asians, we gain a more complete awareness of our "Asian-ness." In addition to all of this, we gain a greater appreciation for our God when we embrace the many cultural reflections of God's image.

How do we become fluent in other cultures? One way this happens is when we live outside of our comfort zones and relate in significant, ongoing ways to people who are different from us. Our fluency expands as we listen to and live with people from a diversity of settings. This helps us gain points of reference for communicating cross-culturally. If possible, we need to be mentored by persons who are from cultural or racial groups different from our own. Also men need to be mentored by women. Such an apprenticeship cannot be underestimated. Our ways of thinking and viewing the world will be radically altered because of this experience. It is also important to be in regular dialogue with those who are seasoned visionaries for unity and reconciliation.

Our Common Humanity

One of the results of multicultural fluency is a greater awareness of our similarities. As signaled at the outset of this book, while there are many cultural expressions, there is only one human family. It is necessary for us to be fluent in a diversity of cultural understandings. Yet there are times when our distinctive cultures must be worn like loose garments. We must be able to interact free from culture in a manner that is simply "human." I have a friend who was raised in Brazil, speaking German at home and Portuguese at school. When she moved to the United States as an adult, she acquired the ability to speak English. She now teaches Spanish at a university. I once asked her in what language she thought. Her reply was that she does not think in any particular language but rather in concepts. We must have this same ability when relating to individuals and groups of people from other cultures. The freedom to interact as sisters and brothers in the family of God, liberated from the impediments of our differences (but not discounting our cultural uniqueness), may be the most important foundation for future community.

9

THE DIVERSITY DILEMMA

Throughout the foregoing chapters, we have had the opportunity to reflect biblically on our fundamental oneness and our cultural diversity as mandates for coming together as Christians. We explored the effect of our own sense of culture on our identity and how we read the Bible. We observed very closely how Jesus entered history as a person living at the crossroads of many traditions and how, as the resurrected Christ, he is a catalyst for blending our various cultural perspectives. The much maligned apostle Paul's views on women and gender relations were reconsidered with a fresh take on Paul as having one of the most redemptive social policies in all of history. We reflected at some length on how liberation, reconciliation, and empowerment are key messages in God's self-revelation, challenging us to address injustice. Finally, we envisioned new ways of understanding how we can come together as the community of God.

Diversity is a much larger topic than culture, race, gender, and class. It includes age, ability, sexual orientation, religion, life circumstances, lifestyle choices, and much more. The Bible has something to say about a wider range of diversity beyond the primary focus of this volume. Discussing a broader range of diversity is a dilemma for many. Some find such conversations uncomfortable. Others feel as if they are not even invited to the dialogue. Children and seasoned adults can find themselves marginalized or feeling invisible, as though they have little or nothing to offer. People with disabilities are set aside as an inconvenience and an uncomfortable reminder of weakness. Or their contribution is defined by their impairment. Certain illnesses exclude people or declare them untouchable. To some extent people with cancer still experience this reality. Sexually transmitted diseases and HIV/AIDS cause stigma. People with mental illness can feel isolated. We need to discover how to make people visible through rehumanizing our perspectives.

Some discussions of diversity produce competing interpretations of the Bible or bring to light various theological positions. Gays, lesbians, bisexuals, transgendered persons, and others whose gender identity or sexual orientation does not fit neatly into a heterosexual box are often marginalized. Heated debates about sexual orientation are fragmenting the Christian community. Religious diversity is a reality in the United States and much of the world. How do we relate to our neighbors who proclaim a different faith? What do we believe about religious pluralism? How is the Bible used to argue various positions on sexual orientation and interfaith interactions? Is there any common ground on these divisive issues?

Today people are also defined by lifestyle choices and life circumstances. More individuals are expressing themselves through tattoos and body piercings. Does this preclude them from engagement in the human family or church communities? There are various living arrangements outside of traditional marital status and extended or nuclear families. Single people are often left out or feel like a "fifth wheel." Growing numbers of people are cohabiting. Gay marriage is occurring legally in some places. Sensational news accounts remind us that plural marriage is still practiced in some cultures or religions. Divorce has also become commonplace in our world and in the church. What is the Bible's message regarding these aspects of diversity? How does the Bible instruct us to relate to people whose life circumstances or lifestyle choices differ from our own?

We live at a time in history when very different worlds (and worldviews) exist side by side. Can we learn to live in community with respect for others in the human family without unanimity of belief or a full understanding of each other's perspectives? As Christians can we live as neighbors with persons whose lifestyles are very different from our own? Can we agree to disagree with others who claim the name of Christ yet hold divergent views from our own? In the midst of our world there are people who feel invisible, like outsiders, or defined by their lifestyles choices and life circumstances. Diversity can be very complex and at times confusing. How can the Bible help us navigate the diversity dilemma?

Embracing the Eunuch from Ethiopia

In Acts 8, Philip was sent to proclaim "the good news about Jesus" to the treasury official from the court of Queen Candice in Ethiopia (vv. 26-39). The royal official had been in Jerusalem to worship. When Philip encountered him, the treasurer of Ethiopia was reading from the prophet Isaiah. The author of Acts noted that the Ethiopian finance minister was a eunuch, that is, a "sexually altered" person.[1] The fact that the man was a eunuch has no relevance for the story itself. It must have been inserted to demonstrate the extent of the inclusiveness of the first-century church. The biblical record regarding eunuchs is mixed. The Mosaic Law excluded eunuchs from access to the temple (Leviticus 21:16-23; see also Deuteronomy

23:1). Eunuchs were considered unfit to serve God. Later God spoke through the prophet Isaiah, announcing the inclusion of eunuchs in the temple (56:4-5). Perhaps this was why the court official acquired the Isaiah scroll. The Acts passage does not say whether the temple was practicing the Mosaic Law or Isaiah's proclamation regarding the inclusion of eunuchs. Certainly Isaiah's word set the stage for the followers of Jesus Christ to practice inclusion and acceptance rather than exclusion and rejection.

Perhaps today's sexually altered persons are transgendered individuals who have surgically changed themselves from one biological sex to another (or are living an altered existence without surgery). While many in the church are still debating sexual orientation, it seems clear that the first-century church had room for sexually altered persons. Should today's congregations welcome people with sexual orientations and gender identities that do not align with heterosexuality? What does the love of neighbor mean?

Issues of sexual orientation and gay marriage have dominated the discussions of many Christian denominations for years. These battles have been brutal. Local congregations have also felt the same emotions. There seems to be no middle ground. For some this issue is simple—the Bible speaks against homosexuality and declares it a sin. Others have determined that the few Scriptures that do speak of the issue are not as clear as they may seem when examined in the light of how they would have been understood in the times they were written. Another approach taken is to address the issue not from a verse-by-verse analysis, but rather by seeking to apply the grand themes of the Bible. A person's beliefs about the Bible tend to direct her or him to a particular approach. Then there is the political battle over gay marriage in civil society in the United States and elsewhere. Often the Bible is used in this contest.

Sexual orientation and gender identity are important issues for the church and society in the United States and much of the world. Perhaps some preliminary questions need to be asked. Does God love bisexuals, transgendered people, lesbians, male homosexuals, and persons who are asexual? Do our discussions about sexual orientation display loving attitudes alongside the search for God's will in the matter? So much of the rhetoric is heated by angry and demeaning taunts thrown back and forth. Some who call themselves Christians even use hateful rhetoric or make derogatory gay jokes, which hardly represents a loving God. Given Jesus' comfort in hanging out with people who others dismissed or avoided, it is surprising how many Christians find it difficult to interact with gays, lesbians, bisexuals, and transgendered people simply as human beings. Where does this discomfort come from?

As we move into the dilemma of wider discussions about diversity, actually having real relationships with the people whom we are talking about will enrich our understanding. We all should know people who are gay, disabled, older or younger, from religions other than our own, and whose lifestyles differ from our own. First-century Christians followed Jesus in building relationships with everyone. Philip exhibited no concerns or discomfort when he met with an Ethiopian treasury official whom he discovered was a eunuch. And he welcomed him into the church.

An Encounter with a Samaritan Woman

Having a real sense of comfort and actual relationships with people whose lives differ from our own is important if we are going to move beyond the diversity dilemma. We need to know the life stories and circumstances of others. Kwok Pui Lan recommends the use of "dialogical imagination," in which one takes the biblical text and a people's history and culture and "brings the two in dialogue with one another."[2] Jesus' use of elements of the culture of those to whom he encountered shows that he studied the history, culture, and life experiences of the communities and people he interacted with. He was familiar with and used agricultural images when in farming communities and aquatic images when in seashore villages.

Perhaps the best example of a time when Jesus engaged in "dialogical imagination" was when he encountered a woman from Samaria (John 4:4-42). He used his understanding of Samaritan culture and religious beliefs to connect with the woman. As a Jewish person, an understanding of Samaritan life was critical for Jesus because of the intense animosity between Jews and Samaritans during the first century. When the ancient Israelites were taken into captivity, poor and working-class Hebrews who intermingled with their captors were left behind in the region of Samaria. When the captives returned to Palestine, they sought an advantage through the claim that the Hebrews living in Samaria had intermarried with the colonizers. Not unlike oppressed peoples in other eras, the people of Samaria had their own story. They claimed that they were the descendants of the patriarch Joseph and his African wife, whose offspring had become the half-tribes of Ephraim and Manasseh. A rivalry between the returning captives (Jews) and the working-class Hebrews (Samaritans) developed.[3]

By the first century the prejudice between Jews and Samaritans was extremely intense. Sometime during the early years of the first century, Samaritan revolutionaries scattered human bones in the sanctuary of the temple in Jerusalem during the Passover Feast as an act of protest and rebellion.[4] This was highly offensive to Jews. So extreme was the bigotry against Samaritans that one rabbi of the time wrote, "He that eats the bread of the Samaritans is like one that eats the flesh of swine." It was also a common belief that Samaritan women began their menstrual cycle at birth. Therefore the ritual purity of Samaritans was always suspect.[5]

Into this environment of mistrust and segregation, Jesus arrived in Samaria well prepared for his encounter with this woman. Jesus must have studied the faith and culture of the Samaritans before making the journey, because he knew that the Samaritans were seeking a Messiah (the Taheb) who would restore belief and reveal truth.[6] When Jesus told the woman that he knew she had previously been married five times and the man with whom she was now living was not her husband, he was not just saying something about her life circumstances; he was disclosing something about himself. By revealing the truth about the woman, Jesus unveiled the truth about his identity. He informed her that he was the Revealer, the Taheb, the Messiah. She immediately changed the direction of the conversation and began to talk about faith.

Jesus' understanding and use of Samaritan history, culture, religious beliefs, and experience of prejudice enabled him to communicate with this woman from Samaria. The Samaritan woman confirmed this when she said to the people in her village, "Come, see a man who told me all that I ever did. Can this be the Christ?" (John 4:29 RSV). The woman took the message of Jesus, couched in her cultural framework, back to her village. Had Jesus attempted to use phrases and images from his own Jewish setting, he would probably not have had much success, particularly considering the tense relationship between Samaritans and Jews.

To find meaningful dialogue on diversity issues, we must follow Jesus into the diversity of local communities and learn to communicate in the language of the people. We can learn to speak the language of people's experience of disability, race, sexual orientation, socioeconomic class, religion, gender, lifestyle, culture, and the like through forming deep relationships and by respecting people enough to know their history, culture, and life experiences.

A Disabled God

A third factor that helps break through the diversity dilemma is the inclusion of the "diverse" persons themselves in the task of assessing the present reality and the work of biblical interpretation. Let us use the perspective of persons with a disability to illustrate. Their challenges are multifaceted. Many places are not accessible for people with disabilities. This is more troubling when these locations are church buildings or other Christian institutions. Yet when these minimal enhancements are in place, this does not guarantee a hospitable environment. And even when Christian communities practice an intentionally representative inclusion in worship leadership, organization staffing, and educational awareness, this does not mean that people feel fully embraced in deep friendships with acceptance as being created fully in the image of God.

There are people with disabilities in the Bible. The Bible's view of disability is mixed. The same Leviticus text that blocked access to the temple for eunuchs also declared that no descendants of the priestly class of Aaron with disabilities were allowed to approach the altar, because they would "profane" God's sanctuary (21:16-24). Yet when King David looked for a member of Saul's family to reward with a place at his table, he found Jonathan's disabled son Mephibosheth. His disability was not seen as in any way problematic by David (2 Samuel 9:1-13). When Jacob wrestled with the messenger from God, he was given a disability by God (Genesis 32:22-32). Kerry H. Winn notes, "The disability was Jacob's sign of the covenant. The blessing was not a result of the disability, nor was the disability a result of the blessing. It is something he took away as a lifelong reminder of what happened there—lifelong for Jacob but, for all of Israel, a sign for all time."[7] Jacob's God-given disability was a symbol of God's covenant with ancient Israel.

Jesus regularly interacted with people who had disabilities, and he dispelled the belief that disability was a result of sin (Mark 2:2-12). The apostle Paul may have had a disability. He spoke of a "thorn" in his flesh (2 Corinthians 12:7-10; see also Galatians 4:13-14). Martin Albl writes:

> Paul himself experienced this condition as a disability. . . . One may perhaps detect a movement in Paul's own thought. He at first stigmatized the disability as a demonic force, a "messenger

of Satan," and he sought to be free from it. But after his revelation from the Lord, Paul interprets the disability as a condition about which he will be content and even "boast." He sees that the disability, even if instrumentally associated with the demonic, is ultimately of divine origin and has a divine purpose.[8]

Like Jacob, Paul found divine meaning in his "thorn" in the flesh.

The fact is we all may be disabled at some point in our lives. Some are born with disabilities. Others may be able-bodied one day and disabled the next through a car accident. We may be going through life seemingly without challenges and then face the disabling reality of depression or other mental illnesses. Remember the blindness of Isaac (Genesis 27:1-45). As Wynn states, "Isaac's visual impairment is the result of the natural aging process. He serves as a reminder that anyone who lives long enough will inevitably become disabled."[9]

We make fascinating discoveries when interpreting the Bible from the vantage point of disability. An often overlooked element of the resurrection of Jesus Christ is that he still had the marks of his crucifixion on his body (John 20:24-29; see also Luke 24:36-39). One would expect that the resurrected Jesus would be healed of the marks of his suffering. Nancy Eiesland declares that the resurrected Jesus comes to his followers as "the disabled God."[10] She writes:

> Here is the resurrected Christ making good on the incarnational proclamation that God would be with us, embodied as we are, incorporating the fullness of human contingency and ordinary life into God. In presenting his impaired hands and feet to his startled friends, the resurrected Jesus is revealed as the disabled God. Jesus, the resurrected Savior, calls for his frightened companions to recognize in the marks of impairment their own connection with God, their own salvation. In so doing, this disabled God is also the revealer of a new humanity. The disabled God is not only the One from heaven but the revelation of true

personhood, underscoring the reality that full personhood is fully compatible with the experience of disability.[11]

Every week churches recognize this in communion celebrations that remember the body of Christ broken for us.[12]

Reconciliation

We must invite persons not like us into our closest relationships, into our communities, into our conversations, into our learning commitments, and into our biblical reflections and theological musings. This is the wonderful work of reconciliation. We need to ask, in the midst of fragmentation, how we as people of faith can be catalysts for reconciliation. Two thousand years ago the apostle Paul summed up our task for today:

> So if anyone is in Christ, there is a new creation: everything old has passed away; see, everything has become new! All this is from God, who reconciled us to himself through Christ, and has given us the ministry of reconciliation; that is, in Christ God was reconciling the world to himself, not counting their trespasses against them, and entrusting the message of reconciliation to us. So we are ambassadors for Christ, since God is making his appeal through us; we entreat you on behalf of Christ, be reconciled to God. (2 Corinthians 5:17-20)

The *Christian Community Bible* provides an additional insight in the interpretation of this text when it comments that "what Paul sees in Christ is the great messenger and artisan of reconciliation."[13] An artisan is a person who is highly skilled at a craft and commits her or his life to excelling at this proficiency. We need to become artisans of reconciliation highly skilled at the craft of bringing people together across the lines that divide us. As artisans of reconciliation, we live as though unity is already a reality. In a real sense, we are already one through our shared humanity and through Jesus Christ. Through the life, death, and resurrection of Jesus Christ, new possibilities for relating to each other were created, new power for transformation was made available, new passion for reconciliation was released. So when our differences take precedent over our oneness, we must step forward as artisans with inspired ideas for promoting unity and creating community.

We live in a world where the need for reconciliation and social justice has never been greater. To sustain efforts at reconciliation, the cadre of artisans must multiply beyond a few "called" individuals. The urgency of this task is great! The Bible's message, in this age of diversity, is an invitation to come together at God's table of fellowship and to go forth into the entire world as God's artisans of reconciliation. In 1990 Steve Charleston predicted:

> In the next century, the Christian church is going to experience a second major reformation. It will be far more powerful than the one we knew in sixteenth-century Europe. For one thing, it will be international, not just regional. It will cross over not only denominational lines, but also over lines of color, class, gender, and age. It will be more important than the last reformation, because it will change the way people think and feel about themselves. While the West will participate in this reformation, it will not play a dominant role. The leaders of the coming reformation will be women. They will be from Africa, Asia, Latin America, and Native America. They are being born right now.[14]

Charleston's babies are now young adults. I pray that they will become artisans of reconciliation and take the lead as catalysts, using diversity as a reason for coming together.

GROUP REFLECTION—
ACTION GUIDE

Robin Bell

Christian communities are facing difficult days. The church as a learning organization is not exempt from the undercurrents of change. We are living "in betwix," a transition from modernity and *postindustrialization*; some call this stage of human history postmodernity. We need to assess what we are becoming. I am concerned for my grandchildren regarding the purpose of Christian communities in five, fifteen, and twenty-five years from now. Will we return to the prophetic tradition of the Hebrew prophets and Jesus? Or will we continue to proclaim a message that seems to represent an elite monocultural orientation in a world that seldom brings people of faith together to create community? Will our ministries continue to function as closed hegemonic operating systems of power and privilege that suppress the proclamation of the biblical message of liberation and reconciliation? The church in the United States may be surprised that in the next generation it will be in a supportive role, with brothers and sisters from other places in the world taking the lead.

In *Coming Together in the 21st Century* Curtiss Paul De-Young and the other contributors cry out that God's people must proclaim the biblical message of liberation, justice, peace, reconciliation, and freedom from dominance, prejudice, racism, classism, and sexism. They write with passion for radical involvement in the biblical message of reconciliation for social justice and liberation grounded in the witness of the biblical authors and the life of Jesus. These gifted men and women have made a difficult subject accessible to all who dare to hear the call of God in a very diverse world. This study and reflection guide is written for those who want to have serious dialogue about embracing a way of life that is discovered through commitment to God's mission of putting on Christ (*imago Dei*) and sharing his transformative contextual orientation in the world of liberation evangelism with others (*missio Dei*).

I have known Curtiss Paul DeYoung for nearly twenty years. He has lived this journey of reconciliation ministry and thus far has not given up. It has been a blessing to break bread with him in ministry and observe his gifts of bringing people together. I have watched God's hand on his life bringing difficult people together to create a better world to live in. I am one of those difficult persons whom he has invited and challenged to proclaim a liberated gospel message. Reconciliation is challenging work, and one can easily become discouraged and give up. I have done this. Yet I have come to realize that the commitment to a ministry of reconciliation is an act of faith that pleases God. It is a liberating journey of learning to be free enough to love others, even the most difficult human beings you may meet along the way in following Jesus' example as a reconciler in a multicultural and diverse world.

Format

The study sessions that follow are written to accompany each of the book's nine chapters. The discussion material helps facilitate challenging conversations and questions individuals' previously held ideas on diversity. Questions are designed to guide input, dialogue, and discussion. The key point noted in each session can be used for keeping a group engaged with a problem-solving activity. The group leader may on occasion need to bring the group back on task.

Objectives

- To understand how the authors' perspectives inform our way of living in a diverse world as people of faith and change agents in society.
- To reflect on the Bible's message of diversity, situated in a broader social and historical context as described by the authors, in order to develop a perspective as problem solvers in the context of the current social-political system operating in one's community.
- To share hopes, dreams, and stories of justice and equity for social change in an increasingly diverse global world.
- To think deeply about how the authors inform the readers' practice of the Bible's message of living for peace, justice, and coming together as communities of faith for social change in a diverse and global world.

Additional Directions

The Bible's message of diversity (from the perspective of the authors) creates a dialogue between the readers and the authors. As participants discuss the key issues that are raised, they will have an opportunity to rethink and move from reflection to action on how to create community. I recommend that the leader assist the group in being clear about what diversity issue(s) is addressed in each chapter. The responsibility of the leader is to present the author's view as a diversity issue the group wants to address in their community from the perspective of the Bible's message on diversity. The group leader has the responsibility for guiding the group through a problem-solving process that contributes to creating community.

Each session should be limited to seventy-five minutes, starting and ending on time. The following is a suggested schedule for each session follows:

Opening: 15 minutes with Scripture
Part I: 20 minutes
Part II: 30 minutes
Part III: 8 minutes
Next Steps: 2 minutes

SESSION 1: ONE HUMAN FAMILY, MANY CULTURAL EXPRESSIONS

Central Question: What are the barriers in your community to seeing the oneness of the human family as found throughout the Bible?

Learning Aim: To engage the participants in choosing between accepting the world as divided or claiming the Bible's message of oneness of humanity.

Introduction

1. Meet each other: have all participants, one at a time, share their name, the name of their community, and an example of a previous group experience.

2. Write "Multicultural Relationships" on the newsprint and make a list of images that this phrase suggests to each of the participants.

3. Ask participants to consider their reasons for choosing to participate in this study. Have each person write down one goal or desired outcome of their involvement.

Scripture Reading

Read aloud Scripture from chapter 1 (Genesis 1:26-27). Take only a few moments (one speaking at a time) to get responses to these questions:

- What prompted the author to include this scriptural passage at the beginning of the chapter?
- What is he trying to communicate to the reader?

I. Understanding the Author's Point of View

Key Point: "One human family, many cultural expressions." Read this quote aloud and make a list of how the world "as it is" is described.

a. Discuss this description by having participants give examples from their world and their own everyday lives. Try to understand what the author is saying from the author's point of view.

b. From reading the author's section on Seeing Today's Diversity in Yesterday's Text and The Biblical Hebrews, why it is meaningful to see today's cultural diversity in the Bible? Is it important to demonstrate that the Hebrews were an Afro-Asiatic people rather than a white European people, as pictured in many Bibles? Why?

c. Discuss the author's experience at college in Anderson, Indiana. How do you feel in the midst of these kinds of negative realities?

II. Living into This Experience

a. Divide the sections Multiracial and Multicultural and Oneness in Christ to different pairs in the group.

b. Have each pair spend a few minutes with the section assigned to them. When the group reconvenes, discuss each section from the author's point of view. How does the author see the world?

c. List on newsprint the ways the participants experience multiracial and multicultural relations in schools, neighborhoods, and places of work.

d. Discuss how your church denomination or congregation experiences multiracial and multicultural relations. What are the issues and problems in churches?

e. Discuss how people can practice reconciliation as people of faith in their personal lives, yet in their public lives restrict that love and adapt to a different ethic.

III. Creating Community

a. Have each person take two minutes to draw a geographic outline (boundaries) of their community or neighborhood.

b. In your own community, where are the tensions with multiracial and multicultural relations?

c. Which of these tensions would you like to begin working to change?

Next Steps: Go around the room and ask for one theme, quote, or short phrase describing today's session. Thank everyone for staying with this discussion about difficult things. In conclusion, ask participants to be prepared next time to talk about chapter 2, "Culture and Identity."

SESSION 2: CULTURE AND IDENTITY

Central Question: How do the authors of chapter 2 inform our understanding of how culture and identity shape our interpretation and application of the biblical text?

Learning Aim: To engage the participants to consider our sameness without losing sight of our differences.

Introduction

1. Meet each other: have all participants, one at a time, share their name and identify their culture/ethnicity and an example of when they have participated in diverse teamwork.

2. Write "Culture" and "Identity" on newsprint, and make a list of images that these terms suggest to the participants.

Scripture Reading

Read aloud Scripture from chapter 2 (Deuteronomy 7:1-6).
Take only a few moments to discuss the authors' purpose in
using this passage. What are they trying to communicate to
the reader?

I. Understanding the Authors' Point of View

Key Point: "Culture, whether it is understood through identity markers such as race, ethnicity, class, gender, or sexual
orientation, affects the way we understand the biblical text."
Read this quote aloud and make a list of how group members
understand culture and identity.

a. Discuss this list by having participants give examples from
their world and their own everyday lives. How do your applied definitions of culture influence your interpretation of the
biblical message?

b. From reading the authors' sections Defining Culture and
Identity Formation, what do they mean when they describe
culture and identity formation?

c. List on newsprint the ways the participants experience
culture and identity formation. How does this lived experience
influence our understanding of a ministry of reconciliation
(2 Corinthians 5:17-21)?

II. Living into This Experience

a. Have group divide into pairs. Have each pair spend a few
minutes constructing their own working definition of culture
and identity. When the group reconvenes, discuss each term
from the authors' point of view. How is this different from
your understanding of culture and identity formation?

b. Discuss the issues and problems for identity formation in
Christ in the national culture in your country, your personal
culture, and church culture.

c. Discuss how understanding national culture and identity informs and organizes our practice of reconciliation in

multicultural and multiracial relations. How do differing understandings of culture and identity affect our attempts at reconciliation in the public space?

III. Creating Community

a. Which approaches to the study of culture and identity are likely to inform reconciliation for a culturally diverse United States and world?

b. To what extent are aspects of national culture perceived differently by different ethnic groups in the country?

c. Which aspects of national culture are most evident in our institutional forms of Christianity?

Next Steps: Go around the room and ask for one theme, quote, or short phrase describing today's session. Thank everyone for staying with this discussion about difficult things. In conclusion, ask participants to be prepared next time to talk about chapter 3, "Jesus Christ: Culturally Human, Inclusively Divine."

SESSION 3: JESUS CHRIST: CULTURALLY HUMAN, INCLUSIVELY DIVINE

Central Question: How does our understanding of the racial and cultural identity of Jesus determine the institutional forms of Christianity in the world?

Learning Aim: To engage the participants in serious dialogue to reconsider our institutional forms and practices of Christianity in the world with a culturally appropriate image of Jesus.

Introduction

1. Have all participants, one at a time, share their name, the places of their family's origin, and an example of how they have participated in global teamwork.

2. Have the group close their eyes and try to imagine what Gods looks like. Do the same with Jesus. Describe the images that come to your mind and list them on newsprint. What is the source of these images? Discuss what they mean.

Scripture Reading

Read aloud Scripture from chapter 3 (Revelation 1:14-15). Take only a few moments to discuss the author's purpose in using this passage. What is the author trying to communicate to the reader? Define what it means to be created in the image of God. How widely is this definition accepted?

I. Understanding the Author's Point of View

Key Point: "A monocultural image of God develops from a faulty understanding of the biblical teaching that humans are created in the image of God." Read this quote aloud and discuss the role of Western imposition of its own image of God on others. What is the issue the author is raising?

a. Discuss this description of humanity created in the image of God (Genesis 1:26-28). What are the questions that we should pose from our reading of Genesis to challenge the dominant image of Jesus as white? What are the effects of a white Jesus?

b. In the section How Did Jesus Become a White European? who does the author say decided that Western civilization determines the image that represents all of humanity?

c. Ask each participant to describe the experience of worship in his or her sanctuary. What kind of cultural approaches are represented in their worship, liturgy, and practice with the community?

II. Living into This Experience

a. Have groups divide into pairs and discuss the author's section on The Effects of a White Jesus.

b. Have each pair spend a few minutes and make a list of what effect a white image of Jesus and the Western image of Christianity have had on the church and society. When finished, have the group reconvene to discuss these issues from the author's viewpoint.

c. Discuss the negative consequences related to the image of a white Jesus in your congregations.

d. Discuss how this issue is related to one's individual faith and practice.

III. Creating Community

a. Ask group members to continue to summarize the issue of constructing a white Jesus and Western image of Christianity and what is required to move toward a call for action.

b. What are the individual and publicly harmful effects that this issue has on your church and in Christian higher education? How is this issue a public matter? How is the issue political? What is the controversy?

c. Identify and discuss the key stakeholders in your faith community. Who among them could you contact to define this problem so that it can be addressed in a tangible manner with measurable results?

d. When will you begin to address this issue as a crisis for your church, Christian school, college, or seminary?

e. What Scriptures will you use to inform and challenge your community to rethink your mission statement and assess whether it needs to be adjusted to address any of the issues the author has raised?

Next Steps: Go around the room and ask for one theme, quote, or short phrase describing today's session. Thank everyone for staying with this discussion about difficult things. In conclusion, ask participants to be prepared next time to talk about chapter 4, "Reading the Apostle Paul through Galatians 3:28."

SESSION 4: READING THE APOSTLE PAUL THROUGH GALATIANS 3:28

Central Question: How does our understanding of Paul's theology of gender restrict the meaning of authority as it is applied to men and women serving in God's covenant community when there is no contextual consideration?

Learning Aim: To understand Paul's theology of gender as grounded in a gift-based perspective rather than a gender-based perspective and to discover how we serve as men and women who share authority from God through the transforming power of the gospel and Holy Spirit.

Introduction

1. Have all participants give an example of how they have participated in teamwork with men and women.

2. Have the group close their eyes and try to imagine what female authority looks like in the church. Do the same with male authority in the church. Describe the images that come to your mind. What is the source of these images? Write the images on newsprint, and make a list of images. Discuss what they mean.

Scripture Reading

Read aloud Scripture from chapter 4 (Galatians 3:28). Take only a few moments to discuss the author's purpose in using this passage. What is the author trying to communicate to the reader? Define what it means to be equal in status with respect of person according to class, gender, and ethnicity. How widely is this definition accepted?

I. Understanding the Author's Point of View

Key Point: "How can you be equal to someone yet without equal authority?" Read this quote aloud and discuss the role of women in authority as a service unto God in the church? What is the issue the author is raising?

a. Have groups divide into pairs and discuss the author's sections The Apostle Paul, In the Spirit of Jesus and Pentecost, and Baptism and the Cross. How would you define *authority*? What does it mean to you?

b. Where do your ideas on authority come from in Scripture? What are your sources?

c. How does our understanding of our baptism in Christ inform our practice of women and men in authority in service to God in the church?

d. Ask participants about their experiences in their congregation, denomination, and/or faith-based learning organization. Who has benefited from the belief that women are not equal to men based on their gender?

II. Living into This Experience

a. Have groups divide into pairs and discuss the author's section Women as Coworkers with Paul. Did the author's perspective cause a shift your thinking? If so, what shifted? Was it difficult to make this shift? Why?

b. In pairs spend a few minutes discussing the author's section Does Paul Silence Women? Make a list of contextual issues that the author raises in applying Paul's theology of gender. When the group reconvenes, discuss these contextual issues from the author's viewpoint. What questions does this raise for the church and Christian higher education?

c. Discuss the negative consequences related to gender segregation in our churches and in Christian higher education. What might be the effect of a leadership model that subordinates women to male authority in the church and in Christian higher education?

d. For many people in ministry, authority is a major part of their identity and multicultural self. How does the author's chapter affect the way you think about the practice of leadership in the church and in Christian higher education?

COMING TOGETHER IN THE 21ST CENTURY

III. Creating Community

a. Have group members participate in a dialogue about how we can prevent dominant perspectives that restrict our understanding of how the Bible addresses gender, class, and ethnicity for the church and Christian higher education in an increasingly multicultural world and diverse church.

b. Dialogue with key stakeholders in your faith community about the issues that affect community and equity in the church and in Christian higher education. Ask for measurable results.

c. Which of these issues would you like to begin to develop into a policy to be lived out in your church, Christian school, university, or seminary? What steps will you take?

Next Steps: Go around the room and ask for one theme, quote, or short phrase describing today's session. Thank everyone for staying with this discussion about difficult things. In conclusion, ask participants to be prepared next time to talk about chapter 5, "Addressing Injustice."

SESSION 5: ADDRESSING INJUSTICE

Central Question: How does our understanding of human nature inform our thinking and practice of being in community with others in a culturally diverse world?

Learning Aim: To begin to understand that our thinking and practice of creating a community of justice and peace must be grounded in the model of transformed humanity that the Hebrew prophets proclaimed and Jesus lived out on earth.

Introduction

1. Have participants take a moment and reflect on a time in their lives when they were mistreated as a human being because of race, gender, or class.

2. Define *justice* and *peace*. Define *prejudice, racism, sexism,* and *classism.* What are people like underneath all of the layers of cultural conditioning? What in your understanding is based on God?

Scripture Reading

Read aloud Scripture from chapter 5 (Jeremiah 6:14; Ezekiel 13:10; Micah 3:5; and Luke 19:41-44). Take only a few moments to discuss the author's purpose in using these Scriptures. What is the author trying to communicate to the reader about the relationship between justice and peace?

I. Understanding the Author's Point of View

Key Point: "Jesus broke nearly every social taboo of first-century society by liberating the victims of injustice and by challenging the individual, institutional, and cultural forms of injustice. Our biblical faith calls us to follow his example."

a. Write on newsprint: "Racism, sexism, and classism are all injustices." Ask participants in what ways these three "isms" are interrelated.

1. How do they differ from each other?
2. Can someone who experiences racism still be a classist or sexist?
3. Can someone who is affected by sexism still practice racism or classism?
4. Can someone be victimized by class and still hold sexist and racist attitudes? Why or why not?

b. Racism, sexism, and classism can be found in at least three forms: individual, institutional, and cultural. Ask participants to identify some strategies for addressing these "isms" in each of their forms in personal attitudes, the community, and the church.

II. Living into This Experience

a. Read the examples of Jesus' action in response to a society that was structured through human actions, institutional practices, and cultural beliefs based on an oppressive system of injustice.

1. Discuss and make a list of how Jesus responded to the power relations based on racism.
2. Discuss and make a list of how Jesus responded to the power relations based on sexism.
3. Discuss and make a list of how Jesus responded to the power relations based on classism.
4. What do Jesus' actions say to us about our responsibility in response to unequal relations of power that dominate individuals and dehumanize a community?

b. Discuss sexist ideology and how it informs gender relations in our community, in our churches, and in our families. The author writes, "The life and ministry of Jesus significantly influence how we understand God's view of women and how men are to relate to women." What is it that Jesus wants us to be liberated from in our gender relations?

III. Creating Community

Racism, sexism, and classism are found in at least three forms: individual, institutional, and cultural. Discuss the root of the problem related to these issues as an individual created in God's image and rooted in Christ.

a. Ask participants to make a list of their issues and share their issues with the group.

b. Ask participants if their church is taking a stance on these issues and to explain why or why not.

c. Ask participants to make a commitment to begin a study group in their churches with their community. Invite church members to spend time together reading what Scripture has to say on these issues of prejudice, racism, sexism, classism, justice, and peace. And then begin to act through biblical models of justice and peace ministries in our communities.

Next Steps: Ask each participant to share the most difficult thing about this session and the most exciting thing. In conclusion, ask participants to be prepared at the next session to talk about chapter 6, "The Source of Liberation and Empowerment."

SESSION 6: THE SOURCE OF LIBERATION AND EMPOWERMENT

Central Question: How can a shift in our understanding of liberation as the central message of the Bible help us reexamine how we proclaim the biblical message?

Learning Aim: To begin to sense our own empowerment through the biblical message of liberation that helps us personally survive life's daily struggles.

Introduction

1. Have participants take a moment and reflect on a time in their lives when they have felt liberated, healed, or empowered. Describe the feeling.

2. How would you define *liberation*? How would you define *empowerment*? What in your definition is based on God?

Scripture Reading

Read aloud Scripture from chapter 6 (Exodus 3:14-17). Take only a few moments to discuss the author's purpose in using this passage. What are the common themes in the exodus event and the jubilee? What is the author trying to communicate to the reader?

I. Understanding the Author's Point of View

Key Point: Is the Bible a source of "liberation and justice at a societal and structural level? Is the Bible a source of liberation and empowerment for people, cultures, and societies? Misuse of the Bible to endorse the domination of one group over another has caused many to see" the Bible as anything but a source of liberation. Read this quote aloud and discuss: Do you agree that liberation is the central message of the Bible? Why or why not? How has Western domination restricted the proclamation of the biblical message of liberation? What is the issue that the author is raising?

a. Read the author's section Jesus as the Incarnation of the Jubilee. Discuss the life and message of Jesus. How can these shared meanings affect our world today?

b. Read the author's section The Power of Personal Liberation. Write on newsprint: "Liberation," "Empowerment," and "Oppression." Ask the participants to give synonyms for each of these words. After you have several for each word, ask for examples of the following:

1. Where the participants see each in the world
2. How they have experienced each of these terms in their own lives
3. What these examples suggest about the reality of liberation and empowerment

c. Next write on newsprint: "A biblical view of power." Make a list of principles of liberation and empowerment (from the Old Testament and the Gospels). Then make a list of statements describing personal liberation.

II. Living into This Experience

Recount the story of Dr. Martin Luther King Jr. from the chapter as a backdrop for this discussion. In light of the story in the author's section on The Power of Personal Liberation, discuss the key points of this section relating the story to the points made.

a. Is the Bible a source of personal liberation? How does the author define it?

b. What did personal liberation mean for Martin Luther King Jr.? What was the source of his personal liberation? What is the responsibility of liberation? Why do people avoid it?

c. Why are good people who believe in Jesus watching on the sidelines in their communities, allowing other people's values and behavior to dominate? What did Martin Luther King Jr. do? What was his approach? What specific practices did he use? How could Martin Luther King Jr. have abused his power in the civil rights movement?

d. Have the group identify a situation in which they are part of a group trying to make a decision. Someone in the group may be on a church or neighborhood committee. Treat it as a case study to examine the issue of power that is present. Describe something the group did once or now has to decide. What does it mean for each person to function as a liberated and empowered person with power?

III. Creating Community

As background for this section, have each person read this quote aloud: "For many Christians, the problem is not one of too much emphasis on the social aspects of a liberating biblical faith but an exclusive focus on the personal aspects of faith in Jesus Christ. Many people consider faith a personal matter without implications for one's society. While this belief is held by some who are powerless in society, it is more pervasive among the powerful."

a. Why is it that personal and social liberation are often not integrated in an individual's life? How do we merge the personal and the social in our world today?

b. Have group members make a list of the groups or associations they are a part of, beginning with the family. Have them rate their participation as an empowered person in the group.

c. Have group members take a few moments to write and discuss how they see themselves—as persons who make decisions without consulting others, or as persons who let others make decisions.

d. Have group members make notes on their list of associations in response to where they intend to make a transformed decision and how they will participate in the future to create a community in their meetings.

Next Steps: Go around the room and ask for one theme, quote, or short phrase describing today's session. Thank everyone for staying with this discussion about difficult things. In conclusion, ask participants to be prepared next time to talk about chapter 7, "A Roundtable on the Bible, Liberation, and Reconciliation."

SESSION 7: A ROUNDTABLE ON THE BIBLE, LIBERATION, AND RECONCILIATION

Central Question: How do we practice our faith as agents of liberation and reconciliation?

Learning Aim: To begin the process of committing oneself to becoming involved in the community as an agent of reconciliation and liberation.

Introduction
1. Share how you encountered the need for reconciliation in your community.

2. What is the most critical issue today in providing leadership as agents of reconciliation in faith-based organizations, churches, or learning organizations?

Scripture Reading
Read aloud Scripture from chapter 7 (2 Corinthians 5:16-18). How does the term *kairos* relate to the ministry of reconciliation? What do the terms *truth*, *justice*, *liberation*, and *salvation* suggest to you about the ministry of reconciliation?

I. Understanding the Authors' Point of View
Key Point: There are times when people must accurately recognize and respond to the reign of God in their midst.

a. Read and discuss Salter McNeil's section, Seizing the *Kairos* Time in Our Generation. What is your understanding of kairos?

b. Do we need a theological mandate calling for the implementation of the ministry of reconciliation in our churches today?

c. Discuss the critical issues of creating new models and practices of reconciliation today based on Salter McNeil's perspective of kairos?

II. Living into This Experience

Activity: Divide the group into two, one being the Reconciliation group, the other the Liberation group. Give each group fifteen minutes to prepare a short drama (about three minutes in length) demonstrating its role, identity, and function. One group could proclaim, "We are reconcilers!" and give a demonstration of what that looks like. The other group could do the same with liberation. The Reconciliation group may take a few minutes to read the section Liberation and the Land by Richard Twiss. The Liberation group may take a few minutes to read the section And Zacchaeus Remained Sitting in the Tree by Allan Aubrey Boesak to inform their dramas.

a. Have each group present its drama. After it is completed, ask the other group's members what they thought were the strengths and weaknesses of the content presented.

b. Bring the whole group back together and ask how they experienced working with one another. What were the issues? What problems are caused if only reconciliation is emphasized? What problems are caused if only liberation is emphasized? How has the group seen this combination misused in ministry? How have they seen it complementary in ministry?

c. Ask the group for any insights that would clarify the nature of these realities. How does the Bible inform us about how to practice reconciliation and address injustices?

III. Creating Community

As background for this section, have each person read Jean Zaru's quote aloud: "Real reconciliation involves a fundamental repair to human lives, especially to those who have suffered. It requires restoring the dignity of the victims of violence. Reconciliation contains four dimensions: political, economic, psycho-social, and spiritual."

    a. Discuss Zaru's story from her section *Sulha*, Reconciliation.

    b. Point out reconciliation and liberation in her section.

    c. Assume we tend to lean one way or another as persons and organizations. Ask each person to identify which direction he or she leans when addressing injustice. What is needed in your life to bring balance?

    d. As you consider living and practicing a faith for reconciliation and peace, how is liberation present? How is it strengthened? How is justice present? How is it strengthened?

    e. Write down one thing you will do this week to explore a new dimension of yourself as reconcilers for peace and justice.

Next Steps: Go around the room and ask for one theme, quote, or short phrase describing today's session. Thank everyone for staying with this discussion about difficult things. In conclusion, ask participants to be prepared next time to talk about chapter 8, "Community in the Midst of Diversity."

SESSION 8: COMMUNITY IN THE MIDST OF DIVERSITY

Central Question: How does our understanding of the body of Christ inform our individual practice of helping to build a just and reconciling community?

Learning Aim: To help create and become an active participant in a just and reconciling community in your congregation and/or neighborhood.

Introduction

    1. Where did you observe or experience community in your own life this past week?

2. Where did you see diversity based on a combination of community and justice?

3. Did you pay attention this past week to your own reconciling community?

Scripture Reading

Read aloud Scripture from chapter 8 (1 Corinthians 12:12-27). Take only a few moments to discuss the author's purpose in using this passage. What are the common themes in 1 Corinthians on community? What is the author trying to communicate to the reader?

I. Understanding the Author's Point of View

Key Point: Misuse of the Bible to endorse the domination of one group's voice over another has caused many to see the Bible as anything but a blueprint for creating community. Read the author's section Contrast Community.

a. Have participants dialogue about the following questions raised by the author.

1. Is the church a model of community that promotes diversity, justice, and equity?

2. Can the Bible inform our thinking and practice for creating a beloved, reconciled community for diverse people, cultures, and societies?

3. What is the issue the author is raising that keeps people of faith so segregated and alienated from one another?

b. Read the author's section Household of God. Write the term on newsprint and ask the participants to give synonyms for this phrase. After you have recorded several, ask the following questions.

1. Where have participants seen the author's notion of koinonia in their congregation?

2. How they have experienced koinonia and/or table fellowship in their congregation?

3. What about these images of community do you find appealing and compelling?

203

c. Use newsprint for the following: (1) write down your image of community; (2) make a list of biblical images of community; and (3) make a list of other images of community.

II. Living into This Experience

Tell the author's story in New York as a backdrop for this discussion. In light of the author's section Spiritual Transformation:

a. What did this teach the author about community?

b. In what ways have you personally experienced community? Cite some examples.

c. Why is "the discipline of dialogue" important to community? How can we ensure that everyone truly has a voice? What are some ways of addressing disagreements without manipulating or isolating someone?

d. What are some concrete ways we can live into a deeper understanding of community? What are the issues and problems? What can we propose to move in a direction that the author suggests for experiencing community?

III. Creating Community

As background for this section, have each person read Multicultural Fluency and Our Common Humanity.

a. Have each person reflect on the author's perspective and discuss the point the author is making.

b. Have group members make a list of how they can improve their multicultural fluency. Have group members take a few moments to write and discuss the issues and problems that keep them from being fluent in other cultures.

c. Have group members discuss what stance they need to take as individuals on community in their congregations.

d. Have group members list three action steps their congregations could do.

Next Steps: Go around the room and ask for one theme, quote, or short phrase describing today's session. Thank everyone for staying with this discussion about community. In conclusion, ask participants to be prepared next time to talk about chapter 9, "The Diversity Dilemma."

SESSION 9: THE DIVERSITY DILEMMA

Central Question: How can our understanding of diversity help us to learn new pathways on coming together as a community of God in a postindustrial and multicultural world?

Learning Aim: To adjust our biblical worldview because the Bible's message of liberation demands we come together to live out the image of God and mission of God.

Introduction

1. Have each person discuss how we relate to and love our neighbor who proclaims a different faith. What do we believe about religious pluralism? How is the Bible used to argue various positions on sexual orientation? Is there any common ground on these divisive issues? Ask people how they are doing in these areas of their faith practice.

2. What was the new pathway of understanding human relations that Jesus introduced to the Samaritan women?

Scripture Reading

Read aloud Scripture from chapter 9 (John 4:4-30). Read aloud and consider the author's questions regarding our diverse humanity.

1. Can we learn to live in community with respect for others in the human family without unanimity of belief or a full understanding of one another's perspectives?

2. As Christians can we live as neighbors with persons whose lifestyles are different than our own? Can we agree to disagree with others who claim the name of Christ yet hold divergent views from our own?

3. Diversity can be very complex and at times confusing. How can this passage from the Bible help us navigate the diversity dilemma?

I. Understanding the Author's Point of View

Key Point: "We must invite persons not like us into our closest relationships, into our communities, into our conversations, into our learning commitments, and into our biblical reflections and theological musings." Discuss the author's section Embracing the Eunuch from Ethiopia.

a. What does "love of the neighbor" mean? How does this relate to freedom for us?

b. What is the underlying problem of the issue of sexual orientation and gender identification that the author wants us to make? Make a list of the participants' responses on newsprint.

c. What approach did Jesus and the first-century church practice in their contacts with human beings, especially those who felt invisible, like outsiders? What is it that is fundamental to being human that the author wants the reader to come away with in our relationship with others?

II. Living into This Experience

With the group discuss the author's section An Encounter with a Samaritan Woman.

a. Why does the author use Kwok Pui Lan's term "dialogical imagination" to help us discover what is embedded in our humanity that links us as one human family? Discuss and share your culture and history.

b. How does Jesus encounter the Samaritan? How has God encountered your culture and personal history that may help you navigate your diversity with others?

c. How does the image of a disabled God inform our understanding of ourselves in the world with others? What is our responsibility and attitude toward others that the author wants us to learn and practice?

III. Creating Community

a. Have each person reflect along on the author's remark about how we must become "artisans of reconciliation and take the lead as catalysts, using diversity as a reason for coming together."

b. Have participants reflect on their churches and discuss what is preventing their churches from being communities of reconciliation that proclaim a message of social justice. What issues and restraints do they need to be liberated from?

c. Have participants discuss the fundamental change they need to make in order to begin a way of life as followers of Christ committed to service for social justice and reconciliation.

Next Steps: Go around the room and ask for one theme, quote, or short phrase describing today's session. Thank everyone for staying with this difficult discussion. Ask the group what they would name this experience they have had during this time together. Then ask each one to share one thing he or she is going to practice in a new way. Conclude by reading 2 Corinthians 5:17-20.

NOTES

Introduction

1. "An Older and More Diverse Nation by Midcentury," U.S. Census Bureau, August 14, 2008. The percentages add up to over 100 percent due to the fact that some individuals identify more than one cultural/racial group.

2. Soong-Chan Rah, *The Next Evangelicalism: Freeing the Church from Western Cultural Captivity* (Downers Grove, IL: InterVarsity, 2009), 14.

Chapter 1

1. Cain Hope Felder, "Out of Africa I Have Called My Son," *The Other Side* 28, no. 6 (November–December 1992): 10.

2. Charles B. Copher, *Black Biblical Studies: An Anthology of Charles B. Copher* (Chicago: Black Light Fellowship, 1993), 133.

3. Cain Hope Felder, "Afrocentric Biblical Interpretation," *The Biblical Institute for Social Change Quarterly* 3, no. 1 (1992): 2.

4. Calvin S. Morris, "We, the White People: A History of Oppression," in *America's Original Sin: A Study Guide on White Racism* (Washington, DC: Sojourners, 1992), 12–15.

5. A. H. Sayee, *The Races of the Old Testament* (New York: Revell, 1891), 174.

6. William F. Albright, "The Old Testament World," in *The Interpreter's Bible*, ed. George Buttrick (New York: Abingdon, 1952), 1:238–39.

7. For an overview of the various views regarding the location of Eden, see David Tuesday Adamo, "Ancient Africa and Genesis 2:10-14," *Journal of Religious Thought* 49, no. 1 (Summer–Fall, 1992): 38–43. At times the issue is avoided, such as in Terrance E. Fretheim, "The Book of Genesis," *The New Interpreter's Bible*, ed. Leander E. Keck (Nashville: Abingdon, 1994), 1:351, where it refers to the Pishon, Gihon, Havilah, and Cush as "rivers and places no longer known to us." There is no acknowledgment of the research of scholars such as Charles Copher and Cain Hope Felder, who argue that these rivers and places can be known and are in Africa.

8. Cuthbert A. Simpson, "The Book of Genesis: Introduction and Exegesis," in *The Interpreter's Bible*, ed. George Buttrick (New York: Abingdon, 1952), 1:495.

9. Cain Hope Felder, "Introduction," in *The Original African Heritage Study Bible*, ed. Cain Hope Felder (Nashville: James C. Winston, 1993), ix. Also, Felder, "Afrocentric Biblical Interpretation," 5.

10. Cain Hope Felder, *Troubling Biblical Waters: Race, Class and Family* (Maryknoll, NY: Orbis, 1989), 37.

11. Felder, "Out of Africa," 10.

12. Alfred G. Dunston Jr., *The Black Man in the Old Testament and Its World* (Philadelphia: Dorrance, 1974), 58–69. See also Copher, *Black Biblical Studies*, 138.

13. Felder, "Introduction," xi.

14. Dunston, *Black Man in the Old Testament*, 82–86.

15. In this section we will address the African presence in the Bible rather than the black presence, which is discussed in the works of Charles B. Copher, Alfred G. Dunston Jr., John L. Johnson, Walter Arthur McCray, William Dwight McKissic Sr., Daud Malik Watts, and others.

16. Copher, *Black Biblical Studies*, 135.

17. For a detailed discussion on the history and various interpretations of the curse of Cain and Ham as "blackness," see Cain Hope Felder, "Race, Racism, and the Biblical Narratives," in Cain Hope Felder, ed., *Stony the Road We Trod: African American Biblical Interpretation* (Minneapolis: Fortress, 1991), 129–32; and Charles

B. Copher, "The Black Presence in the Old Testament," in ibid., 146–53.

18. David Roberts, "Out of Africa: The Superb Artwork of Ancient Nubia," *Smithsonian*, June 1993, 91.

19. Miguel A. De La Torre, *Reading the Bible from the Margins* (Maryknoll, NY: Orbis, 2002), 20. He states: "In the Hebrew Bible, Cush was also used to refer to the Egyptians. In short, Cush (Ethiopia), Nubia, Put (Phut), and Egypt were not always distinct geographic entities, but can be understood as referring essentially to the ancestors of the same group of people, Africans."

20. Copher, "Black Presence in the Old Testament," 157, 161.

21. Felder, *Troubling Biblical Waters*, 22–28.

22. This is the preference of Hebrews' scholar James Earl Massey as stated at the 1986 Newell Lectureship in Biblical Studies, Anderson School of Theology, Anderson, Indiana, June 18, 1986. See also James Earl Massey, "The Letter to the Hebrews," in *The Peoples' Bible, New Revised Standard Version with the Apocrypha*, ed. Curtiss Paul DeYoung, Wilda C. Gafney, Leticia A. Guardiola-Sáenz, George "Tink" Tinker, and Frank M. Yamada (Minneapolis: Fortress, 2008), 1679–80.

23. R. S. Sugirtharajah, "Prologue and Perspective," in *Asian Faces of Jesus*, ed. R. S. Sugirtharajah (Maryknoll, NY: Orbis, 1993), viii.

24. Greece is also mentioned in Joel 3:6 and Zechariah 9:13.

25. C. H. Gordon, "Tarshish," in *The Interpreter's Dictionary of the Bible*, ed. George Buttrick (Nashville: Abingdon, 1962), 4:517.

26. Justo L. Gonzalez, *Manana: Christian Theology from a Hispanic Perspective* (Nashville: Abingdon, 1990), 77.

27. Orlando Costas, "Liberation Theologies in the Americas: Common Journeys and Mutual Challenges," in *Yearning to Breathe Free: Liberation Theologies in the U.S.*, ed. Mar Peter-Raoul, Linda Rennie Forcey, and Robert Fredrick Hunter Jr. (Maryknoll, NY: Orbis, 1990), 37.

28. Virgilio Elizondo, *Galilean Journey: The Mexican-American Promise* (Maryknoll, NY: Orbis, 1983), 51.

29. Fernando F. Segovia, "Reading the Bible as Hispanic Americans," in Keck, *The New Interpreter's Bible*, 1:169.

30. Ibid., 49–50.

31. Robert Allen Warrior, "A Native American Perspective: Canaanites, Cowboys, and Indians," in *Voices from the Margin:*

Interpreting the Bible in the Third World, ed. R. S. Sugirtharajah (Maryknoll, NY: Orbis, 1991), 289.

Chapter 2

1. The section by Frank M. Yamada and Leticia A. Guardiola-Sáenz was originally published as "Culture and Identity," in *The Peoples' Bible: New Revised Standard Version with the Apocrypha*, ed. Curtiss Paul DeYoung, Wilda C. Gafncy, Leticia A. Guardiola-Sáenz, George "Tink" Tinker, and Frank M. Yamada (Minneapolis: Fortress, 2008), 3–12. Used by permission of Augsburg Fortress Publishers.

2. James Earl Massey, "Reading the Bible from Particular Social Locations," in *The New Interpreter's Bible*, ed. Leander Keck (Nashville: Abingdon, 1994), 1:151.

3. Lydia E. Lebron Rivera, "Response to the Paper Presented by Justo Gonzalez," in *Uncover the Myths: Proceedings of the Roundtable of Ethnic Theologians of the United Methodist Church*, Des Plaines, IL, October 20–23, 1988, 15.

4. See Massey, "Reading the Bible," 150–53. See also Randall Bailey, "The Bible as a Text of Cultures," in *The Peoples' Bible*, ed. DeYoung et al., 13–22; and Fernando F. Segovia, "The Bible as a Text in Cultures: An Introduction," in ibid., 23–30.

5. Elsa Tamez, "Women's Rereading of the Bible," in *Voices from the Margin: Interpreting the Bible in the Third World*, ed. R. S. Sugirtharajah (Maryknoll, NY: Orbis, 1991), 61–70. See also Ada Maria Isasi-Diaz, "Solidarity: Love of Neighbor in the 1980s," and "The Bible and Mujerista Theology," in *Lift Every Voice: Constructing Christian Theologies from the Underside*, ed. Susan Brooks Thistlethwaite and Mary Potter Engel (San Francisco: Harper, 1990), 31–40, 261–69; and "Mujeristas: A Name of Our Own," in *Yearning to Breathe Free: Liberation Theologies in the United States*, ed. Mar Peter-Raoul, Linda Rennie Forcey, and Robert Fredrick Hunter Jr. (Maryknoll, NY: Orbis, 1990), 121–28. Of related interest are Fernando F. Segovia, "Reading the Bible as Hispanic Americans," in Keck, *The New Interpreter's Bible*, 1:167–73; and Carolyn Osiek, "Reading the Bible as Women," in ibid., 1:181–87; and Francisco Lozada Jr., "The Bible as a Text in Cultures: Latinas/os," in *The Peoples' Bible*, ed. DeYoung et al., 37–43; and Hee An Choi, "Women, Culture, and the Bible," in ibid., 109–15.

6. Stanley J. Samartha, "The Asian Context: Sources and Trends," in *Voices from the Margin*, ed. Sugirtharajah; Frank M. Yamada, "The Bible as a Text in Cultures: Asian Americans," in *The Peoples' Bible*, ed. DeYoung et. al., 51–57.

7. Tamez, "Women's Rereading of the Bible," 64.

8. Ibid., 67–68.

9. Ibid., 68.

10. Samartha, "The Asian Context," 37.

11. Tissa Balasuriya, "Toward the Liberation of Theology in Asia," in *Liberation Theology: An Introductory Reader*, ed. Curt Cadorette, Marie Giblin, and Marilyn J. Legge (Maryknoll, NY: Orbis, 1992), 34.

12. R. S. Sugirtharajah, ed., *Asian Faces of Jesus* (Maryknoll, NY: Orbis, 1993), x.

13. Samartha, "The Asian Context," 43.

14. Kwok Pui Lan, "Discovering the Bible in the Non-biblical World," in *Voices from the Margin*, ed. Sugirtharajah, 303.

15. See Cain Hope Felder, *Troubling Biblical Waters: Race, Class, and Family* (Maryknoll, NY: Orbis, 1989), 79–101, for rules of interpretation used in the African American church.

16. George Tinker, "Reading the Bible as Native Americans," in Keck, *The New Interpreter's Bible*, 1:174–80; "Native Americans and the Land: 'The End of Living, and the Beginning of Survival,'" in *Lift Every Voice*, ed. Thistlethwaite and Engel, 141–51; "The Full Circle of Liberation," *Sojourners*, October 1992, 12–17; "With Drum and Cup" and "For All My Relations," in *America's Original Sin: A Study Guide on White Racism* (Washington: Sojourners, 1992), 130–37; George Tinker, *American Indian Liberation: A Theology of Sovereignty* (Minneapolis: Fortress, 2008), 7; and George "Tink" Tinker, "The Bible as a Text in Cultures: Native Americans," in *The Peoples' Bible*, ed. DeYoung et al., 45–50.

17. Tinker, "Full Circle of Liberation," 15. See also Tinker, *American Indian Liberation*, 7–8.

18. Tinker, "Native Americans and the Land," 149. See also Tinker, *American Indian Liberation*, 9.

19. Ibid., 145.

20. Tinker, "For All My Relations," 136–37; idem, "Reading the Bible as Native Americans," 176–80; idem, *American Indian Liberation*, 50–53.

21. Tinker, "Reading the Bible as Native Americans," 174.

22. Tinker, "For All My Relations," 136.

23. Tinker, "Reading the Bible as Native Americans," 179. See also Tinker, *American Indian Liberation*, 53–54.

24. Ibid., 176.

25. Homer Noley, "Native Americans and the Hermeneutical Task," in *Uncover the Myths*, 2. See also Tinker, *American Indian Liberation*, 9, 10.

26. Tinker, "Reading the Bible as Native Americans," 176.

27. Steve Charleston, "The Old Testament of Native America," in *Lift Every Voice*, ed. Thistlethwaite and Engel, 49–61, and Tinker, *American Indian Liberation*, 138.

28. Charleston, "The Old Testament of Native America," 54.

29. Tinker, "Reading the Bible as Native Americans," 175.

30. Charleston, "The Old Testament of Native America," 55.

31. Ibid., 59.

32. Ibid., 58.

Chapter 3

1. Albert Cleage, *The Black Messiah* (Kansas City: Sheed and Ward, 1969), 42–43, quoted in Kelly Brown Douglas, *The Black Christ* (Maryknoll, NY: Orbis, 1994), 56.

2. William Mosley, *What Color Was Jesus?* (Chicago: African American Images, 1987), 34.

3. Footnote 6 in the "Book of Revelation," in *The Original African Heritage Bible*, ed. Cain Hope Felder (Nashville: James C. Winston, 1993), 1783: "European and American white Bible translators have intentionally rendered this description in a manner to minimize the Negroid features clearly evident in the original Old Testament Hebrew and New Testament Greek texts."

4. Cain Hope Felder, "Out of Africa I Have Called My Son," *The Other Side*, November–December 1992, 10.

5. There may have been others. Such a possibility is that the mother of Rehoboam could have been Solomon's Egyptian wife, the daughter of Pharaoh. She seemed to be Solomon's favorite wife.

6. Mosley, *What Color Was Jesus?* 5–6.

7. Virgilio Elizondo, *The Future Is Mestizo: Life Where Cultures Meet*, rev. ed. (Boulder: University Press of Colorado Press, 2000), 77–81. Elizondo speaks of Jesus as a mestizo.

8. Anton Wessels, *Images of Jesus: How Jesus Is Perceived and Portrayed in Non-European Cultures* (Grand Rapids: Eerdmans, 1990), 3.

9. Ibid., 3–5.

10. Ibid., 6.

11. James Burns, *The Christ Face in Art* (New York: Dutton, 1907), xx.

12. Ibid., xviii.

13. Bibles that offer visuals using persons of color include Cain Hope Felder, gen. ed., *The Original African Heritage Study Bible* (Nashville: James C. Winston, 1993) with black images; and Curtiss Paul DeYoung, Wilda C. Gafney, Leticia A. Guardiola-Sáenz, George "Tink" Tinker, and Frank M. Yamada, eds., *The Peoples' Bible: New Revised Standard Version with the Apocrypha* (Minneapolis: Fortress, 2008) with a diversity of racial and cultural images.

14. J. A. Mackay, quoted in Saul Trinidad, "Christology; Conquista, Colonization," in *Faces of Jesus: Latin American Christologies*, ed. José Miguez Bonino, trans. Robert R. Barr (Maryknoll, NY: Orbis, 1984), 62.

15. R. S. Sugirtharajah, ed., *Asian Faces of Jesus* (Maryknoll, NY: Orbis, 1993), viii.

16. Aaron Gallegos, "Mestizo Popular Religion," in *America's Original Sin: A Study Guide on White Racism* (Washington: Sojourners, 1992), 148.

17. Virgilio Elizondo, *Galilean Journey: The Mexican-American Promise* (Maryknoll, NY: Orbis, 1983), 11.

18. Gallegos, "Mestizo Popular Religion," 149.

19. Elizondo, *Galilean Journey*, 12.

20. Ibid.

21. Ibid.

22. Chung Hyun Kyung, "Who Is Jesus for Asian Women?" in *Asian Faces of Jesus*, ed. R. S. Sugirtharajah (Maryknoll, NY: Orbis, 1993), 225.

23. Douglas, *Black Christ*, 9.

24. Mosley, *What Color Was Jesus?* 36.

25. Efoe Julien Penoukou, "Christology in the Village," in *Faces of Jesus in Africa*, ed. Robert Schreiter (Maryknoll, NY: Orbis, 1991), 47.

26. Kosuke Koyama, "The Crucified Christ Challenges Human Power," in *Asian Faces of Jesus*, ed. Sugirtharajah, 155–56.

27. Susan Bogg, in *Slave Testimony*, ed. John W. Blassingame (Baton Rouge: Louisiana State University Press, 1977), 420, quoted in Douglas, *Black Christ*, 18.

28. Douglas, *Black Christ*, 12.

29. Ibid., 13–18.

30. Nicholas C. Cooper-Lewter, "My Jesus Was Jim Crowed!" *Colors*, May–June 1994, 18.

31. Douglas, *Black Christ*, 29.

32. Mosley, *What Color Was Jesus?* 42.

33. Steve Charleston, "The Old Testament of Native America," in *Lift Every Voice: Constructing Christian Theologies from the Underside*, ed. Susan Brooks Thistlethwaite and Mary Potter Engel (San Francisco: Harper, 1990), 59.

34. J. N. Sanders, "Gospel of John," in *The Interpreter's Dictionary of the Bible*, ed. George Buttrick (Nashville: Abingdon, 1962), 2:944.

35. Charleston, "Old Testament of Native America," 59.

36. Miguel A. De La Torre, *Reading the Bible from the Margins* (Maryknoll, NY: Orbis, 2002), 104–35. De La Torre has a chapter on images of Christ that includes economically marginalized Christ, Hispanic Christ, Amerindian Christ, Asian American Christ, Black Christ, Female Christ, and Gay Christ. See also Leticia A. Guardiola-Sáenz and Curtiss Paul DeYoung, "Jesus and Cultures," in *The Peoples' Bible*, ed. DeYoung et al., 65–76.

37. Sugirtharajah, *Asian Faces of Jesus*, x.

38. Kim Chi Ha, *The Gold-Crowned Jesus and Other Writings* (Maryknoll, NY: Orbis, 1978), 85–131.

39. C. S. Song, "Oh, Jesus, Here with Us!" in *Asian Faces of Jesus*, ed. Sugirtharajah, 133.

40. Kim Chi Ha, *Gold-Crowned Jesus*, 121–23.

41. Byung Mu Ahn, "Jesus and People (Minjung)," in *Asian Faces of Jesus*, ed. Sugirtharajah, 165.

42. Song, "Oh, Jesus, Here with Us!" 146.

43. Byung Mu Ahn, "Jesus and People (Minjung)," 165.

44. Song, "Oh, Jesus, Here with Us!" 133.

45. Orlando E. Costas, "Liberation Theologies in the Americas: Common Journeys and Mutual Challenges," in *Yearning to Breathe Free: Liberation Theologies in the United States*, ed. Mar Peter-Raoul, Linda Rennie Forcey, and Robert Frederick Hunter Jr. (Maryknoll, NY: Orbis, 1990), 42–43, 46.

46. Elizondo, *Galilean Journey*, 54.

47. Justo L. Gonzalez, *Manana: Christian Theology from a Hispanic Perspective* (Nashville: Abingdon, 1990), 78.

48. Elizondo, *Galilean Journey*, 56.

49. Ibid., 94.

50. Kuribayashi Teruo, "Recovering Jesus for Outcasts in Japan," in *Frontiers in Asian Christian Theology: Emerging Trends*, ed. R. S. Sugirtharajah (Maryknoll, NY: Orbis, 1994), 11–26.

51. Ibid., 15.

52. Ibid., 16–17.

53. Ibid., 15.

54. Ibid.

55. Rigoberta Menchu, *I Rigoberta Menchu: An Indian Woman in Guatemala* (London: Verso, 1984), 130–35, 245–46.

56. Teruo, 19.

57. Anselme T. Sanon, "Jesus, Master of Initiation," in *Faces of Jesus in Africa*, ed. Schreiter, 90.

58. Cece Kolie, "Jesus as Healer?" in *Faces of Jesus in Africa*, ed. Schreiter, 128.

59. Anne Nasimiyu-Wasike, "Christology and an African Woman's Experience," in *Faces of Jesus in Africa*, ed. Schreiter, 80.

60. Kolie, "Jesus as Healer?" 128.

61. Ibid., 131.

62. Ibid., 145.

63. While it could have been any religion, it was Christianity.

Chapter 4

1. All Scripture references in chapter 4 are taken from Today's New International Version (TNIV).

2. One wonders why this argument does not extend to men's authority in culture as a whole. After all, if men are God's chosen arbiters in the church and the home, why not in society? Why draw the line in the church and home?

3. John E. Phelan Jr., *All God's People: An Exploration of the Call of Women to Pastoral Ministry* (Chicago: Covenant, 2005), 38–48. Phelan shows how holiness in the Old Testament was pursued through separation, rituals, and regulations, whereas in the New Testament holiness was acquired not by way of separation or regulations but through relationship with Christ. See also Gordon

D. Fee, *Listening to the Spirit in the Text* (Grand Rapids: Eerdmans, 2000), 58ff.

4. See Phelan, *All God's People*, 38–48.

5. Ibid., 41.

6. Ibid., 42.

7. Fee, *Listening to the Spirit in the Text*, 59ff.

8. Ibid.

9. Ibid, 59.

10. Ibid.

11. Ibid., 60.

12. Catherine Clark Kroeger and Mary J. Evans, eds., *The IVP Women's Bible Commentary* (Downers Grove, IL: InterVarsity, 2002), 621.

13. Ibid.

14. Linda Belleville, *Women Leaders in the Church: Three Crucial Questions* (Grand Rapids: Baker, 2000), 53.

15. Kroeger and Evans, 644.

16. See Eldon Jay Epp, *Junia: The First Woman Apostle* (Minneapolis: Fortress, 2005), 2ff.

17. Linda L. Belleville, "Teaching and Usurping Authority: 1 Timothy 2:11-15," in *Discovering Biblical Equality: Complementarity without Hierarchy*, ed. Ronald W. Pierce, Rebecca Merrill Groothuis, and Gordon D. Fee (Downers Grove, IL: InterVarsity, 2005), 209–10. See also Belleville, *Women Leaders in the Church*, 174–76.

18. Fee, *Listening to the Spirit in the Text*, 74–75.

Chapter 5

1. Justo L. Gonzalez, "Hermeneutics: A Hispanic Perspective," in *Uncover the Myths: Proceedings of the Roundtable of Ethnic Theologians of the United Methodist Church*, Des Plaines, IL, October 20–23, 1988, 11.

2. Steve Charleston, "Victims of an American Holocaust: Genocide of Native People," *America's Original Sin: A Study Guide on White Racism* (Washington: Sojourners, 1992), 47.

3. E. Stanley Jones, *Mahatma Gandhi: An Interpretation* (New York: Abingdon-Cokesbury, 1948), 55.

4. Cain Hope Felder, *Troubling Biblical Waters: Race, Class, and Family* (Maryknoll, NY: Orbis, 1989), 37.

5. For an extended discussion on these various forms of racism and their affect on the church, see Joseph Barndt, *Dismantling Racism: The Continuing Challenge to White America* (Minneapolis: Augsburg, 1991), 51–154.

6. For a detailed description of the experience of women in biblical times, see Joachim Jeremias, *Jerusalem in the Time of Jesus* (Philadelphia: Fortress, 1969), 359–76.

7. No books of the Bible are attributed to women. Some scholars, however, have suggested that Hebrews could have been written by Priscilla.

8. For an overview of the perspectives of women scholars on the Bible, see Carolyn Osiek, "Reading the Bible as Women," in *The New Interpreter's Bible*, ed. Leander Keck (Nashville: Abingdon, 1994), 1:181–87.

9. Renita J. Weems, "Reading Her Way through the Struggle: African American Women and the Bible," in *Stony the Road We Trod: African American Biblical Interpretation*, ed. Cain Hope Felder (Minneapolis: Fortress, 1991), 57.

10. Elsa Tamez, "Women's Rereading of the Bible," in *Voices from the Margin: Interpreting the Bible in the Third World*, ed. R. S. Sugirtharajah (Maryknoll, NY: Orbis, 1991), 62.

11. Elisabeth Moltmann-Wendel, *The Women around Jesus* (New York: Crossroad, 1982), 7.

12. Renita J. Weems, *Just a Sister Away: A Womanist Vision of Women's Relationships in the Bible* (San Diego: LuraMedia, 1988), viii.

13. Cheryl Sanders, "Ethics of Holiness and Unity in the Church of God," in *Called to Minister . . . Empowered to Serve*, ed. Juanita Evans Leonard (Anderson, IN: Warner, 1989), 143.

14. Ibid.

15. Elaine Storkey, *What's Right with Feminism* (Grand Rapids: Eerdmans, 1985), 154.

16. Marie Strong, "The Biblical Vision: An Interpretation of Acts 2:17-18," in *Called to Minister*, ed. Leonard, 5.

17. See Barbara J. MacHaffie, *Her Story: Women in Christian Tradition* (Philadelphia: Fortress, 1986), 10–11.

18. Anne Nasimiyu-Wasike, "Christology and an African Woman's Experience," in *Faces of Jesus in Africa*, ed. Robert Schreiter (Maryknoll, NY: Orbis, 1991), 73.

19. MacHaffie, *Her Story*, 15.

20. Jeremias, *Jerusalem in the Time of Jesus*, 376.

21. MacHaffie, *Her Story*, 15.

22. Mary J. Evans, *Woman in the Bible* (Downers Grove, IL: InterVarsity, 1983), 46.

23. Moltmann-Wendel, *Women around Jesus*, 5.

24. These examples are found in Nasimiyu-Wasike, "Christology and an African Woman's Experience," 73–74, and MacHaffie, *Her Story*, 15–16.

25. Jeremias, *Jerusalem in the Time of Jesus*, 370.

26. Virginia Fabella, "Christology from an Asian Woman's Perspective," *Asian Faces of Jesus*, ed. R. S. Sugirtharajah (Maryknoll, NY: Orbis, 1993), 212.

27. Kelly Brown Douglas, *The Black Christ* (Maryknoll, NY: Orbis, 1994), 91.

28. Jacquelyn Grant, "Subjectification as a Requirement for Christological Construction," *Lift Every Voice: Constructing Christian Theologies from the Underside*, ed. Susan Brooks Thistlethwaite and Mary Potter Engel (San Francisco: Harper, 1990), 213.

29. Osiek, "Reading the Bible as Women," 186.

30. Ibid., 187.

31. For extended discussions on social and economic classism, see Jeremias, *Jerusalem in the Time of Jesus*, 87–376; Felder, *Troubling Biblical Waters*, 51–78, 102–34; and George M. Soares-Prabhu, "Class in the Bible: The Biblical Poor a Social Class?" in *Voices from the Margin*, ed. Sugirtharajah, 147–71.

32. Ronald J. Sider, *Cry Justice: The Bible on Hunger and Poverty* (New York: Paulist, 1980), 3.

33. Soares-Prabhu, "Class in the Bible," 149–51.

34. Ibid., 151.

35. Ibid., 157–58.

36. John R. Donahue, "Biblical Perspectives on Justice," in *The Faith That Does Justice: Examining the Christian Sources for Social Change*, ed. John Haughey (New York: Paulist, 1977), 78.

37. James H. Cone, "Jesus Christ in Black Theology," in *Liberation Theology: An Introductory Reader*, ed. Curt Cadorette, Marie Giblin, and Marilyn J. Legge (Maryknoll, NY: Orbis, 1992), 143–44.

38. John C. Haughey, "Jesus as the Justice of God," in *The Faith That Does Justice*, ed. Haughey, 271.

39. Mercy Amba Oduyoye, "The Empowering Spirit of Religion," in *Lift Every Voice*, ed. Thistlethwaite and Engel, 246.

Chapter 6

1. George Tinker, "With Drum and Cup: White Myths and Indian Spirituality," in *America's Original Sin: A Study Guide on White Racism* (Washington: Sojourners, 1992), 13.

2. From a speech given by Allan Boesak at Luther Seminary, St. Paul, MN, April 21, 1993.

3. Elsa Tamez, *Bible of the Oppressed*, trans. Matthew J. O'Connell (Maryknoll, NY: Orbis, 1982), 60.

4. George V. Pixley, "A Latin American Perspective: The Option for the Poor in the Old Testament," in *Voices from the Margin: Interpreting the Bible in the Third World*, ed. R. S. Sugirtharajah (Maryknoll, NY: Orbis, 1991), 229.

5. Ibid., 230–31.

6. Bernard W. Anderson, *Understanding the Old Testament* (Englewood Cliffs, NJ: Prentice-Hall, 1975), 9.

7. Sharon H. Ringe, *Jesus, Liberation, and the Biblical Jubilee: Images for Ethics and Christology* (Philadelphia: Fortress, 1985), 16–17, 25–28, 32.

8. See discussion on biblical images of freedom and the Galatians struggle to incorporate freedom into their lifestyles in Cain Hope Felder, *Troubling Biblical Waters: Race, Class, and Family* (Maryknoll, NY: Orbis, 1989), 104–9.

9. Ringe, *Jesus, Liberation, and the Biblical Jubilee*, 29–32.

10. Ibid., 32.

11. Cyris H. S. Moon, *A Korean Minjung Theology—An Old Testament Perspective* (Kowloon, Hong Kong, and Maryknoll, NY: Plough and Orbis, 1985), 5.

12. Ibid.

13. Mar Peter-Raoul, "South Bronx to South Africa: Prayer, Praxis, Song," in *Yearning to Breathe Free: Liberation Theologies in the United States*, ed. Mar Peter-Raoul, Linda Rennie Forcey, and Robert Frederick Hunter Jr. (Maryknoll, NY: Orbis, 1990), 12.

14. Howard Thurman, *Jesus and the Disinherited* (New York: Abingdon-Cokesbury, 1949), 33.

15. Virginia Fabella, "Christology from an Asian Woman's Perspective," in *Asian Faces of Jesus*, ed. R. S. Sugirtharajah (Maryknoll, NY: Orbis, 1993), 219.

16. Tamez, *Bible of the Oppressed*, 67.

17. Robert Allen Warrior, "A Native American Perspective: Canaanites, Cowboys, and Indians," in *Voices from the Margin*, ed. Sugirtharajah, 288. See also George E. "Tink" Tinker, *American Indian Liberation: A Theology of Sovereignty* (Minneapolis: Fortress, 2008), 126–43; and George "Tink" Tinker, "The Bible as a Text in Cultures: Native Americans," in *The Peoples' Bible: New Revised Standard Version with the Apocrypha*, ed. Curtiss Paul DeYoung, Wilda C. Gafney, Leticia A. Guardiola-Sáenz, George "Tink" Tinker, and Frank M. Yamada (Minneapolis: Fortress, 2008), 45.

18. Ibid., 289.

19. Arthur Lewis, "Introduction: Joshua," in *The NIV Study Bible*, ed. Kenneth L. Barker (Grand Rapids: Zondervan, 1985), 290. For a different approach for appropriating these texts, see Chan-Hie Kim, "Reading the Bible as Asian Americans," in *The New Interpreter's Bible*, ed. Leander Keck (Nashville: Abingdon, 1994), 1:165–66.

20. Warrior, "A Native American Perspective," 292.

21. Ibid.

22. Amos Niven Wilder, *Theopoetic: Theology and the Religious Imagination* (Philadelphia: Fortress, 1976), 29.

23. Ibid., 27.

24. These ideas were developed in conversations with Nicholas Cooper-Lewter.

25. Warrior, "A Native American Perspective," 294.

26. Vine Deloria Jr., "Vision and Community: A Native American Voice," in *Yearning to Breathe Free*, ed. Peter-Raoul et al., 78.

27. David J. Garrow, *Bearing the Cross: Martin Luther King, Jr., and the Southern Christian Leadership Conference* (New York: William Morrow, 1986), 57–58.

28. Keith D. Miller, *Voice of Deliverance: The Language of Martin Luther King, Jr. and Its Sources* (New York: Free Press, 1992), 138.

29. In many African American churches, the older members of the congregation are esteemed for the wisdom that comes with a long experience in the faith, and they can speak when they feel so moved.

30. Taylor Branch, *Parting the Waters: America in the King Years 1954–63* (New York: Simon and Schuster, 1988), 164.

31. Ibid., 166.

32. Lloyd K. Wake, "Salvation, Struggle, and Survival: An Asian-American Reflection," *Proceedings* (Nashville: Division of Ordained Ministry of the Board of Higher Education and Ministry, The

United Methodist Church, 1989), 31, quoted in Justo L. Gonzalez, *Out of Every Tribe and Nation: Christian Theology at the Round-table* (Nashville: Abingdon, 1992), 92.

33. Donald W. Dayton, *Discovering an Evangelical Heritage* (1976; reprint, Peabody, MA: Hendrickson, 1992), 7–119.

34. Ibid., 18–19.

35. Branch, *Parting the Waters*, 227–28, see also Michael G. Long, *Billy Graham and the Beloved Community: America's Evangelist and the Dream of Martin Luther King Jr.* (New York: Palgrave, 2006), 106.

36. Kosuke Koyama, "Union of Ethical Walking and Theological Beholding: Reflections from an Asian American," in *Yearning to Breathe Free*, ed. Peter-Raoul et al., 111–19.

37. Ibid., 111.

38. James H. Cone, *Martin and Malcolm and America: A Dream or a Nightmare* (Maryknoll, NY: Orbis, 1991), 164–65.

Chapter 7

1. *The Kairos Document*, September 25, 1985, Johannesburg, South Africa.

2. Jonathan Stein, "Contempt from Court: The Blistering Eloquence of Judge Royce C. Lamberth," Mother Jones (September 1, 2005). Accessed on August 5, 2009 at: http://www.motherjones.com/politics/2005/09/contempt-court-blistering-eloquence-judge-royce-c-lamberth.

3. A. Scott Catey, "Cobell v. Norton: Law-Making, Legal History, and the Production and Reproduction of Structural Inequality Among Native Americans," Paper presented at the annual meeting of The Law and Society Association, Renaissance Hotel, Chicago, Illinois, May 27, 2004. Accessed on August 6, 2009 at: http://www.allacademic.com/meta/p_mla_apa_research_citation/1/1/6/8/7/p116878_index.html.

4. Stein.

5. Excerpt from Jean Zaru, *From Occupied with Nonviolence: A Palestinian Woman Speaks* (Minneapolis: Fortress, 2008), 76–79. Used by permission of Augsburg Fortress Publishers.

6. Johnny de Lange, "The historical context, legal origins and philosophical foundations of the South African Truth and Recon-

ciliation Commission," in *Looking Back Reaching Forward: Reflections on the Truth and Reconciliation Commission of South Africa*, ed. Charles Villa-Vicencio and Wilhelm Verwoerd (Cape Town: University of Cape Town Press, 2000), 14-31.

7. Mamphela Ramphele, *Laying Ghosts to Rest, Dilemmas of the Transformation in South Africa* (Cape Town: Tafelberg, 2008), 46-69.

8. Curtiss Paul DeYoung, "The Bible as an Instrument of Reconciliation," in *The Peoples' Bible: New Revised Standard Version with the Apocrypha*, ed. Curtiss Paul DeYoung, Wilda C. Gafney, Leticia A. Guardiola-Sáenz, George "Tink" Tinker, and Frank M. Yamada (Minneapolis: Fortress, 2008), 77–84.

Chapter 8

1. Luther E. Smith Jr., "Community: Partnership of Friendship and Responsibility," in *God and Human Freedom: A Festschrift in Honor of Howard Thurman*, ed. Henry J. Young (Richmond: Friends United, 1983), 24.

2. Howard Thurman, *Meditations of the Heart* (Richmond: Friends United, 1976), 121–22.

3. Leonard Goppelt, *Theology of the New Testament Volume 2: The Variety and Unity of the Witness to Christ* (Grand Rapids: Eerdmans, 1982), 10–11.

4. Paul S. Minear, *Images of the Church in the New Testament* (Philadelphia: Westminster, 1960), 211.

5. George M. Soares-Prabhu, "Class in the Bible: The Biblical Poor a Social Class?" in *Voices from the Margin: Interpreting the Bible in the Third World*, ed. R. S. Sugirtharajah (Maryknoll, NY: Orbis, 1991), 163–64.

6. Ibid., 164.

7. Ibid., 163.

8. Ibid.

9. Steve Charleston, "Victims of an American Holocaust: Genocide of Native People," in *America's Original Sin: A Study Guide on White Racism* (Washington: Sojourners, 1992), 48.

10. Ibid.

11. Soares-Prabhu, "Class in the Bible," 164.

12. Ibid.

13. Charleston, "Victims of an American Holocaust," 48.

14. Cain Hope Felder, *Troubling Biblical Waters: Race, Class, and Family* (Maryknoll, NY: Orbis, 1989), 157.

15. Ibid., 163.

16. Anselme T. Sanon, "Jesus, Master of Initiation," in *Faces of Jesus in Africa*, ed. Robert J. Schreiter (Maryknoll, NY: Orbis, 1991), 85.

17. George E. Tinker, "Native Americans and the Land: The End of Living, and the Beginning of Survival," in *Lift Every Voice: Constructing Christian Theologies from the Underside*, ed. Susan Brooks Thistlethwaite and Mary Potter Engel (San Francisco: Harper, 1990), 149.

18. George Tinker, "The Full Circle of Liberation: An American Indian Theology of Place," *Sojourners*, October 1992, 16. See also George E. "Tink" Tinker, *American Indian Liberation: A Theology of Sovereignty* (Minneapolis: Fortress, 2008), 73–74.

19. Albert Nolan, *Jesus before Christianity* (Maryknoll, NY: Orbis, 1976), 37.

20. Marcus J. Borg, *Jesus a New Vision: Spirit, Culture, and the Life of Discipleship* (San Francisco: Harper and Row, 1987), 101–2.

21. Nolan, *Jesus before Christianity*, 117–18.

22. Ibid., 39.

23. Borg, *Jesus a New Vision*, 133.

24. Jerome H. Neyrey, "Ceremonies in Luke-Acts: The Case of Meals and Table Fellowship," in *The Social World of Luke-Acts: Models for Interpretation*, ed. Jerome H. Neyrey (Peabody, MA: Hendrickson, 1991), 361.

25. Jon Sobrino, "Jesus and the Kingdom of God," in *Liberation Theology: An Introductory Reader*, ed. Curt Cadorette, Marie Giblin, and Marilyn J. Legge (Maryknoll, NY: Orbis, 1992), 114.

26. Ivone Gebara, "Women Doing Theology in Latin America," in *Liberation Theology*, ed. Cadorette et al., 63.

27. Vincent Harding was paraphrased by George Tinker, "With Drum and Cup: White Myths and Indian Spirituality," in *America's Original Sin*, 133.

28. Ibid.

29. Naomi P. F. Southard, "Response to the Paper Presented by Stephen Kim," in *Uncover the Myths: Proceedings of the Roundtable of Ethnic Theologians of the United Methodist Church*, Des Plaines, IL, October 20–23, 1988, 64. She uses imagery from

Audre Lorde, *Sister Outsider* (Trumansburg, NY: Crossing, 1984), 110–14.

30. Howard Thurman, *The Luminous Darkness: A Personal Interpretation of the Anatomy of Segregation and the Ground of Hope* (New York: Harper and Row, 1965), 113.

31. The Covenant House Faith Community, a group of people who volunteer a year of their lives or longer to prayer, community, and service, was created to provide a spiritual core for the work of Covenant House, an outreach to runaway and homeless youth in several cities.

32. Howard Thurman, *With Head and Heart* (New York: Harper and Row, 1963), 9.

33. Dwight N. Hopkins, "Columbus, the Church, and Slave Religion," *The Journal of Religious Thought* (Winter–Spring 1992–93): 35.

34. Southard, "Response to the Paper Presented by Stephen Kim," 61.

35. Justo L. Gonzalez, *Out of Every Tribe and Nation: Christian Theology at the Roundtable* (Nashville: Abingdon, 1992), 54.

36. James Earl Massey, *Spiritual Disciplines* (Grand Rapids: Zondervan, 1985), 71–87.

37. Ibid., 87.

38. Susan Brooks Thistlethwaite and Mary Potter Engel, "Conclusion: Directions for the Future," in *Lift Every Voice*, ed. Thistlethwaite and Engel, 295.

39. Delores S. Williams, "Womanist Theology: Black Women's Voices," in *Yearning to Breathe Free: Liberation Theologies in the United States*, ed. Mar Peter-Raoul, Linda Rennie Forcey, and Robert Frederick Hunter Jr. (Maryknoll, NY: Orbis, 1990), 67.

40. Dietrich Bonhoeffer, *Letters and Papers from Prison: The Enlarged Edition* (New York: Macmillan, 1971), 17.

Chapter 9

1. Ray Bakke, *A Theology as Big as the City* (Downers Grove, IL: InterVarsity, 1997), 142.

2. Kwok Pui Lan, "Discovering the Bible in the Non-biblical World," in *Voices from the Margin: Interpreting the Bible in the Third World*, ed. R. S. Sugirtharajah (Maryknoll, NY: Orbis, 1991), 304.

3. T. H. Gaster, "Samaritans," in *The Interpreter's Dictionary of the Bible*, ed. George Buttrick (Nashville: Abingdon, 1962), 4:190–92.

4. Joachim Jeremias, *Jerusalem in the Time of Jesus* (Philadelphia: Fortress, 1969), 353.

5. Ibid., 356–57.

6. George R. Beasley-Murray, *Word Biblical Commentary* (Waco: Word, 1987), 36:62–63.

7. Kerry H. Wynn, "The Normate Hermeneutic and Interpretations of Disability within the Yahwistic Narratives," in *This Abled Body: Rethinking Disabilities in Biblical Studies*, ed. Hector Avalos, Sarah J. Melcher, and Jeremy Schipper (Atlanta: Society of Biblical Literature, 2007), 101.

8. Martin Albl, "'For Whenever I Am Weak, Then I Am Strong': Disability in Paul's Epistles," in *This Abled Body*, ed. Avalos et al, 157.

9. Wynn, "The Normate Hermeneutic and Interpretations of Disability," 93.

10. Nancy L. Eiesland, *The Disabled God: Toward a Liberatory Theology of Disability* (Nashville: Abingdon, 1994), 111.

11. Ibid., 100.

12. Ibid., 107ff.

13. *Christian Community Bible*, 2nd ed. (Quezon City, Makati, Manila, Philippines: Claretian Publications, Saint Paul Publications, Divine Word Publications, 1988), 369.

14. Steve Charleston, "The Old Testament of Native America," in *Lift Every Voice: Constructing Christian Theologies from the Underside*, ed. Susan Brooks Thistlethwaite and Mary Potter Engel (San Francisco: Harper, 1990), 60.

CONTRIBUTORS

Robin R. Bell is assistant professor of Christian ministries at Northwestern College in St. Paul. He is completing a doctorate in education focused on research in teaching for social justice and equity at Hamline University in St. Paul.

Allan Aubrey Boesak is extraordinary professor of public theology at the University of Stellenbosch in South Africa. He is author of several books, including *The Tenderness of Conscience: African Renaissance and the Spirituality of Politics* (SUN, 2005).

Leticia A. Guardiola-Sáenz teaches New Testament at Seattle University School of Theology in Seattle. She is coeditor of *The Peoples' Bible: New Revised Standard Version with the Apocrypha* (Fortress, 2008).

Mimi Haddad is president of Christians for Biblical Equality (CBE) in Minneapolis. She is coeditor of *Global Voices on Biblical Equality: Women and Men Serving Together in the Church* (Wipf & Stock, 2008).

Brenda Salter McNeil is president of Salter McNeil & Associates in Chicago. She is author of *A Credible Witness: Reflections on Power, Evangelism and Race* (InterVarsity, 2008).

Richard Twiss is president of Wiconi International in Vancouver, Washington. He is author of *One Church, Many Tribes: Following Jesus the Way God Made You* (Regal, 2000).

Frank M. Yamada is director of the Center for Asian American Ministry and associate professor of Hebrew Bible at McCormick Theological Seminary in Chicago. He is coeditor of *The Peoples' Bible: New Revised Standard Version with the Apocrypha* (Fortress, 2008).

Jean Zaru is a Palestinian peace activist and presiding clerk of the Friends Meeting House in Ramallah in the Occupied Palestinian Territories. She is author of *Occupied with Nonviolence: A Palestinian Woman Speaks* (Fortress, 2008).

APPENDIX:
A LIFTING OF THE BURDEN[1]

In his book *The Luminous Darkness* (Harper, 1965), Howard Thurman wrote that "the burden of being black and the burden of being white is so heavy that it is rare in our society to experience oneself as a human being." The election of Barack Obama as the forty-fourth president of the United States lifted that burden for many African Americans and other persons of color. Even if it lifted only for a few hours or a few days, it was a welcome experience. Many whites went to the polls and cast a vote based on the content of their candidate's character. They did not allow the color of his skin to sway their decision. These whites also felt the burden lift, even if only for a short time. The election of Barack Obama was a powerful moment of reconciliation. After five centuries of racial injustice in America, millions of people reclaimed a greater sense of their humanity. The question then, at the commencement of an Obama presidency, is this: Can the moment become a season of reconciliation? And can a season of reconciliation cause a permanent shift toward a less racist and more reconciled society?

There have been moments in U.S. history when a national breakthrough for reconciliation seemed near. In 1968 the multiracial coalitions formed by the Poor People's Campaign of Martin Luther King Jr. and the political campaign of Robert F. Kennedy had great promise. Yet these coalitions did not cause a shift on the landscape of reconciliation. Forty years later the United States is in the midst of a dramatic demographic shift. At the midpoint of the twenty-first century the United States will be a culturally diverse and pluralistic nation with no racial majority. The population will be 46 percent white, 30 percent Latino, 15 percent black or African, 9 percent Asian, and the remainder Native Americans, multiracial people, and others (U.S. Census Bureau). The diverse movement that coalesced to elect Barack Obama signaled this new reality. The flexing of political muscle by Latinos in the election was another sign. Can the Obama coalition become the foundation for a shift in racial dynamics in the United States? Time will tell.

Racism and injustice have not ended because one black person was elected president of the United States. The demographic changes that are producing greater cultural diversity may result in increased bigotry and racial tensions. Economic privilege is still overwhelmingly in the hands of whites. Churches remain segregated by race and socioeconomic class. The singular event of an African American ascending to the most powerful position in the world does not automatically translate into greater access to seats of power in corporate, government, and nonprofit entities for persons of color.

Yet the presidency of Barack Obama is a significant step forward in what he called "the long march...for a more just, more equal, more free, more caring and more prosperous America" (March 18, 2008). It lifts the burden that Howard Thurman claimed was so pervasive long enough for folks to stand up straighter and embrace a greater sense of their humanity. In many ways, the election of Barack Obama as president allows us to take a first step into the Promised Land that Martin Luther King Jr. spoke about the day before he was assassinated. In 1968 King proclaimed, "I've seen the Promised Land. I may not get there with you. But I want you to know tonight that we as a people will get to the Promised Land." Forty years later Barack Obama stated on election night, "If there is anyone out there who still doubts that America is a place where all things are possible; who still wonders if the dream of our founders is alive in our time; who still questions the power of democracy, tonight is your answer." While Obama's words may claim that we are further down the road to reconciliation than reality can support, his election is a significant milestone on the journey.

The election of Barack Obama as president should encourage us to have more of that "audacity to hope," that Obama's former pastor Jeremiah Wright preached about so eloquently some years ago

(Obama borrowed that phrase from Wright to be the title of his book). I believe that the burden has lifted enough so that we can glance into the Promised Land and, with the audacity to hope, come to believe that something has really changed in America.

I now have the audacity to hope that children of color can dream about the future with an imagination less restricted by racism. I now have the audacity to hope that people can discover new spaces and new language for conversing on racism and reconciliation. I now have the audacity to hope that young people will choose to live in diverse communities, dismantle institutional racism, and produce policies of inclusion that lead to the erasure of racism over time so that each generation is less racist and more reconciled. And I even have the audacity to hope that more whites will welcome an African American pastor to oversee their intimate spiritual concerns because of the positive experience of a black president as their leader.

My son, a student at New York University, celebrated both his nineteenth birthday and the election of Obama in Times Square on election night; November 4, 2008. Like Obama, my son has a parent who is white and a parent who is black. The election of Obama opens the door for multiracial people in our society to embrace the fullness of their identity without renouncing the reality of racism. My son, with his big Afro hairstyle, felt some of the burden lift off of his future so that he might more often experience himself as a human being in society. With greater diversity, less racism, and more reconciliation, we will need new ways to blend our cultural realities in what the South Africa antiapartheid activists were calling "nonracialism" in the 1980s, what Latin Americans call the process of *mestizaje*, or what the Caribbean islanders refer to as "creolization." The Obama generation will find fresh ways to blend cultures, and multiracial and multicultural people will be at the forefront of this process.

In his inaugural address, President Obama proclaimed, "We cannot help but believe that the old hatreds shall someday pass; that the lines of tribe shall soon dissolve; that as our world grows smaller, our humanity shall reveal itself." He envisions a time when the burden of racism will be lifted for more than a moment and we will discover our shared humanity as we walk into a promised land of reconciliation. His words echo the core of the gospel of Jesus Christ. The apostle Paul said that through his death and resurrection, Jesus Christ has "broken down the dividing wall...that he might create in himself one new humanity" (Ephesians 2:14–15). Jesus Christ has been in the business of lifting burdens and leading people to reconciled communities since the first century. Barack Obama is the most recent witness on a long journey.

NOTE

1. This article first appeared in a shorter version in the *Christian Century*, December 30, 2008. This essay has been excerpted from the book *The Audacity of Faith: Christian Leaders Reflect on the Election of Barack Obama*, edited by Marvin A. McMickle (Judson Press, 2009), pp. 60-63. Reprinted by permission of the publisher. www.judsonpress.com.

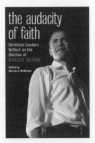